Daughters of Kings

Daughters
of Kings

Growing Up
as a Jewish Woman
in America

EDITED BY
LESLIE BRODY

FABER AND FABER
BOSTON   LONDON

Library of Congress Cataloging-in-Publication Data

Daughters of Kings: growing up as a Jewish woman in America /
edited by Leslie Brody.
    p.   cm.
    ISBN 0-571-19919-4
    1. Jewish women—United States—Religious life.   2. Jewish women—
United States—Biography.   3. Jews—Cultural assimilation—United States.
4. Judaism—United States.   I. Brody, Leslie.

BM205.D28   1997
296'.082'0973—dc21   97-14069
                                                           CIP
                                                           r97

Jacket design by Julie Metz
Text design by Will Powers
Printed in the United States of America

*For our children
and future generations of children,
with the hope that
the differences among them
will not be divisive.*

It was not the custom for a female to study at a yeshiva, because 'the King's daughter is all glorious within' and Jewish daughters are all the daughters of kings.

—ISAAC BASHEVIS SINGER

Contents

Acknowledgments

THIS PROJECT was a personal journey for me, a journey I could not have made without having many people as knowledgeable and caring guides. My Bunting sisters were my fellow travellers as well as my beacons along the way.

I am especially indebted to Rachel Kadish and Ann Koloski-Ostrow, who were always willing to hold my hand when I was distressed, to give wise counsel, and to interrupt their own intensely busy schedules to take time out for my needs. Their editing advice was invaluable.

Karen Fraser Wyche's warmth and her enthusiasm about the project encouraged and supported me—she serves as a role model for me about how you can build bridges that won't collapse. Lois Isenman and Barbara Grossman were extremely helpful to me in lighting the way toward a different view of Judaism than the one I had grown up with, and my relationship with each of them grew in valuable ways as we participated together in this project.

I thank Helena Meyer-Knapp for her wise and heartfelt counsel and encouragement. She frequently gave me a needed reminder about the importance and feasibility of this project. Deirdre Chetham taught me about the possibility of doing many things well, embedding her writing in an array of other activities, including a job change and a relocation from one city to another. Denise Freed, too, embedded this project in a life full of stressful events. Her sound common sense, kindness, and conscientiousness were helpful and much appreciated assets to me during many phases of this project.

Nanci Kincaid liberated and inspired me with her genuine interest in "otherness," her generosity of spirit, and her ability to lessen divisive boundaries and tensions by highlighting the humor in many situations. As a baby-boomer woman raised in New York, Paula Gutlove shared a similar perspective to my own about growing up Jewish, and her poignant writings about these issues helped me to lessen the sense of isolation I sometimes felt.

Ruth-Arlene Howe spent many hours with me in caring, thoughtful, and sometimes difficult discussions, which expanded my consciousness and self-awareness. Our dialogue about the issues involved in interethnic relationships greatly improved the final outcome of this project. Nancy Jones's openness and honesty about the twists and turns her own life as a non-Jew had taken in relation to Judaism and her ability to laugh with me over people's foibles were eye-opening gifts to me, which brought us closer together.

Both the project and I, personally, owe a great deal to Florence Ladd, the Director of the Bunting, who gave of herself and of her wisdom to create a nonjudgmental intellectual community at the Bunting— a community that inspired me and the other Fellows to do our most creative work.

I am also indebted to my cousin and friend Martha Liptzin Hauptman, whose generous willingness to share her incomparable editing as well as social networking skills played an important role in this book project. I appreciate both the absorbing and insightful discussions we had, as well as the superhuman effort she expended in carefully and thoughtfully editing the entire manuscript within a very tight time schedule. The book is far more reader-friendly now than it would have been without her efforts. I also thank my friends who reviewed rough drafts of my chapters, offering me sage and judicious advice: Anne Copeland, Frances Grossman, Marcia Osburne, and David Rothstein. Their perceptive editing recommendations made for a better book, and I treasure the things I have learned from each of them. To Bruce Raider I owe a debt of gratitude for suggesting part of the title for the concluding chapter. Jonathan Huppert and Claudia Yellin, graduate students in the Boston University clinical psychology program, made astute and helpful comments to me. My thanks go to Jeff Gagne for his good-natured willingness to print, xerox, and mail innumerable copies of chapters. Many graduate and undergraduate students whom I have taught over the years at Boston University helped further my understanding of the issues surrounding diversity and multiculturalism in America.

My agent, Lisa Adams, of the Boston Literary Agency, contributed endless hours of hard work on behalf of this project, including researching Isaac Bashevis Singer's work to produce a title for the book.

She also contributed the conviction that the book was important and deserved to be widely read. It is doubtful that this project would have seen the light of day without her help. My gratitude also goes to my editor at Faber and Faber, Valerie Cimino, whose perceptive guidance, clarity of vision, and ability to listen carefully and empathically to even the most unfocused thoughts always kept me and this project on the right track.

And, with love, my appreciation goes to my parents, Shirley and Sydney Brody, and my sister, Marilyn Brody, whose generosity and caring knows no bounds, whose support has been a lifelong gift. The importance they place on family relationships and the delight they take in family connections have enriched my life. They, too, read endless drafts of parts of this book, always with care and encouragement.

My love and gratitude also goes to my husband Lance, who was my close companion on the journey I undertook on this project. He read through and critiqued all of the essays, offering wise and intelligent advice on each one. I am especially appreciative of the pride he takes in my work, since my writing often means that his share of child care and household responsibilities increases above its already high levels. He is truly my life's partner. Both he and I are indebted to our babysitter of the past nine years, Irene King, who has made our work possible with her warmth, her conscientiousness, her ability to take care of us with such good humor, and with the close and caring relationships she has developed with our children. And finally, I thank my precious children, Jennie, Rachel, and Matthew for the daily smiles and joys they bring to my life, and for their creative abilities to involve themselves in some alternative activities when Mommy has to work yet once again. I hope that their futures as Jewish American children will be bright and beautiful.

All stories are printed by permission of the authors.

Preface

Florence Ladd

In THE 1994–1995 cohort of thirty-eight Fellows of the Bunting Institute of Radcliffe College, there were thirteen especially inquisitive women who ranged in age from twenty-six to sixty-three years; they represented a variety of backgrounds with respect to academic training, ethnic heritage, national origin, religious orientation, and regional identification. With the courage to investigate the unknown, they turned their minds and hearts to the intersection of Judaism, feminism, and scholarship. They explored their religious beliefs and attitudes; they re-examined dimensions of their own respective identities. And they were persuaded by psychologist Leslie Brody's openness and sincerity to report the results of their personal recollections and reflections in this superb collection of essays.

In the academic year of 1961–1962, the Radcliffe Institute of Independent Study (renamed the Mary Ingraham Bunting Institute in honor of its founder, Radcliffe College's fifth president) invited the first cohort of scholars, researchers, and artists for a rare collegial opportunity. During the past thirty-five years, more than 1,2000 women have been beneficiaries of the fellowship experience at the Institute. Among the Bunting Institute alumnae are authors Alice Walker, Jayne Anne Phillips, and Gish Jen; psychologist Carol Gilligan; educator Sara Lawrence-Lightfoot; literary scholar Barbara Johnson; anthropologist Mary Catherine Bateson; performance artist Anna Deavere Smith; visual artists Frances Gillespie and Ellen Driscoll; space physicist Margaret Kivelson; composer Augusta Read Thomas; mathematician Lesley Sibner; and social activists Mamphela Ramphele and Linda Stout.

The Bunting Institute offers fellowships to approximately forty women from a wide range of disciplines for the concentrated pursuit of projects they propose. The fellowships are designed to support women of exceptional promise and demonstrated accomplishment in academic and professional fields. Residence in the Boston area and participation in the Institute community are required during the fellowship appointment. A lively cross-disciplinary exchange and a strong sense of community are fostered during the fellowship years. As director of the Institute (1989–1997), I have had the privilege of observing the variety of ways in which scholarly, creative women and their projects are transformed by the multidisciplinary discourse conducted at the Institute.

Imagine the conversations that generated the essays prepared for this volume: the searching questions and candid revelations in some sessions; the strong convictions and evasive expressions of ambivalence; the accusations and denials. Even in the company of well-educated and highly accomplished women, there must have been moments when questions evoked by the subject matter rendered them speechless!

What is the nature of Jewish identity in contemporary, cosmopolitan U.S. communities and, in particular, in the lives of women in the vanguard of intellectual life? And what is the relevance of their sense of identity to other women in their circles, women who are not Jewish? In what circumstances is being Jewish highly salient, and how does the salience of being Jewish make a difference in a society that is predominantly Christian—but growing less so? These are just a few of the questions addressed in some of the essays.

The essayists in this collection who are not Jewish reconstructed the experiences that shaped their understanding of the complexity of Jewish identity. They confessed their naiveté, their exposure to stereotypes, their misconceptions, their insights, and the relevance of their understanding of Jewish history to their own lives. Relating episodes in their lives with reference to minority status, they addressed differences and similarities between their experiences and those of Jewish women. They also offered comparative views of attitudes toward religious and ethnic politics, social conventions, family life, and relations with men.

The Jewish contributors to the volume illustrate variations on the expression of and commitment to one's Jewish identity. There is tension between those who are proud of being Jewish and those who acknowledge ambivalence about their Jewishness as they risk probing it. In Dr. Brody's synthesis of the essays, she suggests that this project afforded the Jewish authors a medium for the exploration of the complexity and diversity of Jewish identification.

All the authors, in their autobiographical analyses of incidents that influenced their self-definitions and recognition of otherness, have offered intelligently revealing material that will expand our knowledge of identity formation. Their accounts reflect aspects of late-twentieth-century experience that are relevant to the social history of this epoch; and they enhance our awareness of the complicated nature of the human condition.

This collection of essays will elicit aspects of one's personal history and evoke memories that have been long forgotten. The personal evidence and unique voice in each of these essays call forth responses. They invite additional voices—statements from other thoughtful individuals, both women and men—to speak of the evolution of their own cultural, religious, racial, and ethnic identities. Inspired by these provocative stories, others may engage their peers or colleagues, relatives or friends in discussions of the varieties of traditions that are represented in our multicultural United States. *Daughters of Kings* demonstrates the social and educational value of cross-cultural discourse, especially when, as in this collection, it is so well articulated.

Cambridge, Massachusetts
May 1997

Daughters of Kings

Introduction

"She Looks Jewish: How Wonderful!"

LESLIE BRODY

M Y HEART RACING, I anxiously thought about what I might say to introduce myself when my turn came to speak. I was seated in a "grand circle" of thirty-seven other Radcliffe College Bunting Fellows, all women, on Orientation Day. Florence Ladd, the gracious and discerning director, had instructed each of us to take a turn introducing ourselves whenever the spirit might move us to do so, using the model of Quaker meetings to set the stage. She had established a personal and revealing tone to the meeting by talking about her own history of affiliation with the Bunting, an affiliation that had encompassed the birth of her son and the untimely death of her first husband some twenty-three years earlier. The Fellows ranged in age from twenty-four to sixty-three; among them were novelists, artists, social activists, and academics from various disciplines, including one, like me, who was a psychologist. We were all there to focus on our work for the year in a stimulating and supportive atmosphere, unencumbered by other professional responsibilities. Harvard University, its home city of Cambridge, and discussions among the Fellows were to provide the inspiration for much creative work. The Bunting Institute is a think tank for women scholars, and women typically feel quite lucky to be selected for yearlong fellowships.

During the introductory grand circle, I felt like a new student at school, wanting to make new friends, to create a good impression, and to learn as much new information as I could. I tried unsuccessfully to talk myself out of being anxious, yet my feelings seemed somewhat justified. When I was not on sabbatical at the Bunting, I taught in the psychology department at Boston University. Almost twenty years in that setting had made me comfortable, almost complacent about my role and my skills, allowing me to take for granted that I would be afforded a measure of respect simply because I was a faculty member. At the Bunting I had no such guarantees: no one really knew who I was, and I felt like I needed to prove my worth all over again.

The tension and excitement in the orientation room were palpable. The first Fellow to speak took off her shoes, rose from her chair, and began to talk passionately about her ambivalence about being a mathematician, or rather, about the ways that she was both a mathematician and not a mathematician at one and the same time. She wasn't exactly sure that she was pursuing the right dream. Other Fellows followed, some matter-of-factly reviewing their proposed projects for the year, others with tears streaming down their cheeks about the opportunity the Bunting presented to them. I was among the more matter-of-fact, but wove into my introduction the importance that feminism had played in my proposed project for the year, a book on gender and emotion.

I listened intently to the other fellows, and three of them planted the seeds from which this book germinated. Several of the introductory comments started a process in which I began to wrestle with my Jewish identity and what it meant to me. My ambivalence about being Jewish, and the pain sometimes associated with Judaism for me, was not the theme I had come to the Bunting to explore, but it was a theme that refused to go away and demanded to be taken seriously. As I entered middle age, my conflicts about my own Jewishness and my indecisiveness about how to raise my children was becoming more and more troublesome to me.

Although the rising tide of feminism in the 1970s and 1980s had helped me dramatically understand and overcome some of the boxes I had been confined to as a woman, there had been no similar expansion of my consciousness about the positive and negative role of Judaism in my life. I felt culturally identified as a Jew in that I celebrated holidays like Passover and Chanukah, but I had never had a formal Jewish education, nor had I ever been part of a formal Jewish community or support group. It was often uncomfortable and difficult for me to publicly acknowledge my Judaism, feelings I needed to come to terms with somehow.

My ambivalence about my Jewish identity was highlighted by my increasing discomfort with the silence about Judaism that prevailed in the academic psychology department in which I work. I teach in a clinical psychology Ph.D. program that has a long and proud commitment to training ethnic minority students. Yet even the Jewish faculty members fail to acknowledge to students and colleagues that to be Jewish is to be a member of a minority group, with all the potential psychological consequences—pain, pride, self-hatred—that may ensue. This book is the result of my own process of "coming out as a Jew," a process that may not have happened in quite the way it did had I not been a fellow at the Bunting in 1994–1995.

What were these comments made at the introductory grand circle that started my personal journey? First, Rachel Kadish ("Living for Export"), a novelist, talked about her personal background as it related to the book she was writing, *From a Sealed Room.* The book involves characters from many different cultural backgrounds, but predominantly Israelis and American Jews. I was amazed that in a room full of strangers, she was able to talk openly about being Jewish, about being the granddaughter of Holocaust survivors. I admired her and was nervous for her at the same time. "What reaction was she evoking in the non-Jewish Fellows?" I wondered. Because I was prepared to see anti-Semitism everywhere I went (a fear that I have since learned is shared by some other Jews), I imagined that it must be there, an unacknowledged presence in our midst. My sense was that Rachel, simply by speaking out as a Jew, must be evoking antagonism in some of the Fellows or, at the very least, caution on their part about what was to be said to her or in her presence. It speaks to my fear that I did not imagine anyone feeling supportive or warmly toward her for this public admission. Much later, responding to a different discussion, Paula Gutlove ("Going Back to Bocki") confessed that she had the same astonished reaction to Rachel's general openness about her Judaism that I did.

In stark contrast to these reactions, other Jewish Fellows were surprised that I should be so fearful. It speaks to the diversity of Jewish experience that some Fellows were quite comfortable with public acknowledgments of the fact that they were Jews and were outspokenly proud of their Judaism. In fact, they were disturbed by my feelings of discomfort.

Ann Olga Koloski-Ostrow ("Hannah's *Teshuvah*"), an academic who studied Roman archaeology and antiquities, shared with the grand circle that she had converted to Judaism twelve years before. I marveled at the pride she took in her statement, at her openness, at her lack of ambivalence. I thought that maybe if I too had made an active choice to be Jewish, I would be able to speak more openly about my ethnic identity, but I wasn't sure. Saying, "I'm Jewish," in an unfamiliar, largely Christian setting felt worlds apart from saying, "I converted to Judaism." The first draws a clear line of difference between you and others and risks their rejection; the second reminds them that since you weren't Jewish by birth, you are less different from them than they might otherwise think.

And the third voice was Nanci Kincaid ("Not a Jewish Woman"), a Southern novelist who spoke poetry and quotable humor every time she opened her mouth. Her theory about crumbling cookies, for example, is one that I try to live by and share with others. It is this: "Think of yourself as a cookie. If you give pieces of yourself away trying to give a bit to all the hungry people in your life, they will all get just crumbs, and no one will have enough to eat." The analogy is limited, but the theory has a certain attraction, especially when you feel so stressed and over-extended that everyone in your life seems to be miserable. Anyway, what Nanci said at the introductory grand circle was that she had been married for many years to a football coach whose kiss had put her to sleep (instead of waking her up, as the fairy tales would have us believe). It was only after her divorce, when she met and interacted with Jewish women for the first time, that she learned that women could actually expect something from men. Jewish women taught her that she could set high standards for the way men treated her, rather than just passively accept whatever treatment men chose to dole out. I didn't know whether to be offended by her characterizing Jewish women in this way, or flattered, since I took her view to be positive. But it got me thinking: non-Jews' feelings about Jews were perhaps more complex than I had acknowledged.

Yet a fourth Fellow highlighted the importance of ethnicity during that grand circle. Karen Fraser Wyche ("What Kind of Name Is Wyche?"), an African American psychologist, talked about how she had come to be at the Bunting that year. Her story had to do with serendipity and professional networking; but the part that stuck out for me was a small incident she relayed. Not knowing who Florence Ladd was, she had met her in the street one day and had nodded to her as she would to any woman of color. Only subsequently did she learn that the woman was Florence Ladd and that she was the director of the Bunting. I thought that this acknowledgment that passed between women of color who were strangers to each other was wonderful. I envied it and thought that Jewish women could learn from it.

After the grand circle, we adjourned for lunch, and I tried to strike up a conversation with another Fellow, Laura Korobkin. I was very taken with her analysis at the grand circle that each of us had multiple stories about ourselves that we could choose to tell. She disclosed that she found it difficult to decide which version of herself and of her history to present as a way of introducing herself to the rest of us. When I approached her after the circle, she seemed preoccupied and distant, and one of my thoughts was that I did not interest her because we were too similar: both Jewish women from New York, both about the same age. I was used to that reaction from some Jewish women: rather than celebrating a connection borne out of similarities, they reacted with distance to me because of a sense that I might remind them of who they were, or where they had come from, associations they wanted to escape rather than be reminded of. As a psychologist, however, I know that much of what I believe to be insightful interpretations about others' behavior are sometimes reflections of my own issues: projections, so to speak. Perhaps it was I who was uncomfortable with being too close to Laura at that point because of our perceived similarities. I realized all of this in a flash, and, not for the first time on that orientation day, recognized that I had a lot to come to terms with.

These issues simmered in the background for me throughout my Bunting year, since my primary focus was to finish the project I had come there to complete. But the open and stimulating friendships that developed among the Bunting women eventually led me to share my struggles about my Jewish identity with them. In one inspired night, I feverishly wrote an essay about growing up as a "not-so Jewish" woman and showed the piece to my "sister" Fellows. They responded with interest and enthusiasm, and I invited both Jewish and non-Jewish women to write about their own encounters with Judaism. The result was an explosion of ideas, group discussions, and autobiographical essays. The energy in our discussions and in our essays became the core of this book. Through the power of shared feelings, we were able to recognize that what we had each assumed to be our own individual struggles about ethnicity had a larger social context. For some of us, this shared understanding and confirmation made our struggles less painful. And at the risk of sounding maudlin, I'll go one step further: the conversations that developed gave many of us hope for a future in which different ethnicities, and even different feelings about the same ethnicity, become not a barrier to common understanding, but a fascinating entry into true communication.

The essays we wrote, now part of this book, are personal stories about Jews through the eyes of Jewish and non-Jewish women. In a sense, to di-

chotomize the women into Jews and non-Jews is too simplistic. Some of
the women have both Jewish and non-Jewish roots and question whether
or not they are Jewish. One of the women is Jewish by choice, having
converted to Judaism from Catholicism in her thirties. The non-Jewish
women come from diverse geographic regions of the United States, including New England, the South, and the Midwest. These regions have
unique cultures that were formative for the women's own ethnic identities as well as for their feeling about Jews in distinct ways. Two of the
women are African Americans, a minority identity that provides a lens
through which they view the Jewish experience. The Jewish women themselves have diverse and multidimensional feelings about their backgrounds, ranging from ambivalent and confused to positive and celebratory. These eloquent and passionate essays were an unanticipated
growth experience for me. They allowed me to share my pain, to see
the humor in some situations I had previously found only somber, and
ultimately to acknowledge and begin to rejoice in my Jewish identity.

The Jewish women's essays convey feelings of pride, but also of difference, which is sometimes powerfully internalized as self-hatred. We
relate a sense of being haunted by intergenerational stories of persecution, especially the Holocaust, which inevitably relate to worries about
the future and the lives of our children. Without exception, we have
each experienced firsthand the effects of ongoing anti-Semitism, a force
that has been both painful and growth inducing.

The Jewish women's feelings are mirrored and elaborated in the essays by non-Jewish women, who reveal the stereotypes they held about
Jews when they were growing up. They consider the ways in which their
own identities have shaped their reactions to Jews and other ethnic
groups. These essays raise interesting and powerful questions about the
nature of ethnic identity itself. It seems that group identity is as much a
process of defining what you are *not* as defining what you are. Many of
the Jewish women came to feel Jewish only with the recognition that
other people treated them as "different." And the non-Jewish women
discover their feelings about Jews only by exploring the ways in which
their own ethnic identity feels both similar to and different from what
they learned about Jews as they grew up.

Living with the Legacy of the Holocaust

The journey I undertook in search of my Jewish identity included grap-
pling with sometimes painful, often surprisingly vivid childhood memo-

ries. But simply remembering did not feel satisfying enough. Perhaps because being a psychologist is such an integral part of my identity, I needed a psychological framework to help guide me through my sometimes seemingly inexplicable and confusing experiences. I began to search for insightful perspectives on Jewish identity, to read widely, and to become involved in many absorbing discussions. Participating in this project eventually enabled me to see beyond my pain, to gain some distance from it, and to begin to feel pride and dignity about being a Jew.

A baby boomer, I was born in the early 1950s and grew up in New York City in a predominantly Jewish neighborhood. The neighborhood, contrary to stereotypes about rich Jews, was predominantly lower middle class. Many fathers held two jobs to earn a decent living, and few children were able to afford summer sleep-away camp or the cost of tuition at a private college.

My first recognition that people might hate me simply because I was Jewish came when I was seven. My best friend Alice, also Jewish, spoke to me in a chilling whisper about the Nazis. "They came with pitchforks to the doors of Jewish children and twirled Jewish babies on them. They speared them through." She spoke with an intensity that could not be disbelieved. "It was just because they were Jewish. They hated Jews. They killed millions and millions of Jews." I wanted to doubt her, but there was something about the urgency with which she spoke that made me realize she must be telling the truth. In the way children do, she avoided looking directly at me when she told her tale, darting her eyes around the room, a sign of how important her story was to her. I'm not sure how she learned about the existence of Nazi Germany—perhaps it was from her sister, five years our senior, someone I thought was a model of sophistication and the source of indisputable wisdom.

My first conversation with Alice about this event was so powerful that it is indelibly marked in my memory. Like a trauma victim, I experienced a sense that time had momentarily stopped. Only the sound of my heart, thumping loudly in my ears, reminded me that I was still in the same world I had been in the instant before Alice's words were uttered. The conversation marked an abrupt loss of innocence I can never reclaim, a sense of before and after that few events have the power to delineate. To this day I can remember where we stood as we spoke. The image of her living room comes back to me, small, dark, and oppressively hot, the attempts to cool it with drawn window blinds and whirring floor fans only partly successful. The noise made by the rickety fans masked the content of our conversation to anyone else in her family who happened to be there at the time.

I remember being scared by what Alice told me, so scared I was almost frozen with horror and dread. Her story also had the quality of furtiveness, like an important secret: something you wouldn't talk about with others because it was so far removed from normal, everyday life. I can't remember whether or not I asked my parents to verify her story, nor, if I did, what they said in response to me, their seven-year-old daughter. This was only twelve years after the end of World War II, and the issues surrounding the Holocaust were so new they were raw: tending to them at all reopened the wounds and hurt. What is so amazing about our sense of fear at age seven was that neither Alice nor I had close relatives who were killed in the Holocaust: we simply identified with the experience as Jews. Perhaps we absorbed the unspoken horror that our parents must have been experiencing.

Not until our Bunting group discussed these issues did I realize that my early exposure to information about the Holocaust was insidiously formative for my sense of self. More important, this was probably true of all American Jews born in the 1940s and 1950s. In fact, most of the Jewish women writing for this book learned about the Holocaust and about hatred directed against Jews at very young and impressionable ages. Some learned about these things in secretive ways. Our families reeled from the atrocities of the Holocaust and often would not speak of what had happened, but the knowledge filtered down anyway, through the media and, as in my case, through peers, who revealed the horrors of what had transpired. These early experiences resemble a "vicarious victimization" experience in that we so closely identified with the victims of abuse ("this could have happened to me") that we experienced feelings of terror that recur and continue to pervade our relationships with others.

The non-Jewish women, too, learned about the Holocaust at young and impressionable ages. Sometimes the information seemed unreal and weirdly fascinating in the way that horror often is; it was a way of learning about the reality of evil. At other times the events of the Holocaust were too distant to be of much personal significance. To most of the non-Jewish Fellows, learning about the Holocaust shaped their vision and understanding of what it means to be Jewish. The Holocaust helped them understand why Jews feel fearful, an emotion that they view as otherwise inexplicable in the light of the very solid middle-class status that Jews have achieved in this country.

Feeling Different

The Holocaust in and of itself would be enough to introduce a sense of wariness and fear, as well as despair, into the lives of Jews. But it must be considered against the backdrop of a long history of being hated and stereotyped in negative ways, a hatred that has taken various forms at various times, such as pogroms and the Crusades, to name two. What all these various forms of hatred have in common is the intent to either convert Jews to other religions, or in more recent history, to annihilate the Jewish people. Apparently, being different is painful not just to the ones who are "other," but to the majority, the ones who set the standard for what "difference" is.

It is never easy to be a member of a minority group. Jews are a minority both in numbers (constituting only 2.5 percent of the American population, and ⅓ of 1 percent of the world population) as well as in the nature of the hatred directed against them and the oppression they have experienced. Peter Langman, in an article on Jews and multiculturalism,[1] makes the point that if the world population were reduced to 1,000, there would be 331 Christians and only three Jews. Moreover, although America is 83 percent white, it is 95 percent Christian, making Judaism a more uncommon phenomenon than non-whiteness.

Despite their long history of persecution (or, as Alan Dershowitz[2] points out, perhaps because of this history of persecution, which often forced Jews to band together against a common enemy), Jews have survived and thrived for four thousand years. Max Dimont, in his best-selling book, *Jews, God and History*, writes that "the Jews are heard of totally out of proportion to their small numbers. No less than 12 percent of all the Nobel prizes in physics, chemistry, and medicine have gone to Jews. The Jewish contribution to the world's list of great names in religion, science, literature, music, finance, and philosophy is staggering." Such a history of accomplishment is a source of pride for Jews, as is their historical and current commitment to social activism and ethical behavior.

But being a member of a small minority group can also be painful, sometimes even shameful. Modern Jews live with a conscious experience of being "different" and vulnerable. Many live with the conviction that persecution will return, as it has so often in the past. Some cope with these fears by hiding their Jewishness to public eyes; others also try to hide it from themselves, perhaps going so far as to convert or to raise their children with no sense of their Jewish history.

For my parents' World War II generation, American anti-Semitism was a powerful social force that placed restrictions on where they could live, study, and work. Being Jewish meant not being admitted to colleges and medical schools because of a religious quota system. It also meant not being allowed to buy houses in certain neighborhoods. And, perhaps most important, it meant not fully being a man in America, in that you could not aim for the same positions of power that non-Jewish white men could take for granted. When combined with the Holocaust, the effects of this anti-Semitism were to encourage Jews to assimilate, minimizing their Jewishness, sometimes attempting to "pass" as non-Jews. Changing your name to make it sound non-Jewish and to avoid anti-Semitism was commonplace. My mother's maiden name was Davidowitz, and her two brothers, without consulting each other, changed their names to Davis and Davids, a fact that to this day makes my mother angry and sad. "They couldn't even choose the same name for the family," she mourns.

My parents, I think, typify others of their generation, in that they both grew up in religious homes, children of Russian and Polish immigrants who fled Eastern Europe because of the pogroms there. My parents' connection to their Judaism underwent many transformations as they themselves came of age. Despite, or perhaps because of, his religious background, my father had no use for organized religion of any kind. His disaffection for organized religion may have been due partly to his agnostic beliefs, but it also arose from his feeling that organized religions carried with them a history of fomenting hatred and promulgating murder and strife (particularly against the Jews). Such a view is not uncommon among secular Jews. My father substituted a humanistic philosophy for religion. One of the most helpful things he taught me, for example, was that "people are people" no matter what their race or religion. For him, emphasizing the humanity common to all people was a preferable alternative to the divisive boundaries organized religions have created throughout much of history.

Despite his antipathy to organized religion, my father was full of ambivalence about Judaism. For example, to this day he fasts on Yom Kippur to atone for his sins and to cleanse his soul for the New Year. But he never goes into a temple if he can help it, unless it is to attend a wedding or a bar mitzvah. He believed that my sister and I should not receive a formal Jewish education because of his feelings about organized religion, so we didn't.

My mother mildly protested his adamant stance, but probably because we were girls, and therefore not expected to receive religious training to the extent that boys were, her protests were neither very serious nor very effective. She herself had grown up in a religious home but had not received extensive religious training because she was a girl. As an adult, she tried to reteach herself the rudimentary Hebrew she had learned in high school as a way of feeling part of a community, but I'm not sure she ever fully succeeded. Like my father, she taught my sister and me the importance of compassion (partly just by modeling it herself) and the usefulness of understanding the basic human motives and needs that drive all people's behaviors, regardless of their religion. These ethical lessons were often given in the form of personal stories she would recount about people she worked with, or grew up with, or went to school with, stories that captured people's foibles and troubles and took on a vivid life of their own.

The upshot of all the intergenerational issues surrounding Judaism that my parents inherited and struggled with was that I did not receive a Jewish education, and so I did not feel particularly Jewish, nor did I learn much about the formal aspects of the religion. To this day, my failure to learn Hebrew and to have a complete knowledge of holidays and rituals makes me feel somehow left out of the Jewish community. On the other hand, my parents celebrated some of the more popular Jewish holidays, including Passover, Rosh Hashanah, Yom Kippur, and Chanukah, and occasionally made a Sabbath dinner, all of which felt special and a part of my world. I also absorbed and felt proud of Jewish values: an emphasis on education, intellectual achievement and curiosity, family closeness, social activism, and tolerance for others.

However, looking back I can see more clearly that my parents' attempts to assimilate, common among their generation, made me more, rather than less, ambivalent and confused about who I was. Because I had no exposure to a formal Jewish community taking pride in its heritage, nor to the spiritual and intellectual underpinnings of Judaism, I was left to define Judaism in the way the majority defined it, internalizing all of the negative stereotypes about Jews that I was exposed to.

How has this affected me? For one, I almost never reveal that I am Jewish to a non-Jewish audience without some trepidation about the response that will ensue: will they hate me, immediately pigeonhole me with negative stereotypes, or worse, will they hurt me?

I was moved to tears recently because I witnessed in my Jewish college students similar needs to hide their Jewish identity. I teach a course on the Psychology of the Family at Boston University, which has an

enrollment of about one hundred students, and I invited a guest lecturer to talk about ethnicity and the family. She started the lecture by
asking for students in the course, mostly junior and senior psychology
majors, to shout out their ethnic backgrounds. "Irish, Italian, Pakistani;
Colombian; Greek; Irish-Catholic, African American; Latina . . ." Probably fifteen different ethnic backgrounds were called out in a few seconds. But no Jews called out, although there were probably more than
ten in the class, and despite the fact that the lecturer had made it clear
that religion, like country of origin, could constitute an ethnicity. After
a few minutes, she queried, "Are there any people of Jewish descent
here?" Several students silently nodded. She and I talked afterward
about how shocking it was that the Jewish students needed to hide their
heritage and did not feel they could shout it out like everyone else. That
this was true in Boston University, known to have a large Jewish student
population, makes it even more likely to be true elsewhere. I have since
given the same lecture to three different classes at BU, and each time I
get the same reaction: the Jewish students do not identify themselves.
When this happened for the third time in a course I was teaching in the
fall of 1995, I unwittingly started to cry, silently waiting for at least one
Jewish student to speak out. Not one did. I could not stand the unspoken pain of my Jewish students' need to hide their identity, a pain I
shared, when most of the other students were being so open.

Hiding one's Jewish identity is nothing new for Jews: admitting to
being Jewish has often been foolhardy and perhaps dangerous in certain contexts. "Passing" or hiding one's Jewishness has historically been
a way of gaining social status and avoiding hatred, discrimination, and
even murder. What is noteworthy, however, is that hiding and passing,
and the conflicted feelings that accompany such processes, are still
going on, despite an American multicultural "revolution" in which ethnic minority groups are encouraged to celebrate their "otherness." Jews
have become, or perhaps always were, the "silent" minority in the multicultural revolution.

Some of the Jewish fellows writing for the book do not seem conflicted or scared about openly acknowledging their Jewishness. On the
contrary, for them, being Jewish is such a rich source of pride that they
find it easy to speak out as Jews. I marvel at these women, at their
brazenness; I envy their ability to be open. I wonder where it comes
from: Did they have more formal religious training than I did, which
was a greater source of solidarity and identity? Did that somehow em-
power them to "come out"? Is it easier to be Jewish when you are recog-

nizably Jewish, and therefore cannot hide? My frequent nonacknowledgment of my Judaism is made easier by the fact that I do not look stereotypically Jewish, especially to non-Jews. I am ashamed to admit that I have often considered it a compliment when some people exclaim, on learning that I am Jewish, "Oh, you don't look Jewish at all." (Of course, the implication is that looking Jewish is somehow unattractive.) My last name sounds Irish, although in fact it is a non-Anglicized name, the name of the town in Eastern Europe from which my grandparents originated. (The town of Brody is currently in Poland, although at the time my grandparents emigrated here it was apparently within Russian borders. It was in a geographic area to which Jews were restricted, known as the Pale of Settlement.)

When I was young, even in elementary school, I remember feeling grateful not to have a stereotypically Jewish last name, like Greenberg, because I assumed that with a name like Brody, people would not stereotype me in negative ways so quickly. I naively assumed that in being identified as Irish, I would not be judged on the basis of predetermined stereotypes, but on the basis of how I acted. In actuality, an Irish ethnicity is associated with an entirely different set of assumptions from those of a Jewish one, but they are assumptions nonetheless. It's hard to escape from being categorized.

I have, to a large extent, internalized some of the negative stereotypes that adhere to Jews, constantly struggling to maintain an awareness that I'm doing so. In fact, psychological research[3] suggests that if I had more of an identification with Judaism, I might feel better about myself and about my fellow Jews. A strong minority identity allows people to use self-protective strategies and sometimes to overvalue the attributes of their own group, while at the same time devaluing the attributes of the majority.

The Power of Anti-Semitism

I first realized that there was anti-Semitism in America when I left my predominantly Jewish elementary school to attend a religiously mixed junior high school. Many of the children there came from an exclusive and upper-middle-class section of New York City called Douglaston Manor. Although this community was only one or two miles away from my own almost exclusively Jewish neighborhood, it was commonly known that no Jews were allowed to buy houses there at the time. This did not escape my attention, and at the tender age of eleven or twelve, I began to feel both angry and bitter not only about how Jews were treated, but sometimes about having been born Jewish at all. Had I not been born Jewish, I wouldn't have had these feelings, I thought. On the other hand, there was a certain righteous indignation and sense of moral superiority I had toward the non-Jews in my class. They were immoral and I was not. I would throw this up to them on occasion. I guess I felt safe enough to do that.

Going to college, Cornell University, was another experience entirely. Although there were many Jewish students there, there were also many non-Jews. And many of them made anti-Semitic remarks to me, sometimes not knowing that I was Jewish. Many students would use the phrase "jew you down" to mean unfair and cheap bargaining. Once, when a student was confronted with how offensive the phrase was, she said, "Oh, okay. Jewish you down. Is that better?" Another student, a friend of mine who was Catholic, came home from a disappointing and frustrating meeting and said to me, "Oh, the meeting was worthless. Jews and cripples—that's who turned out." (One of the participants in the meeting had attended with a broken leg.) When I confronted her with how hurtful the comment was to me, she replied that in her family, Jews were considered inferior to Catholics and were always put down. She hadn't thought much about the significance of her statement until I brought it to her attention.

When I experience anti-Semitism, I feel a mixture of things: rage, confusion, awkwardness, and fear. Often acquaintances share anti-Semitic remarks with me, not knowing that I am Jewish. They believe us to be in a secret conspiracy, bonded by our common superiority to Jews. I am often at a loss in the face of such behavior. I weigh alternative consequences. What will they do if I confront them? Do I tell them I'm Jewish and hope they won't hate me? Or do I hide and harbor a secret knowledge about them that they didn't know they were revealing? How will I feel about myself if I choose to hide? How do I handle my contempt and anger toward them? Defeated by the very questions themselves, I usually wind up letting anti-Semitic remarks pass without confrontation, sometimes simply because it is easier for me. As a well-socialized American female, I have learned and overlearned the lesson that it is best to avoid confrontation and friction; I invariably try to smooth out relationships. But this strategy has had its costs: I am often in a great deal of internal conflict, and frequently I berate myself after the fact.

As the essays by the Jewish women document, anti-Semitism is very much a reality in the United States. Perhaps not institutionalized anti-

Semitism as was commonplace in the 1950s, since Jews are no longer openly prevented from working or living in certain areas, nor are they actively excluded from university admissions. (Although some would argue that the geographic diversity that some universities aim for in their admissions process works to discriminate against Jewish students.) But anti-Semitism in social and interpersonal relationships continues to exist: negative stereotypes about Jews abound; the idea of a Jewish American president is still unthinkable; Jews are still excluded from certain private clubs; and the Jewish American Princess stereotype actively haunts and demeans Jewish women.

Perhaps more important, because of their history of persecution, some Jews see anti-Semitism lurking around every corner. Growing up in the wake of the Holocaust, many Jews report that the unspoken question they ask themselves when interacting with a non-Jew is, "Would she or he have saved me from the Nazis?" I have asked myself this question innumerable times: sometimes I surprise myself by answering, "I don't know," when asking this question of a non-Jewish friend I had otherwise assumed was close to me. The answer is the ultimate standard by which to measure trust in a non-Jewish person. Many Jews believe that most non-Jewish Americans (or non-Jewish people of any nationality, for that matter) are anti-Semitic. The Israeli novelist Amos Oz writes about his experiences growing up in Jerusalem: "Microbes were one of our biggest horrors. They were like anti-Semitism: nobody actually saw them but everybody sensed them lurking everywhere."

And, in fact, the non-Jewish women writing in *Daughters of Kings* confess to encountering anti-Semitism in their own worlds as they were growing up. One Fellow recalls taunting Jewish children because she learned that they had killed Christ. Another, growing up in the Bible Belt, describes her Christian friend not being allowed to sleep overnight at a Jewish friend's home. Other non-Jewish women express surprise, doubt, or pain at the extent of the anti-Semitism reported by Jewish women, either because they do not see themselves as anti-Semitic, or because they perceive Jews to be financially successful and assimilated into the American mainstream.

Lest anyone doubt that private anti-Semitism still exists, as some of the non-Jewish Fellows did when this project began, let me share some of the more recent anti-Semitic remarks I have been privy to. I am always shocked by these remarks, no matter how many I hear. I assume that for every anti-Semitic remark I hear, there are undoubtedly many more said in private among non-Jews.

My husband and I were recently entertaining a couple from India, who apparently did not realize we were Jewish. We were discussing a well-known, somewhat histrionic person in a very negative light. The husband of the couple we were entertaining said, "Well, you know what his background is, don't you?" "No, what?" we asked innocently. "Oh, I hear he's one-quarter Jewish or something like that," he said lightly, as if that explained the person's erratic behavior fully.

The second anti-Semitic incident concerns a friend of mine who is an experienced psychotherapist, someone who is highly educated and whose work I respect a great deal. She was raised Catholic, along with her sister, and recently found out that her maternal grandmother was probably Jewish, a fact she was pleased to learn, as she was married to a Jewish man. However, she told me, "I couldn't possibly tell my sister that she was Jewish. She couldn't take it. It would be too stressful." (According to Jewish law, her sister is actually Jewish because anyone with a Jewish mother is Jewish.) "Would it be stressful for people to find out that they were Jewish?" I asked, astonished. She made it sound like it was the equivalent of finding out your parent had murdered someone. "Oh yes," she said, "my sister would be so ashamed." Her feelings, and my strong reaction to them, were an unintended consciousness-raising experience for both of us.

Yet another incident concerns a passing remark made to a Jewish friend of mine who has an Italian last name because she is married to an Italian man. (The assumption strangers make about her is that she is not Jewish, although there are in fact Italian Jews.) We both live in a community that in the past has had few Jews, but to which increasing numbers are moving. A neighbor said to her, "There are too many Jews moving here. The community is changing." He advised her not to vote for the Jewish man who was running for town selectman.

The feelings that non-Jews harbor about Jews in my New England town may actually be a microcosm of what exists on a more national level. For many years at Christmas, a crèche complete with Virgin Mary and Baby Jesus has been displayed on public land, the town green. This has been a sore point with Jewish town residents for many years because it seemingly violates the separation of church and state and imparts a message of exclusivity to non-Christian groups. It would not be offensive to Jews if the crèche were publicly displayed on church property, supported with private monies. The controversy over this issue has become quite heated within the last two years and has been aired publicly in the local town newspaper. While some non-Jews have agreed that this religious symbol does not belong on town land, others have vociferously disagreed. The first spate of letters written to the editor tended to be thoughtful and reasonable. The next set, however, quickly deteriorated, giving way to name-calling and divisive attacks. Just this year a non-Jewish resident questioned in his letter to the editor whether a tyranny of the minority (namely, Jews) existed in the town.

Anti-Semitism also takes the guise that Jews have certain negative stereotypic "traits" that are internal and possibly genetic. This is an idea that has been historically commonplace. The idea continues to exist even among Jews themselves. I recently reviewed textbooks for potential assignment in my course the Psychology of the Family, and one of the books, published in 1993, had a chapter on ethnicity and families. It discussed Irish American families, Italian American families, Chinese American families, and Jewish American families. I was happy to see the chapter in the table of contents because so many psychology textbooks ignore the power of culture and ethnicity in shaping our family lives. To my dismay, the subheading for Jewish American families was "Jewish Traits," referring to family values and an emphasis on education and achievement. When discussing the values and characteristics of other ethnic groups, the word *trait* was never used. Even though the book referred to positive values and characteristics among Jews, it was disconcerting to see values and motives subsumed under the word *trait*, implying some immutable disposition that Jewish people have in contrast to other ethnic groups. Furthermore, many traditional, long-standing values of Jews, including the emphasis on social activism and charity toward others, were underemphasized.

Anti-Semitism and Jewish Women

Anti-Semitism directed against Jewish women is so commonplace as to be hardly noticed. It is well known that on many college campuses, Jewish female students are labeled as "JAPs," Jewish American Princesses, a pejorative term meaning that they are spoiled, entitled, and demanding. They exist only to find the Jewish Prince Charming, preferably a physician, who will marry them and take care of them. This is a demeaning and insulting stereotype, one I have often heard Jewish women use to characterize themselves or other Jews. In fact, when I was a college student, many Jewish men would not date Jewish women, because they felt they were too "JAPPY"—they wanted "down-to-earth" WASP women, who didn't remind them of their own minority status.

And not only does the label *JAP* exist on college campuses, but you can also hear it almost anywhere. I was recently in a women's clothing store, searching through the racks of clothing for some appropriate gift, when a woman emerged from the dressing room, displaying the outfit she was trying on to a male friend who was waiting outside. He looked her up and down. "No, it looks too JAPPY," he declared. She looked down. "Yeah, you're right," she said. "Especially these sequins." There was an immediate common understanding and acceptance of what the term *JAPPY* meant. Was this couple Jewish? Maybe, maybe not.

That the term *JAP* is such an accepted part of American vocabulary attests to how widespread, often unconscious, and socially acceptable anti-Semitism is. It is hard to think of an equivalent ethnic or racial slur used to describe another ethnic group that does not immediately brand its user as racist. In contrast, somehow saying, "She's a JAP," is considered okay in common parlance.

In an astute analysis, Rachel Siegel,[4] a psychologist, argues that the devaluation and negative stereotypes of Jewish women, including both the JAP label as well as our stereotypes of Jewish mothers, are sexist caricatures of the traditional roles assigned to all women. In particular, ambition, self-assertion, and aggression, seen as inappropriate traits for *all* American women, are labeled as "Jewish" female traits. Moreover, the stereotypical overprotective and intrusive Jewish mother is really just an extreme form of the limited traditional role assigned to all American mothers. Protecting children, a longstanding role for all women, may have been especially adaptive for Jewish mothers in the face of the historical persecution their families suffered. Stereotyping Jewish mothers' protectiveness as "overprotectiveness" may have been a way for immigrant children, particularly sons, to distance themselves from their mothers in an effort to assimilate into mainstream America.

As Siegel writes, both JAP and Jewish mother caricatures allow us to overlook "the humanity, the dignity, the suffering, and the individuality of the real woman." The Jewish American Princess stereotype flies in the face of massive evidence of the accomplishments and political activism of Jewish women. In particular, two of the leaders of the feminist movement in the United States, Betty Friedan and Gloria Steinem, have Jewish backgrounds. Furthermore, the Jewish American Princess stereotype ignores the diversity of social class experiences among American Jews, stereotyping all Jewish women as rich and privileged, a stereotype far from accurate.

In another analysis of the Jewish American stereotype, Evelyn Torton Beck[5] reasons that the stereotype derives from the anti-Semitic images once ascribed to Jewish men, including being "manipulative, calculating, avaricious, materialistic, sexually perverse, ugly (hook-nosed) and foreign in speech." She writes: "The litany of historical accusations against Jews here takes on a decidedly 'female' cast, and the Jewish woman as J.A.P—'a Shylock in drag'—is made to carry the burden. . . ." Both by excluding men and by using the word *JAP* (with its Asian implications, rather than explicitly using the word *Jew*), the stereotype has become socially acceptable, and its anti-Semitic and dehumanizing aspects have been largely unrecognized in popular culture. Beck recounts a chilling series of episodes in the 1980s and 1990s on college campuses involving the Jewish American Princess stereotype, in which Jewish women were either publicly humiliated (being the objects of finger-pointing accompanied by shouts of "JAP—JAP—JAP") at a football game at Syracuse University, or in which they were the object of allegedly humorous jokes and songs centering on the extermination of JAPS, some of which appeared on a national talk show.

Jews Internalize Anti-Semitic Stereotypes

Unfortunately, many Jews internalize the anti-Semitic stereotypes that are part of the common parlance in the culture. Siegel describes how Jewish women defend against anti-Semitic stereotypes by avoiding women whom they perceive to personify "JAPpiness," by rejecting their Jewish backgrounds, or by overtly distancing from the image of themselves as "Jewish mothers," stating, "I'm not like that. I'm not that kind of Jewish mother."[6]

As the social psychologist Kurt Lewin,[7] writing in the 1940s, eloquently put it, Jews begin to see "things Jewish with the eyes of the unfriendly majority." In fact, more than one of the non-Jewish contributors to *Daughters of Kings* point out that they originally heard the term *JAP* from Jewish women themselves, who categorized other Jewish women in this demeaning way. This name-calling most likely stems from Jews being overly sensitive to and rejecting of "offensive" behavior in themselves and other Jews. It may be that they begin to imagine characteristics that don't really exist, a process first described by Lewin.

I am reminded here of a conversation I had with a Jewish friend, who is a physician and quite religious. We were discussing biological versus environmental causes of behavior, and she told me she thought that Jewish aggression was genetic. "Jewish aggression?!" I said, stunned. "What are you talking about? You don't really think Jews are more aggressive than other people, do you?" I asked. She was surprised that I had actually questioned this: It was a stereotype she had taken for granted. Not only did she believe that Jewish people were more aggressive than others (and there are absolutely no data to support such a belief), but somehow she had determined that the cause of this difference was biological and, in her mind, immutable. That she, an educated person, could have internalized such a negative stereotype suggests that such internalization may be commonplace. There is a saying that if you repeatedly broadcast lies, they become truths.

In an all-too-clear example of Jewish self-derogation and distancing from the "offensive" behaviors of other Jews, one of the Jewish residents in my town recently wrote an apologetic and disheartening letter to the editor of the town newspaper. He was seeking to respond to the controversy over having a crèche displayed on public property. After identifying himself as Jewish, he derogated the motives of his fellow Jews for wanting the crèche removed, labeling them elitist and self-serving, and asked his neighbors' forgiveness for other Jews' objections.

Psychologists point out that people not only come to believe what others say about them, but that they come to act in ways that are consistent with those beliefs: the "self-fulfilling prophecy" theory. Or they may attempt to overcome a stereotype by bending over backward and acting in an opposite way in order to prove the stereotype wrong. This may actually be quite self-defeating. For example, my friend confessed that she had not gone to her child's teacher to complain about something happening in the classroom because she did not want to be viewed as an "aggressive Jew." This was clearly not in the best interests of her child.

Blaming the Victim

Recently, I was painfully reminded of the all too common tendency to blame the Jews for their long history of being persecuted. I read about Steven Spielberg's movie *Schindler's List*, which was being shown to Japanese schoolchildren in an effort to educate them. The movie, a gripping and moving portrayal of some aspects of the Holocaust, gives no sense of German history before World War II. When a young Japanese adolescent saw the film, she said, "I'd like to know what the Jews did to deserve such treatment." That was her reaction to the film—that the Jews must have done something; that this couldn't just have happened to an innocent people. In fact, it's entirely possible that many Christians around the world still believe that Jews deserve death, either because they didn't accept Jesus' teachings or, worse, because they were taught that Jews were responsible for killing Jesus, a belief that ignores the historical complexities of that time. Perhaps it is unthinkable to most people that evil would happen for no reason at all: that an entire group of people would be hated just for being different, not because they were inherently inferior or bad. A less generous interpretation is that if people stop blaming victims, then they are obligated to act for justice. Seeking justice is a risky and time-consuming process. It is a process that may also involve some painful feelings, in that the persecutors may be forced to reevaluate their view of themselves, seeing themselves in a more negative light. Few people volunteer to participate in painful processes.

I think Jews take on the attitude of "victim-blaming" as well, searching for clues as to why there is such a long history of anti-Semitism. Often, Jews are uneasy about calling too much attention to themselves or becoming too visible as a group. They worry that their successes and their obvious presence may result in victimization. One example of this is the worry that some Jews feel about the placement of the Holocaust Memorial Museum in Washington, D.C. They fear—rightly or wrongly—that the attention paid to the Jews because of the national visibility of the museum will eventually backfire and worsen anti-Semitic discrimination.

Sometimes Jews' explanations for why they are so negatively stereotyped gets turned into a positive attribute: "People hate us because we're smarter and more successful than most people, and they're envious of us," I've heard many Jews say. Although these arguments may indeed have some merit statistically, they are the equivalent of saying that there are in fact reasons Jews are hated, only they're good reasons instead of bad. They sidestep the real issue, which is that people learn to hate Jews simply because they are Jews, a vulnerable minority group. It's easier and safer to blame a minority than to blame someone in power for everything that's wrong. Freud, an expert on anti-Semitism, taught us that it makes you feel better about yourself if you can feel superior to someone. As one of my Irish friends said to me about the history of anti-Semitism, "It's always the same story. Whenever anything goes wrong, blame the Jews." And Kurt Lewin said, "It has been recognized long ago that the basis of anti-Semitism is partly the need of the majority for a scapegoat."

Because majority groups are taught not to identify with Jews, but to treat us as "the other," they cannot identify with Jews when Jews are professionally or financially successful. In contrast, when a Protestant, for example, is successful, fellow Protestants can partially "own" the success, or view an equivalent success as possible for themselves. When a Jew is successful, majority groups can only be rueful, furious, or envious, because there is no basis for identification. By virtue of being seen as "different," Jews are seen as competitors, not as fellow sisters or brothers.

White and Jewish

Because we are mostly white, American Jews are in undefined territory: on the one hand, identified as part of the white majority, not currently experiencing much discrimination and persecution, yet, on the other hand, having a history of experiences as the "other" that has marked us out for special, often horrifying treatment. This is a tough situation. Jews' pain as a minority group is frequently unacknowledged and delegitimized.

In a social science and political context, minority refers to those who are disempowered—who not only have relatively less status and power than does the majority, but who also have less *access* to power and money than does the majority. So the American government includes under this category women and those of African American, Hispanic, Asian American, or Native American descent. It does so mostly as a way of addressing the inequities in economic opportunities that have plagued these particular minority groups. This system of categorization is done primarily for economic and political purposes, such as affirmative action policies, which I believe continue to be necessary in order to redress the longstanding underrepresentation of some minority groups in critical areas of American life. However, the failure to acknowledge the minority status of Jews has not only political, but also psychological consequences. Jews are left out: their minority status becomes inconsequential to others, although it is just as real. It is, in fact, arguable whether American Jews have historically had equal access to money, status, and power in this country. More important, Jews are privy to all of the psychological effects of being members of a minority group: the feeling of being different and of being treated differently by others, sometimes in subtly, and sometimes in openly, contemptuous ways.

The difficulty in defining precisely what Judaism is has perhaps contributed to the sense that Jews should be viewed as part of the white majority. Classification systems that attempt to categorize ethnic or racial groups are notoriously uncomfortable with ambiguity. As any Jew knows, Judaism is more than a religion. In fact, many American Jews are secular, meaning that they are not members of a temple or religious body. Moreover, not believing in God does not exempt one from being Jewish, and in some sense, even converting to another religion does not change the fact that one was Jewish by birth, leaving a lingering sense of a "different" identity. At times, Judaism has been incorrectly defined as a "race," an argument that has been mostly used to serve political ends. As Langman points out, Judaism is not a race: there are African American Jews, Asian Jews, even Native American Jews. What comes closest to a valid definition is that Judaism constitutes a shared identity, history, and system of values, unconstrained by racial and national boundaries. The very nature of this definition is so ambiguous and imprecise that it is perhaps easier to consider Jews as "white," consistent with their largely European origins.

The assumption in America that to be Jewish is to be white and therefore, by extension, to feel okay, has affected the way in which modern psychologists view the Jewish experience. Self-hatred, fear, and the effects of the minority experience for Jews are not popular research topics among modern-day psychologists. I did a recent survey of a computerized psychology database, entering *Jewish* as the keyword. There were 616 entries since 1974. This is a relatively small number of studies compared to other minority groups I looked at. For example, the number of studies on African Americans since 1974 was over 5,000; on Asian Americans it was well over 1,200. What's especially interesting about this is that most of the studies on minority groups are relatively recent, representing long overdue attention given to the diversity of the groups being studied within psychology. The increasing numbers of women and minority groups who have become part of the academic establishment have put pressure on the psychological community to do studies that include people like themselves, namely women and minorities. These groups have not been able to find their own experiences mirrored in the psychological research literature, which has up until only recently been based on white males.

A sampling of the current computer entries on psychology research with Jews indicates that the studies tend to be of three types: the inter-generational effects of being a Holocaust survivor; various aspects of psychological functioning using Israeli people as the subjects in the study, but not focusing on their Judaism as the primary issue; and case studies of Jewish patients in psychotherapy. In fact, the large number of studies about Jews in psychotherapy contrasts dramatically with the dearth of case studies about other minority groups in psychotherapy. This speaks to several issues: the continuing issue of the effects of the trauma of the Holocaust on Jews; the high percentage of Jews who are in the mental health field, both as practitioners and as patients; and perhaps a subtle message that views Jews through the lens of pathology rather than mental health. Furthermore, it is individual pathology that is emphasized, not the effects of minority status on Jews as a group.

Almost never is there an assumption underlying recent psychological studies that minority status in and of itself may have powerful effects on the Jewish experience. Notable exceptions are recent works by a few feminist Jews, who write about the ongoing effects of anti-Semitism as well as of traditional Jewish values on the psyches of Jewish women.[8,9] I also found a recent unique, somewhat surprising paper[10] that looked at the citation patterns of published social science research and documented the fact that those researchers with noticeably Jewish last names more frequently cited others who also had noticeably Jewish last names; whereas researchers with non-Jewish sounding last names less frequently cited others who were recognizably Jewish. This pattern occurred not just for people citing the work of others whose research areas differed from their own, but also for people citing the work of others whose research area was the same as their own, namely work on prejudice. This paper speaks to the process of favoring those with whom you share an ethnic identity. On a darker note, it may speak to the ongoing effects of anti-Semitism.

Just by chance, I came across a psychology research paper published in 1980, titled "Ethnic and Social Class Differences in Children's Sex-Role Concepts."[11] The authors of the study compared African, Jewish, and Italian American children's concepts of stereotypic male and female sex roles, including how competent they felt themselves to be in their own roles. As consistent with my argument about the negative effects of minority status, Jewish children described themselves as not very competent compared to the other two ethnic groups, a result the authors attribute to the long history of discrimination against the Jews. Yet these results were buried deep within the details of the paper and were never mentioned in the abstract, the part of the article that would most likely be read by other researchers. Perhaps because the results were not widely publicized, subsequent studies did not pursue these provocative results. Although the paper focused on feelings of incompetence among Jewish children, it is likely that Jews have developed not only weaknesses, but also strengths because of their minority status, processes not acknowledged by most current psychology researchers.

In most recent popular psychology writings, especially in the family therapy literature, Judaism is considered an "ethnicity," along with groups such as Italian Americans, Irish Americans, and even white Anglo-Saxon Protestants. It is certainly acknowledged that as an ethnic group, Jews have a long-standing history of persecution, which has affected their values and attitudes. But there is a subtle lack of emphasis on how Jews' current status as a minority group is of the utmost importance in understanding their lives and relationships. In contrast, the vast majority of psychological writings about other minority groups work with the basic assumption that the fact of being a minority is one of the primary determinants of identity and adjustment. This contrast is dramatic: it is clear that Jews are thought to blend in with the white majority.

It is perhaps good news that Jews have become part of the huge "melting pot," no longer considered different enough to be worthy of study. But the news is deceptive, because hatred against Jews and negative Jewish stereotypes are still rampant and insidious, making Jews very much a minority. We are left with a paradox: Jews want to be part of the majority, to avoid discrimination, yet they share the experiences and feelings of other minority groups, without any social or legal recognition that minority status is important for understanding a major part of the Jewish experience. Where does this leave us as Jews? Often with painful feelings that have no outlet, which are never legitimized.

Jews and Multiculturalism

I am frequently in a great deal of conflict when I am invited to attend psychology workshops on multicultural issues in personality and psychotherapy, because almost never do these include the Jewish experience.

"Wait," I want to shout to the panel of experts at one of these workshops, "why haven't you included Jews? We are a minority group, too, and we have a history of suffering and oppression just as you do." But another part of me, calm and logical, says, "Be quiet. You are white, after all." The last thing I want, surely, is to start a competition for which group has been more oppressed. Mostly what I am yearning for is some recognition of shared suffering. A different part of me, frightened, knows that I would have to stand up as a Jew in a forum of people who might not have positive feelings toward Jews, an ironic feeling in the context of a multicultural setting. So I do not shout out loud, but contain my anger and my fear, which fester within. This ambivalence and my tendency to cope by staying silent are so familiar to me that they have become a painful part of my identity, part of what it means for me to be Jewish.

The irony about all of this, in fact, is that for me as well as for others, a Jewish identity often results in shared empathy for minority suffering and a commitment to working for equal rights. When I was growing up, I read an enormous amount of literature about slavery and American blacks, and both identified with them and advocated for them. In high school I spent many hours volunteering and working with inner-city black children. Did they know I was Jewish? Probably not. Only that I was white. Kathleen Cleaver, also a Fellow during the 1994–1995 Bunting year, shared with me her surprise when she learned that about half of the civil rights workers with whom she had worked closely in the 1960s were Jewish. Again, Jews who considered it irrelevant, difficult, or perhaps even dangerous to speak out as Jews.

The other paradox inherent in the "white and Jewish" issue is that some liberal Jews, who have sometimes worked so hard for civil rights, have at times been afraid to champion Jewish causes and have been in the position of actually denying their importance. This was especially true for those of us who were politically active in the 1960s. Students on campuses all across the country were mobilizing for civil rights and against the war in Vietnam. In the Middle East the Palestinians were seen as the minority group needing support, and it was their cause, not the Israeli or Zionist cause, that was championed. Although Zionism and Judaism are not the same thing, to many non-Jewish Americans there is little difference. Many Jewish students were aware that if they had a Jewish identity, they would be earmarked by others as also being Zionist, and therefore as nonsympathetic to leftist, Palestinian causes.

The solution? Deny that Judaism was important to you; deny that it was at all part of your identity. And many of my friends did just that. They denied their Jewish heritage and deliberately took the route of castigating Israel and Israeli society, regardless of the specific issues. This was an issue I tended to watch from the sidelines, but I remember feeling simultaneously angry with and compassionate toward my friends who were caught up in anti-Zionist sentiments at the time.

Judaism and Feminism

In the 1960s, I was conflicted about two alternative dreams for my future: the stereotypic notion of the ideal Jewish woman, homemaker and mother, versus the vision of an independent woman, ambitious in her own right, a vision which emerged out of the feminist movement. I vividly remember being a sophomore, going out with a Jewish man who said to me, in all seriousness and with every good intention, "Why are you studying so hard? You need to have more of a social life. That's where your real life is going to be. You'll find when graduation comes around, your real priority will be finding a husband. It happens to all the women around here." Worse, when I interviewed for admittance to a prominent graduate school, the Jewish professor interviewing me said, "Oh, we like to take women students here. It gives the male professors good students who won't flood the job market. Most of the women will get married and won't be serious scholars anyway." I was enraged by this sexist remark and chose not to attend their program, although the program I chose to attend (at Harvard) was no better in how they treated their female students; just less open about their sexism.

Although these sexist values were imposed on all women in the 1950s and 1960s, not just on Jews, the Jewish emphasis on the importance of family, especially for women, made the issues personally burdensome. I felt like I was fighting not just institutions and male professors, but generations of family values. They were particularly embodied by my extended family members, who took years to broaden their vision about the role of women. My parents took great pride in my academic successes, but it was pride always overshadowed by concern that I should be married, too. Every conversation I had with my parents during my twenties had either the direct message or the indirect subtext that if I did not get married (and soon), I would be a failure in life. Even worse: my mother would be a failure too, for having an unmarried daughter. The simultaneous guilt and resentment I experienced in these conversations were almost too much to bear.

Most traditional Jewish writings and teachings consider women's roles to be family caretakers. Women have played a very marginal role in the formal aspects of religious services, which are traditionally male-oriented and male-dominated. In the Orthodox tradition, for example, women are literally not "counted" when it comes to constituting a "minyan," a ten-person minimum needed to engage in some religious services. Women are also not allowed to become rabbis in the Orthodox movement, and only recently have they been allowed to become rabbis in the Conservative movement. The morning prayer in the traditional prayer book includes thanking God for "not making me a woman." Because of the sexism inherent in the religion itself, Jewish women who are given a Jewish education are continually confronted with the dilemma of how to embrace a religion that formally excludes them. Some branches of Judaism, most notably the Reform and Reconstructionist movements, are currently seeking to transform the religion to make it less sexist, but long-standing patriarchal traditions have left an uncomfortable legacy for many Jewish women.

Some Jewish women, particularly baby boomers, were made to feel that Jewish sons were more valued and more precious in the eyes of their parents than were Jewish daughters. Sons were often revered and idealized, treated as special. They were educated when daughters were not, protected from the everyday drudgery of household responsibilities when daughters were not, and allowed many freedoms that daughters were not. Here again, Jews were probably no worse in their relative treatment of sons versus daughters than many other ethnic groups, in which preferential treatment of sons was socially acceptable. It is hard for some Jewish women to disentangle their experiences as Jewish daughters from their experiences as simply daughters, females in the larger American culture.

Identity and Being a Parent

My understanding of and relationship to Judaism underwent a radical transformation once I had children, as I was forced to decide what kind of religious identity I wanted to give to my children. Part of me felt that it would be a lot easier to raise my children as something other than

Jews. Why expose them to the suffering of being "different"? In fact, was religion necessary at all?

How to raise one's children, that is, whether or not to teach them to identify with Judaism, may be especially troublesome for Jewish women in light of the endless persecution to which Jews have been subjected. In a brilliant analysis, Sara Ruddick[12] discusses two of the primary goals of parenthood: (1) preserving the lives of one's children (that is, ensuring that they are safe), and (2) raising children who are socially acceptable to others, who will also be well liked. Raising children who identify with Judaism threatens the attainment of both of these goals. Jewish children may, in fact, not be safe or socially acceptable to others. This may put parents in a great deal of conflict: do you raise children in a manner that will best keep them safe, or do you raise Jewish children?

I was painfully reminded of these issues by two recent events in my own family. My six-year-old daughter, who is growing up in a predominantly non-Jewish neighborhood, came home from school one day in bewilderment. "Mommy," she said to me, "I asked in school for everyone who was Jewish to raise their hands, and only one other kid did! No one else is Jewish." Well, this is it, I thought. The dawning of the recognition that she is different. How will I tell her that there are people in the world who will hate her because she is Jewish, who will wish to see her dead? How does one tell children such things?

My innocent six-year-old daughter is, in fact, slowly integrating the news that Jews are not well liked. We recently attended a family reunion held on Ellis Island to commemorate the ninetieth anniversary of the family's arrival in America. A powerful family story told at the reunion was that our great-uncle had been killed in a pogrom in Russia when he was seventeen because he was Jewish. This incident had precipitated the family's decision to emigrate to America. At our reunion, we said a silent prayer in honor of this young man. What broke my heart, however, was that the next day my daughter came home from school and asked, "Did you know that Russia isn't the only country that hated Jews?" "What do you mean, sweetie?" I responded. "Well," she continued, "we learned about Christopher Columbus today, and he was from Spain, and Spain didn't like Jews either." In fact, Christopher Columbus set sail during the same time period that the Jews were expelled from Spain. How does this knowledge of global anti-Semitism impact my daughter's development? The thought frequently crosses my mind:

would I save her from suffering or hurt if I were to raise her as something other than Jewish?

One of my friends has, in fact, chosen to raise her children as non-Jews. Although she was raised with a Jewish education, she married a Catholic man and raised her own children as Presbyterians. Her children occasionally came home saying that they hated Jews on the basis of whatever sermon was being delivered that day by the minister. They didn't make the connection back to their mother, who almost never publicly admitted to being Jewish. Her mother-in-law, who lived with her, called her Jew-girl, and never let her forget that her successful son had married a Jew (supposedly, beneath him) when he didn't have to. I didn't know how she tolerated this treatment when I visited her; but then I realized how (or at least I think I did). In her mind, she was no longer Jewish. She said to me, "We had to pick a religion for our children. We didn't want to pick Jewish, because Jews think they're the chosen people or something. And Catholic, I just wasn't comfortable with it. So we picked Presbyterian. That was in between." Her children have no Jewish identity at all. Perhaps this is my friend's way of dealing with the fear that some form of Nazism will return. Her belief is that her children will be safe because they are Presbyterians, despite the fact that converts to Christianity remained Jews to their killers in the Nazi regime.

Embracing a religion different from that of your parents', and raising your children differently than the way you were raised may also be a way of asserting your independence from your parents. I have known many people who repudiated Judaism, or for that matter, other religions in which they were raised, because they felt religion was "forced" upon them by their parents. In other words, rejecting your parent's religion is one way of rejecting your parents themselves, of distancing from them. It may help to establish a separate identity, enabling you to feel better about yourself, even if you're not fully aware of why this is the case.

My fleeting thoughts about raising my own children as non-Jews could never be serious: although I am quite dubious about the value of formal religion in the same way that my father is, Judaism is not really a religion to me—it's a way of life. My fear and reservations about being Jewish are overshadowed by my pride in Judaism and its intellectual, social, and moral values, including its emphasis on social justice, tolerance, and the life of the mind. There is something else I have realized recently, too. Despite all of the negative stereotypes I have internalized about Jews, I feel a rich sense of connection to my fellow Jews. To leave

Judaism would be to abandon the meaningful legacy left to me by the many generations who preceded me, some of whom were killed for their beliefs. I also have come to believe that there is strength to be derived from the courage it takes to be different, a courage I am only now finding. I have heard some people use the term *pediatric Jew*, and in fact I feel that is what I have become: I am newly learning the lessons and strengths of Judaism through teaching them to my children.

My hope for my children is similar to something Kurt Lewin wrote: "Jewish self-hatred will die out only when actual equality of status with the non-Jew is achieved." He advises that children should be brought up in contact with Jewish life in such a way that "phrases like 'the person looks Jewish' or 'acts Jewish' take on a positive rather than a negative tone." My hope for my children is that they can take pride in announcing to the world that they are Jewish, without experiencing fear and shame, something I still cannot easily do.

Motherhood raises identity issues not just for the Jewish Fellows writing for this book, but for the non-Jewish women as well. Some have chosen to raise their children with no religious affiliation. Others watch interactions between their children, Jews, and other minority groups, which seem different in quality to the types of interactions they themselves experienced growing up. All hope that their children will create a more tolerant world in which in-group/out-group differences will be less important to identity, and in which personhood and character take precedence over ethnic or racial identity.

In-groups and Out-groups

For my parents, as well as for the parents of many of the Jewish Fellows in this book, the world was divided into two groups: Jews and non-Jews. Non-Jews were "different," "other," "foreign," and "suspicious"—not to be trusted. They drank, or were straitlaced, or had no sense of humor—they lacked Jewish warmth. Jews have special words for themselves, such as "Landsman" (a Yiddish word pronounced LONTS-*mon*, meaning someone who came from the same hometown[13]), "M.O.T." (pronounced as three separate letters, meaning member of the tribe); or "one of ours." They also have words to refer to non-Jews, labels that have become pejorative, such as *shiksa* or *goy*. "Is he Jewish?" was often the first question my parents would ask if I described a new person I had met. This question was especially important for potential romantic involvements, but was asked about everyone, male or female, young or old. Furthermore, when my parents met someone, they would characterize him or her as Jewish or not within minutes. They taught me to do the same when I was young.

Because Jews have lived all over the world, do not actively attempt to convert non-Jews to Judaism, and until very recently discouraged conversion to Judaism, the very survival of Jews as a people is thought to depend on Jews marrying only other Jews. In many families, there was and is a great deal of pressure put on young people to marry only within the Jewish religion. This rigid in-group/out-group distinction affected me quite intensely as an adolescent. My parents, even my agnostic father, felt very strongly about my marrying a Jewish man, and they would become intrusive and critical and, worse, depressed whenever I went out with someone who was not Jewish. I resented what I perceived to be the limitations placed on my freedom of choice and the lack of respect for my judgment. In addition, it felt quite hypocritical to me, since my parents had raised me with no formal Jewish education. It might have helped if I had been able to understand my parents' motivations for wanting me to date only Jewish men, but they couldn't articulate the reasons very well, even to themselves, so to me it felt like a narrow and limiting worldview. Did dating non-Jewish men feel like a personal rejection of what their values were? Were they scared of anti-Semitism in the families of the boys I would date? That I would not be accepted by non-Jewish families? That my children would not be Jewish? Leftist and liberal that I was, I could not agree with their perspective that this would be a loss.

Interestingly, as more and more of my relatives have married non-Jews, the issue of marrying only other Jews has become almost a non-issue in our extended family. My parents are openly accepting toward, even welcoming of, non-Jewish in-laws, people they would have considered outsiders three decades ago. This may be because anti-Semitism is less prevalent now than it was for my parents' generation. When anti-Semitism is higher, there are good reasons to care whether you're interacting with, or perhaps even marrying, another Jew: it's safer.

The non-Jewish women in *Daughters of Kings* also discuss insider-outsider themes. Many have, at times, felt like outsiders to Judaism and had a sense of being actively excluded, even those whose families were half-Jewish, and especially those who married Jewish men or converted to Judaism. Jews' discouragement of would-be converters and of religious intermarriage is perceived by some non-Jews to be, at best, unwelcoming and, at worst, outright hostile, taking on overtones of smugness and superiority.

Jews, of course, are not the only group with insider-outsider issues. Far from it. In fact, groups tend to define themselves, to take on an identity, not only by who they are, but by who they are not. Groups actually emphasize how they are distinctly different from other groups as a way of making themselves feel superior, sometimes defensively superior. For many of the Fellows who grew up in the fifties, "us versus them" was not "Jew versus non-Jew," but "black versus white." The African American women describe "insider" themes in the African American community, including special words like *girlfriend*, that black women have for each other; or the fact that people of color who are strangers will often acknowledge each other while passing on the street. During the war in Vietnam, some insider-outsider distinctions centered on age. "Don't trust anyone over thirty" was a widely accepted maxim for the under thirty age group. Even now age is an important criterion for outsider status among certain adolescent groups.

Such insider-outsider issues are widespread and often unconscious and unacknowledged in their effects. While they have the benefit of garnering support, bolstering self-esteem, and even helping to ensure survival for "insiders," they also have the potential risk of limiting choices, of categorizing both insiders and outsiders in stereotypic and dehumanizing ways, and of fomenting conflict between groups. We have seen evidence of these consequences all too often in the twentieth century.

Daughters of Kings is an attempt to cross bridges between in-groups and out-groups. Reading and sharing these poignant and engrossing stories has enabled me to recognize my own personhood as a Jew. In openly acknowledging and talking about my Judaism I was able to get over some of the pain I had experienced. My pride became stronger than my fear and even my shame, and I am learning anew about the beauty contained in my Jewish heritage. Other Fellows, both Jewish and non-Jewish, were also powerfully affected by their participation in this project, discovering things about Judaism, about other ethnic backgrounds, and ultimately about themselves. I'll expand on these themes in the last chapter of this book, in which the participants elaborate on how this project transformed and affected them. These essays and our conversations about them were an inspirational gift to each of us. I hope they will be a gift to you as well.

Living for Export

RACHEL KADISH

A S ANY TEMP on a quiet assignment knows, straightening up one's desk is the last resort of the underutilized office worker. *Look busy* might as well be stamped in boldface on the contract of the temporary employee. So it happened that while straightening up my desk last summer in the human resources department of a large firm, I ran across a training manual designed to instruct corporate employees in the ways of cultural diversity. The manual outlined workshops, discussion groups, scenarios for playacting. No discriminatory stone, it seemed, was left unturned. And, in a paroxysm of delicacy, the author of this cultural diversity training manual had coined a euphemism to solve once and for all the problem of how to refer to women, minorities, and the handicapped.

"People who are diverse."

I sat in my nearly all-white work environment and contemplated just how profoundly someone had missed the point.

I was struck of course by the tremendous arrogance of the phrase, with its implication that diversity is a graciously tolerated disease of which only certain people are carriers. I wondered, when will these folks realize that diversity is *contagious*: if I'm in a group and I've got it, then don't look now honey but you've got it too. We're in this one together.

I have laughed and cringed at that phrase for over a year, but there is something in it that strikes me these days as perversely accurate. "People who are diverse." It sounds like a euphemism for some sort of multiple personality syndrome, and sometimes I think that that's not such a bad way to describe what it means to live as a minority in a majority culture.

So, on with it. I am a "people who are diverse." I am Jewish, American, and the granddaughter of Holocaust survivors. Half my family lives in

Israel. I think in two languages, most of the songs I know are not in English, my speech often trips over associations that I must explain if I want my friends (mostly non-Jewish) to understand the major issues in my life. As for mainstream American culture, it often feels unnervingly foreign, and all too often I find myself fending off acquaintances' alarmed reactions to my ignorance of some apparently earthshaking event in American pop culture ("Pretend I'm from another planet," I tell them). But perhaps the most telling of my symptoms of "diversity" is this: my sense of my own safety is profoundly uneasy. The sense of personal security that one might assume I would possess—being white, educated, and middle class—does not at all match the dimensions of my private fears.

Let me say right off the bat that I would not trade my own multiple personality condition for the world. Perhaps more important, I would have no idea how to navigate the world without it. Internal contradiction can, after all, be a wonderful foundation on which to build an identity. ("I don't know," to quote Robert Frost out of context, "where it's likely to go better.") While I am not religious, Jewish history and Israeli culture have been constant, tangible, beautifully if at times infuriatingly complex presences in my life. Mostly, I feel that my life is blessed with a wonderful and indelible richness. Mostly, I feel strengthened by a sense of (sometimes grudging) love for the close Jewish communities in which I spent much of my childhood. I feel thankful for the nine years I spent attending a Jewish day school: learning Midrash, shouting my lines in school plays in Hebrew, computing equivalents for my name and my friend's name (and the names of the boys we had crushes on) using Jewish numerology. Moving from this sheltered and relatively uniform environment into a public high school with gangs and security guards and knife fights was eye-opening and even exhilarating. To see the world through layered lenses is a precious thing.

That is the part of my "diversity" that doesn't raise too many eyebrows. Jewish nostalgia and humor and sometimes overbearing warmth, colliding gloriously with the aesthetic of the "outside world": we know all about these things; we've seen them in Woody Allen movies.

What I want to talk about right now, though, is another aspect of my "diversity": an aspect that often makes both non-Jews and Jews—including me—distinctly uncomfortable.

The year when I was twenty-four, the release of *Schindler's List* set my telephone ringing. *Tell me again how your family got out of Cracow,* old friends began. I had rarely heard that sort of vulnerability in their voices: suddenly, stories they'd heard from me years before urgently needed retelling. My friends were curious and genuinely moved. For them, *Schindler's List* was eye-opening: they had never before seen the images that I had grown up with on a casual and day-to-day basis.

You see, my family was in Poland when the war started. Cracow was their home. Itzik Stern (played by Ben Kingsley in *Schindler's List*) was my grandmother's cousin. Beginning in 1939, my family hid and fled and bluffed their way through Poland and into Lithuania, where they were arrested for illegal border crossings and thrown into a Russian border prison. They fled across Europe to Japan (yes, Japan), where they boarded a ship bound for Curaçao. And when the ship docked in Mexico, they bribed a local doctor to quarantine them with bogus diseases. Forcing my family, naturally, to be detained ashore until the boat had to sail on. Then, of course, there were the Mexican immigration police to contend with . . .

In 1940s Europe, the preferred destination for a European Jew was Anywhere. One did not bother being too picky. In 1942, the year my family finally managed to get permission to cross the Mexican border into Texas, Anywhere was America: a final destination for some family members, for others only a stopping point en route to Israel.

The story is, of course, much more complex than that; it feels infinitely complex at times, more terrifying and miraculous, devastating and humorous, every time I turn around.

But it's also a very simple story: my family just barely got out. It's a fact a child does not forget.

With all the current talk about the fiftieth anniversary of the liberation of German concentration camps, our attention rightfully goes to survivors, to the preservation of their stories, to the German people and the ways in which they have absorbed all that has passed. And so it feels somewhat frivolous to call attention to what the experience of the Holocaust can mean to grandchildren of survivors. Still, the Holocaust has had what I can only describe as a persistent and at times overwhelming presence in my life. As the grandchild of survivors, I feel that I grew up with a brand of internal "diversity" that would make the euphemists of corporate Manhattan seem downright visionary.

When you grow up with the Holocaust, the most horrifying situations are readily absorbed into the realm of the possible. Children's imaginations conform to the contours of the world they know. Lying in bed at night, they see scenarios of the world ahead; preparing them-selves is the only natural thing to do. My childhood speculations were absolutely matter-of-fact. If I were in Amsterdam like Anne Frank, would I wear my yellow star or try to take it off?

If I were in a gas chamber, would I stay high or crouch low?

Should I try to put something over my mouth?

A child's speculations fade over time, but perhaps they never fully disappear. To this day I have a lingering discomfort with the fact that what I do is language-bound: as a writer, I feel particularly vulnerable to dislocation. If I were a doctor, my skills would be universal. I could read-ily transplant them anywhere, in any culture.

It is only now that I understand that most Americans don't carry around the sort of thoughts I've been walking around with all my life. It is only recently that it has hit home: most American children of my gen-eration did not routinely speculate about how they would know if geno-cide were coming. Most American children did not keep a matter-of-fact ranked list in their heads of the countries they would flee to If. . . . Most of them did not wonder which friends would turn against them and which would help hide them; most did not come into adulthood with two very distinct paths stretching out before them: the path their lives would take in the United States and the path their lives would take when they had to run. Most did not know, know with as complete a cer-tainty as they know anything about the world, that if they did not re-member the past their lives might be in danger.

In my family my grandfather was the pillar of memory, the teller of stories. He charged us, everyone charged us, in and out of school, di-rectly and indirectly, never to forget the stories of what had happened in Europe. To forget was to let those people die all over again. To re-member, to remember actively, was to ensure that these things could not happen again.

As a child, I would argue mightily with my grandfather. He was a striking presence in any company, educated and charming, didactic and overbearing. Today I know that he must have relished our arguments— he relished an argument with anyone, even a ten-year-old. Quick to in-struct his grandchildren in the ways of anti-Semitism, he told me that I couldn't trust people around me. I couldn't trust people who weren't Jewish. They had turned on the Jews in Poland, and I should know that Jews weren't safe here in America either. The only place we were safe was in Israel.

I countered that it wasn't true. We were safe, we were safe here in America.

But how could a child argue with this man's experience in Poland, how could I refute stories of the Catholic colleagues with whom he had studied and worked, who had turned blank and stony faces to him when he tried to ride in their wagon while fleeing the German attack? He was not to be allowed a seat; he was a Jew. And when my Jewish day school was spray painted with swastikas one night, when non-Jewish neighbors threw rocks at a classmate while she and her family walked to synagogue, how could I differentiate between these events of my own childhood and stories I'd heard of anti-Semitic propaganda in Poland, of the time when my grandfather, then only nine years old, was hit in the head with a rock by a group of Jew-hating children in Cracow?

As a child, I couldn't win the argument. As an adult, it still stymies me. How do I learn to feel safe in the world I live in, how do I learn to differentiate between "*Mort aux Juifs*" spray-painted on a Paris Metro wall in the 1990s and the anti-Semitism of 1930s Poland?

The short answer is that I don't.

Judaism, for me, has always been synonymous with a certain kind of vigilance. It is a vigilance not in fashion these days, a vigilance that seems strangely out of step with modern American culture. It is a vigilance, too, that makes me uncomfortable because it is so often coupled with myopic conservatism and even self-absorption. *Just who do Jews think they are, going on about how their problems are worse and their situation more precarious than anyone else's?* Still, the counter-message is clear and insistent: *Keep your eyes open. The tide can turn at any time.*

I understand that my experience is unusual for someone of my age (twenty-seven). Jews of my generation in this country simply aren't expected to have this sort of connection to the Holocaust. Most of my Jewish peers are descended from immigrants who left the Old Country in the 1910s; the vast majority of those left behind were never heard from again. Besides, Americans of my generation aren't supposed to be hung up on the past. We're Generation X, immune to scandal: we're rootless and comfortably numb. We don't *do* history.

My sister and brother aside, I've met only two American Jews of my generation who grew up with survivor grandparents. Both seem to share a sense of urgency I recognize in myself. Both seem to see themselves as the repositories of family stories; it is as if, in the wake of the rush to Americanize, which prevented many of our parents from asking questions about the war, we cannot help but ask and ask and ask, and be indelibly marked by the answers. Both of these friends seem to share my own compulsion to hold on to stories. We are well aware that the generation of survivors is dying. If those of us who grew up in their presence, who still can pick up a telephone and ask questions, do not save up the memories, then what will prevent the stories from being lost?

And yet, how can you tell all the stories that need to be told, how can you be sure all these things live on? It is an impossible burden.

Sometimes I don't know why we need to bother. Why remember pain, why this Jewish compulsion to cherish the past? I rebel against all of it. I am irritated by my own vigilance, by the voice inside that needs to weigh and measure: is it Good for the Jews or Bad for the Jews? I am sick to death of the subject of anti-Semitism. "Funny, that's not my experience," an American Jewish friend comments when I tell her about my upbringing, and I want to agree with her, shrug my shoulders and with that single motion shrug away the entire burden of memory.

But memory is not a choice. That much, at least, I have known all my life. Memory haunts, memory insists; it is never safe to believe one can leave it behind. And even if one could, what would be lost might well be more important than what would be gained.

A telephone call from my friend late one night this fall, and I was once again awash in ambivalence. My friend is also the granddaughter of survivors, and when she spoke her voice was a mix of bemusement and pain.

"Remember the games they played with us on *Yom HaShoah* [Holocaust Remembrance Day] at [Jewish] summer camp?" she said. "We were divided into groups. Do you remember? It was a game. We had to pretend to be Danish children in hiding from the Nazis. We had to find ways to survive."

I had forgotten. As she spoke, I recalled the image of cobwebs under cabin floorboards.

My friend went on. "We used to hide under the cabins. I was talking about this," she laughed, "and my husband couldn't believe what he was hearing. But that's what we did; those were the games they had us play at camp to teach us about the Holocaust. And—well, what *should* you teach children? On the one hand you need to give children something they can understand. But couldn't they have found a better way to do it?" My friend's voice, reasoned words edged with bewilderment. "Still we all played those games then. We had to hide in one place, then run to the next without being caught by the guards." She hesitated. "And, do you remember? It was a really fun day."

And then, I did. I remembered those games. I remembered running. Crouching, peering around corners. Whispering. Running.

I told my friend about the ways I remembered learning about the Holocaust. I told her about an assignment to make a board game for my seventh-grade English class. The game, set in concentration camps, followed the plot of Elie Wiesel's memoir *Night.* If you picked a card you were presented with a moral dilemma: whom would you feed if there were only one crust of bread?

"Oh God." My friend's pained laughter. "*Night: The Board Game.*"

"Yeah, I know. Pretty awful, huh."

I hung up the telephone still thinking about the question: what *should* you teach children?

As an adult raised in the shadow of the Holocaust, I am driven to remember, to gather up testimonies, gleanings on the edges of a devastated field. And yet I don't want to be that token sufferer, the widow wearing black for the rest of her life so no one will forget that she lost the husband of her youth. It is an impossible problem: how do you hold on to the stories with which you are entrusted, and at the same time keep from becoming a backward-looking shrine, a caricature of your own intent? In *The Sun Also Rises,* Ernest Hemingway's characters lash out against the persistent seriousness of the Jew Robert Cohn. "Go away, for God's sake," they tell him. "Take that sad Jewish face away." Jewish suffering has become an institution, a way of seeing the world. Sometimes I worry that as a people we have the capacity to lovingly caress every detail of our own sorrow. As if we and we alone are qualified to wear that proud badge of persecution. (Yet, in fact, so often and so vocally do people in this country assume Jews have nothing to worry about, that even here I find myself falling reflexively into the habit of explaining exactly why there are indeed many reasons to worry: the publication of *The Turner Diaries* and the recent popularity of *The Protocols of the Elders of Zion* are two handy examples. Anti-Semitism is alive and well in many parts of America, no doubt about that. But I must set aside my Good-for-the-Jews reflexes long enough to state what seems obvious to me as well: Jews don't have it worse than most other minority groups in the country, and we have it a lot better than many.)

At its best, the Jewish emphasis on memory evolves into an expansive worldview, an understanding that peace is fragile, that chaos is never as far away as anyone might think, and that it therefore behooves us as citizens of the world to understand the mechanics of hate and to fight prejudice wherever, however, and against *whom*ever it manifests.

At its worst, such intense focus on one's own past is no nobler a form of jingoism than any other. It has taken me a long while to realize this one thing: many of the pillars of the community who charged me to remember the Holocaust when I was growing up are, for all that, no less racist and no more openhearted where other people's suffering is concerned.

My grandfather once said to me that he cherished his hate of the Germans—it was all he had left.

If I have a declaration of independence to make from the complications and contradictions of my upbringing, then this is it: I cannot live in a world where pain is cherished. I am not willing to paint the corners of my universe that small. I cannot live in a shrine. And I refuse not to trust the people around me. That's the prescription for a sort of world in which I'm not willing to live.

But still I hear my grandfather's stories. I cannot simply walk away from them.

So how do I move forward and be a whole person living as a Jew in America, trusting my friends ("diverse" and otherwise) with all my heart . . . and at the same time hold on to my knowledge of other times and worlds now lost?

I have found only one solution that works for me, only one way to make the world feel safe, and it is the one on which I stake everything. I tell stories.

In a German prisoner-of-war camp in Algeria, American and British soldiers befriend the Jewish doctor whom the Germans have pulled from the ill-fated Cracow ghetto to serve their medical needs. The Jewish man becomes so popular with the soldiers that they keep him from being sent back to the ghetto. They save his life. Of course, there is the practical joke they play on him, for it *is* true that one of the American soldiers bears a striking resemblance to Adolf Hitler. . . .

A boy growing up in an ultra-Orthodox family in Poland is expected to revere the community's rabbi. Instead, ten years old and fearless, he replies to every one of the esteemed rabbi's mealtime belches with a resounding one of his own. Much to the mortification of his family. He sneaks out of the house to play soccer. He climbs the walls of the monastery and steals the monks' pears.

It is a world that is gone. The story matters.

A Jewish man deliberately breaks his nose; in its unbroken state it looked too Jewish and he would have been unable to "pass." A Jewish woman buys a big dog and takes refuge in the countryside; everyone knows only Gentiles have dogs.

A mob of peasants wait on the hillside, ready to loot the town of Luniniec. A red-haired woman passes through them unremarked; she is a Jew and no one knows. A Jewish man, greeting old friends in the street three weeks into the war, is told that this is no time for jokes: the assembled friends are members of the Polish Communist Party, waiting to greet Russian troops as they march into Poland. "Well, if the Communists can't tolerate jokes, then Heil Hitler," the Jewish man calls out.

A young man is heartbroken when his old girlfriend marries another. Trying to get over her, he travels to England in the summer of 1939. His heartbreak saves his life.

With all this storytelling, I sometimes feel as if I am living for export. That is, the things that I experience, the issues that move me and matter to me, turn up in some form in stories I send out into the world. Stories are doves sent out from the ark to test whether the storm waters have receded. They are emissaries sent to map out new possibilities for understanding and even peace. A world without stories is, it seems to me, not only a less beautiful place but also a dangerous one.

For me, storytelling goes beyond remembering the Holocaust (in fact, I write mostly about other subjects). Storytelling is my way to feel that people of different backgrounds can be safe around each other. This, perhaps, is a twenty-seven-year-old's best way of waging the argument she's been having with her grandfather since she was ten. Over and again, I find myself telling stories that force me to cross ethnic lines. In order to tell an Ethiopian immigrant's story, I have to educate myself about the circumstances of her life. In order to tell a Russian woman's story, I have to do my best to be sure that I'm not stereotyping Russian women. Likewise, when I read I am drawn most strongly to the literature that brings me into a world unlike my own. Amy Tan, Toni Morrison, Anton Shammas make the world safer for me. If we can tell and hear stories across these seemingly uncrossable lines of ethnicity and race, then perhaps we can all lay down some of our godawful vigilance and trust that there is now an understanding of our common humanity. Storytelling is, to me, the way in which people can best guarantee a place in each other's hearts. I don't want to be Pollyanna-ish about this. But more and more I believe that reading about another person's experience is the surest way to guarantee that we will look each other in the eye when we meet.

Perhaps I am simply imposing my own exaggerated sense of vigilance on others, but there are times when I feel that much of our human impulse for storytelling boils down to a question of safety. Living for export is a way to send one's own personal and cultural "diversity," one's own fears and joys and sorrows, out into the world, in the hope that the very act of speaking will guarantee them safe haven somewhere. Sometimes I wonder whether this is why the "people who are diverse" of this world—that is, those who have been forced to reside in the margins of their nations' histories—have been some of the world's most avid storytellers. Stories strengthen one's own people, that's true. But they also, inevitably, extend a welcoming hand to those outside. In a hostile world, narrative is perhaps the highest measure of optimism: a form of purposeful trust. Maybe for those reviled for their "diversity" such storytelling is more than a symptom of trouble: it is the beginning of a solution.

If it is naive to believe that stories can actually change how we understand and behave toward each other, then I am intentionally naive. I choose not to imagine a world without that belief; it is not a world I would want to inhabit. So I trust in the power of stories: my own, other people's. I trust aggressively. All this living for export feels like the bare minimum, the only way I can look around with wide-open eyes and not be overwhelmed by fear. The stories hold joy and wonder and a promise, however ephemeral, of safety.

The year when I was twenty-four, something happened that seemed designed to test many of my vague hopes about trust and storytelling. A new friend, not Jewish, was embarking on a project. He was preparing to write something about Holocaust survivors, about Holocaust survivors living in Israel. Did I know anything about the subject?

There are times when you simply feel: this is one of the reasons I'm here on this planet.

I have deluged my poor friend with bibliographies, books of photography, family stories. Over time we have developed an easiness of dialogue about subjects most people usually avoid or tolerate only briefly. I have sent my friend articles and books; I have translated song lyrics by Israeli pop singers. We went, together, to see *Schindler's List*. We went to the Holocaust Museum in Washington, D.C. The crowds were predominantly Jewish; my friend is black. You might say we stood out in the crowd.

On several occasions my friend has thanked me for my help with the process of researching and thinking through these issues. It's true that I've brought to his attention material that might otherwise have been inaccessible. Sometimes I flatter myself with the thought that he couldn't have found a more committed research assistant. But just as often, I find myself laughing internally at the notion that *he* is thanking *me*. I feel at times that I'm unloading stories on him. I feel at times that in pointing out this story and that anecdote, I am lifting some of my own burden of memory and placing it on his shoulders. I myself walk a bit lighter for the knowledge that someone else cares; I wonder, does he feel more burdened?

Recently I've begun to realize how important my friend's project is to me. I am stubbornly committed to the idea that understanding is possible, and I find that I do indeed have complete confidence that when he sits down to write he will do a good job. Any "errors" will be honest mistakes, not malicious ones. Knowing this, I can lay down one small corner of my vigilance. In this era of uproar about the state of re-lations between blacks and Jews, a friend's honest curiosity makes the world safer for me. It is a haven, and something more. A bolstering of the supports of the world. Lately, I've begun to think that perhaps I have more hope than I used to. I feel easier, and feeling easier gives me more energy to focus on something other than the same old tired sub-ject of the past.

Memory is both strength and hobble; I don't know whether my own so-lution to the contradictions it imposes can hold. All I know is that I ex-port stories. I trust deliberately, aggressively. Sometimes I turn around and look at my relationships with non-Jewish friends, relationships in which we have spoken and, I think, begun to understand the different ways we experience the world. At those moments I see, I am relieved to see, that in the process of remembering painful stories I haven't con-ceded my ability to trust. I am relieved to see that I have staked every-thing, with the stubbornness of a ten-year-old child, on the idea that people can understand each other.

Or, rather, *almost* everything.

Perhaps I haven't been completely honest.

For all my comforting optimism, my claims of making the world safer through storytelling, "living for export" can never feel like complete safety. When I told my late-night telephone friend the title of this essay, she assumed that I was referring not to the habit of storytelling, but to another persistent sensation we both acknowledge: that of living with one foot out the door. Living with 99 percent of one's resources committed to one's life in America, yet with a keen ear to the ground for signs of the slightest anti-Semitic tremor. Living ready to flee, living vigilantly, living ready to export *oneself.*

I am not proud to admit that beneath my strongest political convictions to work for change in this country of my birth there remains a capacity for wild-eyed panic. If things turn bad, I'm out of here. It has always felt that simple to me, and in this I know I am anathema to most American Jews of my age. Sometimes I wish that I could feel more stick-to-it patriotism. But, you see, in my heart I know that storytelling requires the luxury of time to work its magic. Storytelling is a way to instruct polite company and combat gentle ignorance. And hate is neither polite nor gentle.

If everything I have counted on fails, then storytelling will not save anyone. I know I can trust my non-Jewish friends. I have that much faith. But beyond my friends . . . Common experience and common sense mandate paying close attention to the first glimmerings of fear. In an odd way, it makes me think of Eddie Murphy's comic routine on why no one bothers to make horror movies starring black people. It goes, in loose paraphrase, like this:

> Black man (moving his family into new home): Nice house . . .
> Disembodied voice: *Get out.*
> Black man: . . . too bad we can't stay.

Common sense and common experience can convince you to keep flight handy in your repertoire. I could, I would, stand poised to flee given a frightening enough set of election results, a convincing enough wave of hate. It is a family legacy to ignore at one's own risk, a lesson learned with searing clarity: Leave now. Ask questions later.

Such fear, surely, has no basis in America?

But my friend and I, we remember running. Crouching, peering around corners. Whispering. I say to her over the telephone, "How much did we understand about the games we were playing in those days?" She says to me, "I wonder what it's like to grow up without knowing what a concentration camp is." Murmurs of bewilderment, layerings of wonder. Who could have known we held so much sorrow, knotted snugly into the turns of our sinews, knitting bone to bone so that we cannot be sure who we would be without it.

It is late at night and my friend and I are saying our good-byes. We have exchanged good wishes and weary laughter. Still, before I lay down the receiver, I find myself reaching to her once more for companionship. "Am I remembering right?" I want to know. "When we played those games on *Yom HaShoah*, didn't we have to wear yellow Jewish stars on our clothing?"

Setting off for the night's dreams, we heft the bundle of memory on our shoulders; stray feathers drift loose around us. A story of practical jokes in a prisoner-of-war camp, a story of a man who broke his own nose. A story of mobs on a hilltop, barren faces in a jolting wagon. *Tell me again how your family got out,* a voice insists, and it is the voice of a friend. *I want to understand.*

The response comes in low and steady syllables—my own, someone else's?—weaving stories across lines, weaving stories between people understood to be enemies, weaving stories through time. Listening like a child, I want it to go on and on and on.

Going Back to Bocki

PAULA GUTLOVE

WHEN I FIRST HEARD that I was going to Warsaw I didn't know that my father had been born in Poland. I had been invited to be a member of an official U.S. State Department delegation to a conference on security and cooperation in Europe. The conference was to address "preventive diplomacy"—and my work in conflict resolution in the former Yugoslavia was of interest to the organizers. I reported my upcoming journey to my father, as I usually do, expecting little more than his usual passive interest in my comings and goings. Instead, he became animated at the news of my impending trip to Warsaw and told me that I must go to Bocki, where he was born, not far from Warsaw. Animation in my father, who is ninety-three years old and now lives in a nursing home, is such a rare occurrence that I had to take notice. I had always thought he had been born in Russia. "Bocki," my father told me, "is near Bialystok," as though that would explain everything.

While I prepared for my journey during the intervening three weeks I periodically called my father. Every conversation brought up more names, new crumbs of information, new directives. I was to travel to Bialystok, then to Bielsk and then to Bocki. But what would I do once I arrived? Would anyone be there? "I want you to find my sister, Malkah," said my father as he pulled out tidbits of information that had been lying dormant in his memory for the last seventy years. I had an image of him probing into the dark and dusty corners of his mind, cleaning cobwebs off relics from a very distant past. I pointed out that he was ninety-three years old, the youngest of five children. Even if his sister miraculously survived the Holocaust, she would be more than one hundred years old, and she probably wouldn't be in Bocki. Our conversations began to take on a surrealistic quality. "She has many children. Someone will be there." I had to mention the Holocaust.

It was implausible that he simply forgot that the Jewish population of

Poland, and most of Europe, was eradicated in World War II. The suffering of the Jews in the Holocaust was the most salient aspect of the
Jewish education my parents gave us. We did not belong to a temple or
observe the Sabbath, nor did we celebrate any of the traditional Jewish
holidays. But my parents spoke Yiddish to each other (not to us kids),
and one of my two most memorable family excursions into midtown
Manhattan was a trip to the Jewish Museum to view a special exhibit on
the Holocaust. (Curiously, my other memorable family journey into
midtown Manhattan was a visit to Radio City Music Hall to see the Rock-
ettes kick up their heels in their annual Christmas show.) At the Jewish
Museum the life-size black-and-white photos, of the emaciated skeletal
figures who survived until the liberation of the camps in 1945, dwarfed
my ten-year-old body and led me into a passionate reading binge of
everything I could get my hands on that described the devastation of
the Jews. As I learned about anti-Semitism throughout history I felt
more and more inclined to relinquish or deny my Jewish identity. There
seemed to be little to gain in claiming it and a great deal to lose. Making an issue of one's Jewish identity made me feel uncomfortable, vulnerable, and isolated. I sometimes thought the phrase the "chosen
people" was a bit of a sick joke, as if we chose discrimination and abuse.

My identity was further complicated because I was a white person living in an explicitly black/white world. I grew up in New York City in the
1960s, in the northwestern part of Harlem that borders Washington
Heights. My world was a black/white world much more than it was a Jew-
ish/Gentile one. When I was seven years old my best friend Andrea, who
was black, told me that her family was going to a civil rights march in
Washington, D.C. I asked what was that and could I join her. Her response was not only that I could not come but that I would never be able
to understand what civil rights were all about. She patiently explained
to me that, being white, I would never understand her pain as a member
of an oppressed people, and, therefore, I would never really understand
her. I vividly recalled her words nine years later, when a man was shot
outside my window, the evening after Martin Luther King Jr. was assassi-
nated. When I asked my parents to call the police to report the injured
man they admonished me to stay away from the window. "We must not
be seen, we must not get involved." I understood we were afraid because
we were white and we did not belong in Harlem; we were not supposed
to be there. We were also afraid on this horrifying night in Harlem because we were Jews, and fear was a justified, conditioned response.

"I was there during World War Two," my father told me when I tried to argue that Malkah, and everyone else, would be gone. "No, Daddy. You came over in the 1920s. Hitler was in the 1940s. You were there during the First World War. The Holocaust was after you left. You were living in New York during the Holocaust. Have you been in touch with anyone from over there since you left?"

I knew that he hadn't. I hoped the absurdity of the task would become clear to him, as I felt it was to me. I felt myself trapped in a web of fantasy that I was allowing him to weave around me. I didn't want to raise his expectations, to build him up for disappointment. And yet, I began to look forward to talking to him, to discovering more about him and hopefully, more about myself. After some discussion I heard in his voice the realization that he had endured one war in Europe, but a second war in Europe took place while he was living in New York. However his belief that family would be in Bocki remained unshaken. "She had a very large family, my sister Malkah did. And there are cousins on my mother's side of the family, Liepe and his daughter Beila Klein. And then my good friend Nacha Farber, he will be there. No one could make Nacha leave Bocki." My father's unbending conviction persuasively caught me in its illusory veil. What did I know about Bocki anyway? Almost against my will I felt myself drawn into the fantasy, the dream, to go, to see what was there, to see who was there, to touch the soil of my father's childhood, to look for my own roots.

"I want you to bring some money to give to the family," my father told me, continuing to weave the spell. "Bring two hundred dollars cash. Give it to family. Or Farber, give it to Farber. Give it to their children. Just two hundred dollars. No more. If you give too much it would embarrass them. Find out if they need something." The sinking feeling returned. Even if I found Bocki, so far not on any of the maps I had procured, how would I find "family"? "If no one is there, shall I give it to the synagogue?" What was I saying? What synagogue? Any synagogue that had been there would surely have been razed. But my father would not be deterred. "Go. Someone will be there." Somehow I could hear him smile over the telephone. "Have a good trip."

The practical aspects of making my way to Bocki kicked in. First I had to get a detailed regional map so I could find it and prove to myself, after all, that it really did exist. How far was it from Warsaw? My business travel routine is usually in and out, completely work focused, so I can get home to my family, my husband and my two daughters, ages ten and five, as soon as possible. How long was it going to take to get to Bocki? How would I travel there? "From Warsaw you can take a train to Bialystok. From Bialystok, well . . ." my father paused. "I guess now you would go by car." I had a vision of my father as a small boy sitting on a horse-drawn cart. The thought of renting a car in a strange city where I did not speak the language was not a pleasant one. When I drive around my own country, in my hometown, I often find myself hopelessly lost. "How long would it take? An afternoon?" "No, no, it's too far," my father corrected me. Too far? I thought this town was supposed to be close.

It dawned on me that for this excursion to Bocki I could not go alone. I would have to assemble a small expedition. This was awkward for me as I tried to think about who to ask to join me on this personal journey, and what the implications might be. One obvious implication was that my professional colleagues would learn about an aspect of my identity that I had always kept to myself, namely that I have roots in Eastern Europe, Jewish roots. While I have never lied about my history, I have never gone out of my way to point it out. Working on ethnic conflict issues in Europe and the Balkans, I have strived to clothe myself in an armor of neutrality and impartiality. In my professional persona my identity is that of the third party, the facilitator, the convener. If anything is salient it would be my identity as an American, in a roomful of Central and Eastern Europeans. This persona allows me a sense of invulnerability. It casts me as one who is present to help others, not someone who is in need of help myself. Claiming my Jewish identity in this context would cast me as a member of a minority group that has been the object of one of the most devastating ethnic cleansings the world has ever witnessed, at the hands of the ancestors of many of the people who are my clients. To seek my roots in Bocki would be to publicly shed my armor and to acknowledge my Jewish identity.

As I pondered my ambivalence, an incident that occurred at a party I attended some fifteen years earlier came to mind. The party was hosted by a wealthy colleague of mine at the New York City hospital where I was a medical resident. I had never before been to a party in a Fifth Avenue penthouse, and I dressed with extraordinary care, not certain what the occasion called for. The penthouse was crowded, the food light, and the drinks strong. Early in the evening I found myself conversing, and flirting, with a well-known, somewhat notorious, Manhattan attorney. I thought he was about to make a pass at me when he said: "You know, you are so attractive, if it weren't for your nose you wouldn't look Jewish."

I was so shocked I couldn't say anything for a few moments and then responded: "You know, if it weren't for your mouth you wouldn't sound stupid." I left the party in a blur of confused emotions, pleased that I had the last word, annoyed that "looking Jewish" was pejorative, and disappointed with myself that I had tried to "pass," that I had failed, and that I cared. Nonetheless, I reflected that I often dated non-Jewish men and eventually married one.

I also wondered how many of my current professional colleagues thought of me as a Jew. Was it pretense, was I actively trying to pass? If anyone knew about the trip to Bocki, everyone would know, as I would have to make inquiries about getting to Bocki and take time away from the conference to travel out of Warsaw.

I broached the subject with a colleague, Bob, with whom I would be traveling to Macedonia after the conference in Warsaw. I had no reason to believe that Bob would be more or less interested in the venture than any other of my non-Jewish colleagues. To my utter amazement he greeted the prospect of seeking out Bocki with great enthusiasm. "This sounds like the kind of adventure I really enjoy. I've always wanted to look for the small town in Sweden that my great-grandparents came from, but never got around to it. You just find out absolutely everything you can from your father, write down every detail, and we will sort something out after the conference. No problem."

I borrowed a detailed map of the northeastern part of Poland from a friend and found Bocki exactly where my father said it would be—about 200 kilometers northeast of Warsaw, near to the border of Belarus, in a part of Poland that had been Russia until 1915. Bocki was in a region called the "Pale of Settlement," an area in which many Jews settled because Russian laws prevented them from living in other parts of Russia.

After that I tried to put the journey to Bocki out of my mind. I needed to prepare for the conference. This was an occasion that brought together threads of the work I had been doing since 1985, first promoting dialogue between Soviets and Americans and now, since 1991, as the director of the Balkans Peace Project, a project to promote dialogue and the nonviolent resolution of conflict in parts of the former Yugoslavia. After the trip to Warsaw I would be traveling to Macedonia with Bob, where we were setting up an office for a nongovernmental organization to promote conflict resolution there. If this weren't enough, I was also organizing a training workshop for a group from Serbia, Bosnia, Croatia, Slovenia, and Macedonia. This workshop was to take place in

Austria only two weeks after I returned from the Poland/Macedonia trip. I tried to juggle all of these tasks and prepare myself and my family for my busiest work and travel schedule in memory.

During the four days of the conference I was so busy that I had little time or energy to think about my plans to travel outside of Warsaw. As the conference drew to a close, Bob asked someone he knew in Warsaw for assistance in arranging an expedition to the countryside. We soon found Marylla, a bright young woman who worked for an international agency, spoke good English, and had a large (by Polish standards) car.

All week long the weather vacillated between snow and sleet and rain. The gray skies and the chill didn't affect me as I spent my days in meeting halls and my nights in restaurants or reception rooms. Saturday morning dawned as gray as the previous mornings, with a very fine mist of rain that was almost welcome because a heavy snow would have stalled the entire venture. The assembled entourage included Marylla, who was driver, translator, and tour guide; and Bob, bright-eyed and enthusiastic, surveying the weather and pronouncing it perfect for the journey. (As Bob lives in Santa Rosa, California, I wondered how far he had to reach to pronounce those dismal skies perfect.)

We set out due east on the Berlin-Moscow highway. "A very good traveling road," Marylla told us. Sitting in the front passenger seat I started to make conversation with Marylla, explaining to her that I was intrigued to have discovered a new aspect of my identity—a Polish identity. Marylla looked at me in confusion and said, "But I thought your father was Jewish." I had never told her that my family was Jewish. It must be my nose again, I thought, or maybe it's the region of Poland. Putting that question aside I mulled over the fact that it was not possible, in her mind, to be both Jewish and Polish. I didn't pursue the matter, but thought about a story I had read in *Newsweek* earlier that month about experiences that the crew making the movie *Schindler's List* had when they were filming in Cracow. Apparently an older woman came up to one of the actors portraying a high-level Nazi official and told him that "they had done a good thing, it's just too bad they couldn't finish the job." I felt intensely vulnerable without my armor and was comforted that Bob, a blond, blue-eyed Aryan, was with us. Did I perceive him as a witness, or as a protector?

As we left Warsaw the gray faceless housing blocks of the outskirts of the city gave way to open fields, blocked off in neat rectangular patches by small fences every three hundred yards or so. The snow-covered fields were broken by occasional orchards of an unusual dwarf apple tree. There were small flat country houses of wood or cinder block lining the road. In time the four-lane road, with a single center white line, became a two-lane road as the outermost lanes were frequently snow-covered and unusable. The small houses were farther apart, as were the towns we passed through.

In Siedlce we turned off the Berlin-Moscow road onto a smaller road to Losice and then to Bocki. Here the towns virtually disappeared, aside from an occasional sign telling us what we had just passed through. Low wooden houses that were either homes or field houses looked bleak and cold in the snow-covered fields. An occasional horse-drawn cart clumped along the verge. The driver sat swaddled in woolen blankets and heavy hats, soggy in the cold rain that fell intermittently. Patches of snow and ice appeared on the road, making the driving slippery and slow.

As we passed Siemiatycze, heading north to Bocki, the landscape abruptly changed. Bob said we were moving out of Iowa and into Minnesota. We were suddenly driving through tall pine forest broken only by the occasional collection of small wooden houses that meant we were passing through a town. Once we spied an old windmill on the side of the road beyond a clearing.

Marylla had taken her job as tour guide very seriously. She had gone to the library the night before, searching out information about Bocki. The only references she found were in an old Jewish archive where, in a book from the nineteenth century, she read that Bocki was a city of ten thousand people, of whom 70 percent were Jewish. Much later, at the turn of the twentieth century, Bocki lost its status as a city and became a village.

After we passed the Bocki town sign we pulled into a gas station, a new, fairly large tarmac affair that felt out of place in the pine forest landscape. The gas station could have been a self-service gas station on a rural road in the United States. Marylla grilled the attendant in the small glass booth, but he had no information for us. How could he? He had only been in Bocki for two years and knew few people in the town. I felt compelled to buy something in Bocki, and not knowing if this gas station would be my only opportunity, I looked over the collection of American candy bars and chewing gum and spied a can with the words POLISH KOSHER BEER written on it in Hebrew and in English. Not in

Polish. I pushed a collection of Zloty bills under the glass partition to the attendant and pointed to the can of beer.

The gas station attendant directed us to the city council office—maybe we could look up some information in the ancient registry books. As we drove along the road the trees gave way to wooden houses, and on our right, about one hundred yards off the road, stood a large, stuccoed, white-and-blue Catholic church behind a circular driveway. On either side of the church were low wooden buildings. I saw no cars parked nearby. The city council building was locked, as one might expect on a Saturday afternoon, and we followed Marylla around it, trying side and back doors.

Next we went over to the church and, after trying its door, followed Marylla to a wooden building next to the church. The home of the priest, she told us. Bob and I waited in the alley on the side of the house, surrounded by friendly white chickens and geese, while Marylla disappeared into a small side door in the back of the house. She emerged about ten minutes later and invited us in to meet the priest's housekeeper. The housekeeper, a woman of nondescript middle age, told us that she knew of no Jewish community in Bocki, but alas she had only been living here for twenty-five years. She felt certain that the priest, who was out, would have no more information to add as he was quite new, having replaced a much older priest less than ten years ago. The older priest could probably have given us some information, she told us, but alas he was dead. She directed us to the home of a woman in her nineties who had lived in Bocki all her life.

Handzia Srobowska lived in a one-story wooden house on a street of ancient wooden houses not far from the Catholic church. Some of the houses looked abandoned, but others appeared to be inhabited, and I wondered how the wooden walls could possibly keep out the damp winter chill. We entered Handzia's house through a side door in the rear, and after passing through a small back entryway found ourselves in a small kitchen. I felt distinctly alien as my five-foot-nine-inch form folded onto a tiny stool offered to me and I met Handzia's eyes. Handzia had to be less than four feet tall. As we sat on tiny stools and began to talk to Handzia I imagined myself in my daughter's kindergarten classroom, sitting at child-size tables on scaled-down chairs.

The small kitchen was heated by a wood stove built into a part of the interior wall. The wall was lined with ceramic tiles on which a small rectangular iron door hung. Another part of the kitchen had a separate cook stove with iron pots on it or hanging over it. We kept our coats on as we sat, partly because it was chilly and partly because there didn't seem to be anyplace to hang them up. Handzia wore several woolen knit sweaters, a woven wool scarf on her head, and boiled wool boots with leather soles on her feet. She inspected us with deep-set gray eyes coming out of a very wrinkled face that lit up frequently with a broad smile as she spoke. And she spoke a lot, to Marylla, in Polish. Marylla had to struggle to get her to stop long enough to translate at least some of what was being said.

Marylla explained to Handzia about who we were and the lost family that I was looking for. Soon Handzia's daughter-in-law, Maria, joined us in the tiny kitchen. Maria and Handzia seemed to vie with each other for Marylla's ear or simply spoke at the same time, regardless of the fact that Bob and I couldn't understand the Polish they were directing to us.

Marylla presented them with the names of the people we were seeking information about: my father's sister and her husband, Malkah and Hyman Epstein, my father's mother's brother, Liepe Klein, and his daughter Beila Klein, and his childhood friend, Nacha Farber.

Handzia told us that when she was a young girl she worked for the Jewish families as a "Shabbos Shiksa," lighting their fires on Saturdays and making them bread. She tried to remember the names of families for whom she had worked but was unsuccessful.

Maria reported that she thought she knew the son of Nacha Farber, Mortko Farber, as she went to school with him. Mortko was born in 1926, she told us, as she was. Mortko and his mother died in the war, but Nacha escaped while being transported to Treblinka. He made his way to the United States and remarried. She knew all of this because several years ago Nacha's son, from his second marriage in the States, came to Bocki. He came as I had come, looking for remnants of his father's family. Handzia added that this "son of Farber" was supposed to send them photographs he had taken while in Bocki, but he never did. This was the reason she did not have his U.S. address, something Handzia felt terrible about, because if she had it I could contact him and find out more about his family. Handzia told Marylla that Farber's son gave them chocolates while he was there but she would have preferred that he kept his promise to send them the photos they took. She said this with a sidelong glance at me and the camera I had been using. I promised to send photos promptly and asked them to write down their address for me. I also gave them my address and my business card.

We learned that there was no Jewish population in Bocki now. Handzia spoke tearfully of the "ghettos" in Bocki during the war and how she saw Jewish girls behind barbed wire fences, starving. "And I couldn't even give them bread. These girls didn't even have bread, and I used to help them light their fires on their Sabbath." The street we were on was one of the few remaining streets in Bocki that had original houses from the old Jewish section of town. The house Handzia lived in had belonged to a Jewish family, but she couldn't remember their name. "A textile trader, whose family had lived in Bocki for centuries," Handzia said. "He wasn't a very wealthy textile trader. He had a horse and he went to the villages and bought rags and then sold them in Bialystok." When he didn't come back after the war they bought his house from the State.

Handzia was curious about my business card, which read DIRECTOR OF THE BALKANS PEACE PROJECT, and she wanted to know about my work. She was intrigued at the prospect of teaching conflict resolution in the former Yugoslavia. She came to where I was perched on the tiny stool and looked at me, our eyes level. "Be careful. It's very dangerous," she told me. Her bony fingers reached out and rested firmly on my shoulders. "Don't let them do there what they have done here." Handzia's eyes filled with tears and she turned away.

As we thanked Handzia and Maria and prepared to leave, Handzia looked up and said there was something she wanted to show us. Quickly she put a coat over her sweaters and almost ran out the back door. We followed her for about half a mile and found ourselves in the parking area adjacent to a pair of faceless seven-story apartment towers, looking very incongruent with the old wooden houses in this small, rural town. Behind the towers were fields, the pine forest, and a creek. On a rise near the towers was a bit of a clearing, in the middle of which was what appeared to be a boulder.

The boulder was rectangular, roughly three feet by two feet, and about fifteen inches thick. It was lying on its side in the snow, and we followed Handzia as she wiped the snow off the face of the stone. Barely discernible, we saw the stone was covered with Hebrew letters, and Handzia explained that this spot had been the Jewish cemetery, a cemetery that had contained stones hundreds of years old. Most of it had been destroyed in the war. Stones had been used to pave roads and make foundations for buildings. A small part of the cemetery remained until four years ago, when someone decided to build these apartment towers on the cemetery site. Handzia told us that groups had come to Bocki from Warsaw, and from other places she didn't know, to protest the desecration of the Jewish cemetery, but the construction took place anyway. We looked at the only stone that remained. This was the only sign that a community of Jewish people had ever lived in Bocki.

Back in Bocki we met with the mayor, went to the town hall, and scoured the official records office, searching for any trace of the large family my father left behind when he came to the United States in 1920 at the age of sixteen. There was no record of Jews in the town hall records office, although the birth, death, and marriage records went back to the mid-nineteenth century. No trace remained of any of the people my father had left behind.

As each effort to uncover information about the Jewish people in Bocki, and my family in particular, turned up empty, I felt the Jewish aspect of my identity growing larger, stronger, more significant. I felt more and more separate from my American colleagues and from anyone who did not share with me this history of familial loss and horror. As I stood on the remains of the Jewish cemetery on that gray, cold February afternoon, I felt more connected to and identified with the person whose name was inscribed on the stone at my feet than with anyone I saw around me. I envisioned myself in the detention camp, freezing in a bitter wind, starving, praying, despairing, dying. My identity was that of a Jew, a Jew from eastern Poland, a Jew from Bocki. As it had long ago, this identity made me feel different, separate, vulnerable, and alone.

I mourned the loss of a family I had never known. Later that day, after we returned to Warsaw, I stood on the steps of the memorial to those who had perished in the Warsaw ghetto. I wanted to grieve and be done with it, so that I could go back to my safer professional identity. The Jewish identity that had clothed me in Bocki felt like a horsehair shirt: coarse, scratchy, and ill-fitting. I wanted to take it off and return to the armor of ethnic-less identity that I usually wear in my professional milieu.

I was surprised at how easily I was able to reenter my professional persona. Back in Warsaw, at the conference with my colleagues, I could smile and go about my business with, if anything, a greater than usual efficiency. Nothing seemed to have changed, in me or in them. I traveled to Macedonia with Bob and then home briefly to make the final arrangements for a workshop I was organizing to take place in Austria in less than one month. I had myriad details to attend to as my project involved bringing together people from Serbia, Croatia, Slovenia, Macedonia, and Bosnia for a training workshop on conflict management skills.

In Austria my two colleagues and I began the workshop as we usually do, with introductions and a series of small group exchanges to allow the participants a chance to get to know each other before diving into the theory and practice of conflict management. As a part of this introductory phase of the workshop we broke the group of thirty-five people into smaller subgroups of eleven or twelve, and in each group people discussed what brought them to the workshop and what they hoped to achieve. I joined one of the subgroups as a facilitator, to assist participants in carrying out their assigned task.

The participants in the small group included a psychologist from Macedonia, a physician from Bosnia now living as a refugee in Slovenia, a teacher and (underground) peace activist from Serbia, an academic from Slovenia, and a relief worker from Croatia. There were students and retired professionals, men and women. Each spoke about their reasons for coming to the workshop, many citing the war, the personal losses they sustained, and their wish to do something to curtail the spread of violence.

One of the participants asked me why I was there. I was not prepared for the question, seeing myself as the facilitator, rather than a participant. I resisted at first, feeling that it was important to maintain my role as an uninvolved facilitator. But I soon capitulated, and I found myself telling the group about my journey to Bocki. When I was done, I realized my throat was tight and my eyes were moist. I looked up and saw that everyone in the group, without exception, was teary-eyed or outright sobbing. There was no more need for discussion, as we mourned together the trauma and loss experienced by each person in the group and the pain that is a part of being human in a violent world. Furthermore, we confirmed our desire, indeed our need, to do something to change the violent course of events we saw taking place around us.

For the first time, I found that I wore neither my professional armor nor the hair shirt that had represented my Jewish identity. I felt proud of my roots, I did not feel vulnerable, and I felt connected rather than cut off from others. My Jewish identity had been transformed so that it was no longer isolating, no longer excluding of others, but, remarkably, had become somehow inclusive. This identity had stretched like a rubber band to include and bind together the Jew from New York, the Muslim from Bosnia, the Catholic from Croatia, and the Orthodox from

Serbia; the men and the women, the old and the young, the East and the West. There was a coming together in the shared pain, the shared vulnerability, and the common purpose that crossed the boundaries of each person's ethnic identity and bound us in a common future. I marveled at this miracle, this acknowledgment and embracing of diversity. I wondered how it might be possible to retain this connection and understand its source and its sustenance. It is the essence of the work that I have chosen to do and the key to making civilization possible in the twenty-first century.

When I returned from Austria I was finally able, physically, emotionally, and spiritually, to tell my father about my journey. With my husband and two daughters I walked into his room in the nursing home armed with the can of Polish kosher beer and a carefully assembled photo album that chronicled my travels from Warsaw to Bocki and back. My husband and my elder daughter Anna were fascinated by the story. Anna held my father's hand and hugged him as I spoke. But my father seemed impatient. He searched the photos for a familiar sight, then closed the album and put it aside in disgust. Either his eyes were too weak or the memory too dim, but nothing looked the way he thought it would. He asked me several times how it could be that nobody remembered his family, that Bocki had no Jews. He closed the subject and turned from it as he had the photo album. He didn't want to discuss it anymore.

I thought he had erased the whole thing from his mind until I found out that for several months thereafter he had nightmares that I had perished in Bocki, and he asked my sister to tell me never to go back. However, he was pleased when I told him I had written to Handzia and her family and sent them photos. When they responded to my letter some months later, he asked me to write back to see if I could find more information about Farber's family. The can of Polish kosher beer found a permanent home on top of his television set, sitting amid a clutter of photos of his children and grandchildren.

Not a Jewish Woman

NANCI KINCAID

WHEN I WAS growing up in Tallahassee, Florida, as far as I knew, there was only one Jewish boy in town. He was older than I was and I didn't know him. The reason I knew he was Jewish was because my friend, Pat Sharkey (who was Catholic and therefore fairly exotic herself), told me.

"How do you know he's Jewish?" I asked her.

"Because," she said, "his last name is Goldberg."

I pretended that this made sense to me.

"Besides," she said, "he looks Jewish."

It was nearly impossible for me to be sure he looked Jewish since I didn't know what Jewish looked like. The truth was he looked like he could be Pat Sharkey's cousin. He had the same physical characteristics as her family—dark hair that sometimes rioted in the humidity and somewhat dark skin like a person born with an uncommonly good tan. My aunt looked like that too, so did my mother and so did three of my four brothers.

When my aunt moved North people occasionally mistook her for Jewish (she said it was because she was so smart). People sometimes mistook my mother for Native American. Because we had six children in our family people often mistook all of us for Catholic. (I thought that was very strange. For the life of me I could not figure out what about us looked Catholic. There was not a redhead among us.) When my dark-skinned twin brothers hit adolescence and sprouted sudden unmistakable Afros people mistook them for proof that my mother was—just as she seemed—a radical liberal with a secret past.

My dark-skinned family members were declared to be Black Scots. We claimed this heritage like it was something to be very proud of. Most people I knew traced their ancestors back to Scotland, Ireland, or England. Or, of course, Africa. The white South of my childhood was mostly a blond-haired, blue-eyed world. I fit right in—even if my brothers didn't. So did most of the other girls I knew. Anybody who wanted to be blond and wasn't could correct that easily enough with a bottle of peroxide. Peroxide was a staple of the culture, an essential part of the coming-of-age ritual. It went hand in hand with getting a good tan. It gave us a fairly uniform look of dark tans and sun-lightened hair (which ranged from brassy gold to snow white). Golden skin, golden hair, golden girls. We were taught that this was beauty. And we believed it.

As I write this now I think back to the not-so-subtle Southern insistence that the world *should be* blond and blue-eyed—right down to the portraits of Jesus that hung in homes, churches, office buildings, and just about everywhere. Fair-skinned, blue-eyed, soft-haired Jesus with streaks of sunlight in his fine, fine hair. Jesus was feminized in the Southern culture. He was soft and beautiful and he glowed. It was the way girls—women—were supposed to look. At least the good and holy women.

For many Southerners, Jesus was the only Jew we knew in what the evangelists called "a personal way." And his picture said to us over and over again that being Jewish looked just like being Southern. We were happy to believe that. We didn't ask any questions.

Just recently I was at the YMCA in Charlotte, North Carolina, working out in the women's gym, waiting my turn to torture myself on the StairMaster, when I looked around and realized that every woman in the gym was blond. Half of them were still cultivating tans, too. It was one of those Southern moments that startles me a little now, but for the years when I was growing up such moments went almost totally undetected.

I am just beginning to understand the full import of being a Southern woman. It fascinates and frustrates me. The notions of what it is to be a Southern woman are complex, sometimes oppressive, occasionally liberating. Like so many Southerners growing up I had longed to be a citizen of the world, thought I was one—then I went out into the world and found out once and for all that what I was, was Southern. And that wasn't all. But it was the label that seemed to fit me best "out there," the one applied to me by people I met, that I accepted, that I came to believe explained something about me.

No matter how twisted and knotted the label is, underneath it is the intriguing and remarkable place where I live my life. I embrace being a Southern woman—and all the history and mystery and heartache that go with it. I have never wished to be other than a Southern woman.

In this way I think perhaps being a Southern woman is not unlike being a Jewish woman. Yet, if I believed my label explained something about me, did that mean other people's labels explained something about them? This is where the trouble starts—isn't it?

Southern women, black women, Jewish women all operate under labels, sometimes ill-fitting, often irritating—labels that establish invisible dividing lines. Most of my life in the South I'd been reaching across that line to touch the hands of black women also reaching across. I think there has always been a very strong yearning (along with fear and mistrust that is legendary and makes for such good literature) of each group for the other. A longing to peel the labels back a little, to hold sticky hands in Birmingham, Alabama—and to really mean it. In the Deep South black and white women are not just well versed in the stereotype of the other—we are also well versed in our own stereotypes. Together we struggle not to be totally reduced to cartoon characters. I swear to God I know something about the black woman's struggle.

But I didn't know Jewish women until I was grown. I am just now running headfirst into their stereotype, which I've already been told I've got all wrong. That's probably true. The great majority of Jewish women that I know are in the arts or in academics—so I think I might confuse characteristics of artists and academics with characteristics of Jewish women. I stand accused.

I grew up in Tallahassee, Florida, in a black-and-white world. I mean this literally and figuratively. Half the people in my world were black, half were white. I don't remember that we broke the white category down into many subcategories, but maybe I was just too young to know. Multiculturalism was too far-fetched a concept to have any impact on me at the time. Mine was a dual culture. An either/or world. One could be

1. black or white;
2. rich or poor;
3. male or female (if you wanted to be something more original than either of these you had to move to New York—or at least to Atlanta—to do it);
4. saved or unsaved (saved meant Protestant; it did not apply to anything as misguided and far out as Catholic);

5. ignorant or educated (ignorant meant you could not read; educated meant you could read—even if you never did);
6. Southern or not (which in the end might have been the most important category of all).

As a child growing up in the Bible Belt, it never occurred to me to think of the Belt in terms of geography. I thought of it in terms of the implied beating sinful people would suffer at the hands of an angry God. The Bible Belt was like a symbolic leather arm of the leather-bound Bible itself. The Bible Belt was God's weapon against sin—God, the ultimate father whose job it was to whip us into shape, to discipline us into submission, to motivate us with fear, to lash out at us for our own good, just like any mortal father who lived on my street, in my neighborhood, and kept his own family in line with the threat of his belt. "Am I going to have to take off my belt?" was the familiar refrain of fathers of my friends. "You're going to get a whipping" was the singsong threat we, as children, used to try to keep each other from giving over entirely to evil. To me, the success of God's plan for humankind seemed heavily dependent on corporal punishment. Men used their belts to keep order and obedience in their homes. I thought they got this idea directly from God and his own terrifying Bible "Belt."

The Bible, we were taught, had all the answers. In my family, thanks to my mother, we were not necessarily required to believe this. This was partly because we were Methodists—a milquetoast variety of Christian that generally claimed to be economically and educationally elevated over the "If-the-Bible-says-it-I-believe-it Baptists."

My daddy was raised Baptist. But by the time I was born he was more or less a Baptist gone wrong. In a misguided moment he had married my Methodist mother and subsequently yielded to her religious affiliation. As far as I know he never read the Bible himself—at least not much of it—but was willing to swear (on a stack of Bibles) that it was God's word, every bit of it true, every bit of it beyond question. It made him nervous to contemplate any other possibility or to be in the company of people who did—like my mother, his wife, his helpmate gone haywire.

Like nearly everybody else in Tallahassee our family of eight went to Sunday school every week and to church afterward and to Morrison's cafeteria for lunch after that where we were allowed to select one meat, one vegetable, and one dessert from the long, steamy line of fantasy foods. School began each morning with a class devotional followed by pledging allegiance to the flag with our hands over our pounding hearts. Every afterschool club meeting began with prayer led by an elected chaplain. (It was the simplest job you could have as an officer. All you had to do was read the twenty-third psalm aloud once a week, which was easy because most people already knew it by heart.) All ball games (of which there were endless numbers) were preceded by communal prayers on the loudspeaker and/or witnessed prayers in the huddle or the dugout. Sports were a primary religious vehicle with a direct route to heaven. I thought it was the only hope many boys had of getting there. Every meal was preceded by prayer. We said ritualized and free-form prayers before bed. Nobody (*nobody*), no matter how much of a heathen he might be or wish to be, escaped the Bible. *Jesus loves me, this I know, for the Bible tells me so* was the regional anthem.

When I was growing up, I could not get into focus the small picture of my own life, or that of my family or my neighbors. I was always mystified by my neighbors—the smells of their houses, the pictures on their walls, the music on the hi-fi, the plastic Tupperware cups they drank milk from, the beer in the back of the refrigerator, the whiskey on their breath, the pendulum-tailed dogs roaming through their houses knocking ashtrays to the floor, the secret magazines under their beds, the photographs on their coffee tables, the guns in their closets, the smiles on their faces.

Growing up I had enough trouble trying to understand what was going on on the street where I lived, in my own hometown, in the hot Florida fantasy land, the swampland where my life simmered. I had trouble knowing what was going on with my own two parents—decoding their body language, translating their simple sentences, trying to make enough love for all of us out of the soft scraps of their troubled lives. I had trouble understanding my four brothers in their Superman capes and guns and holsters—their need to jump off things and land hard, their need to climb things so high they couldn't get down, to crawl into dark places they couldn't see their way out of, to prove their lives with the threat of pain, the thrill of danger. I wasn't much better at understanding my baby sister—her cotton white hair, closet full of pink tutus, bedroom full of gerbils—who stopped being a baby long before I noticed, long before I stopped thinking of her as one.

Not until I left the South—and people said, "Say 'oil.' Say 'towel.' Ya'll? You're fixing to do what?" did images begin to make sense. Out of a sense of being defined as different by others, I could begin to define certain parts of myself and my history: they were Southern. Now I have moved west again. Arizona this time. The desert is beautiful with sunsets like the inside of a peach near the seed. I love it here—maybe because once more, far away from the South, I become Southern again. Whatever that means.

And it sure feels good.

One thing becomes increasingly clear to me—the experience of being a member or a group that is well represented numerically can be totally different from being a member of that same group when it is notably underrepresented. To be Southern in Alabama is totally different from being Southern in Boston. I think to be Jewish in New York City is very different from being Jewish in Columbus, Georgia. To be of the culture, but without the culture, can be an eye-opening experience.

If there was a temple or synagogue in Tallahassee (I assume there must have been) I never knew about it. Because I knew no Jews personally I knew almost nothing about "Jewishness." The best dress shop in town was owned by the one Jewish family I knew of, the Goldbergs. People said they were rich and I believed it, since I assumed they owned all the dresses in that store, not a single one of which I could ever come close to affording. We lived more of a Sears and Roebuck sort of life.

There were Jews teaching at Florida State University—people said so—but we never knew any of them, never recognized them, never noticed or identified them. Never gave them a minute's thought.

Not long ago when I commented to my mother that I had grown up without knowing any Jewish people she proceeded to name various Jewish families in Tallahassee to prove to me that I did indeed know some. And it was partly true. I knew a few of the families she mentioned, but had not known they were Jewish. My mother went on to designate those Jewish families who were members of the Tallahassee Country Club. (We were not members ourselves but were well aware of who was.) I guess membership in the country club was supposed to serve as proof that there was little or no anti-Semitism in Tallahassee at that time.

Here was what I knew about Jews when I was a child:

1. Jesus was one.
2. Jews were the chosen people.
3. Jews did not believe Jesus was the Savior.

4. Jews believed in the Old Testament, but not the New Testament.
5. Jews did not celebrate Christmas. No decorated trees, no presents, no nativity set up on the lawn. (This was the saddest thing I'd ever heard.)
6. Jews lived mostly in New York City. Sometimes they moved to Miami when they retired. (I was vague on Israel.)
7. Jews did not play football. (We didn't know if it was because they didn't want to or because they were no good at it.)
8. Many comedians on TV were Jews. Sometimes we didn't catch their jokes, didn't think they were funny. "So what am I? Chopped liver?" We listened with totally blank expressions. "Jewish humor," my mother explained.
9. Jews ate strange foods we had never heard of—like lox and bagels and who knows what else.
10. Jews did not eat pork. (That included barbecue!)
11. Jews had to marry other Jews.
12. It was not nice to call anybody a Jew—even if they happened to be a Jew. It was more polite to say, "He is Jewish."
13. Lots of Jews were rich.
14. The expression "to jew somebody down" meant to outsmart them in a money matter. It took a while for me to understand that there was no verb *jue*, that the word was *jew*—and it was intended as an insulting compliment. (The insulting compliment is an art form in the South.)
15. In World War II Hitler killed thousands of Jews.

Regarding this last piece of knowledge, I was not sure why. My mother said it was because Hitler was the Devil personified. If we could believe Jesus was God treading the earth in human form then it was easy for us to believe Hitler was the Devil treading the earth in human form. Hitler seemed to us—just like the gospel did—to be something that had happened in some other sphere. Something terrible—proof of evil—that floated all round us like dust. We could barely detect it or identify it, could not grab hold of it, but we breathed it in and out unknowingly and were quietly poisoned by it. And not knowing can be as lethal as knowing. It simply manifests itself differently—the way an overdose of sleeping pills manifests itself differently from a bullet to the brain. Either way the damage is done.

I was in college before I ever remember hearing the word *Holocaust.*

I was unsure what it meant. We had grown up hearing talk of World War II. We heard about the atrocities Hitler had committed against the Jews—but only in the sketchiest terms. My mother whispered when telling us. My father thought she shouldn't tell us at all. It was an abstraction to us—like Satan's evil deeds were an abstraction. Germany was some distant, imaginary continent, like hell, where evil was allowed to flourish. (Quite unlike the South, of course.)

We had a book on World War II that was published by *LIFE* magazine. The photographs were terrifying. My brothers and I studied them for hours with the worst kind of curiosity and horror. If our mother thought we were looking at the book too long she took it away from us and made us go outside to play. The pictures in the World War II book did not seem like they could be real—but we knew they were. They looked like something that had happened far, far away from us on the other side of this huge, spinning world, in a place where we would never go if we could help it.

We had friends whose fathers had fought in World War II but hardly talked about it. If they did they mostly said things about the "Japs bombing Pearl Harbor," and not really very much about that. I never knew a Holocaust survivor. And I didn't know anybody else who did.

The first time I ever heard the word *JAP* I was visiting a friend in New York City. Her daughter spoke of "all these JAPs" at a store where her sister worked—and I'm ashamed to say I conjured up the image of upscale Asian girls with credit cards, for I knew for a fact that she was talking about a very pricey store. Somewhere along the line I guess the daughter caught wind of the fact that I really didn't know what she was talking about. "JAPs," she said, "you know, Jewish American Princesses." I was lost. "You know," she said, "their fathers buy them everything. All they do is shop and have their nails done."

Actually, I knew these girls/women, but they mostly lived in Atlanta, direct descendants of Scarlett O'Hara. I didn't think Jews should take all the credit for indulging their daughters. Certain Southern "daddies" are masters of the art of spoiling their daughters, in every meaning of the word.

The odd thing was that I am fairly certain that the daughter telling me this was herself Jewish. (It never occurred to me because—this is a confession—the mother and daughter were both very, very blond, and if I thought anything I thought they were WASPs of the privileged variety.) I didn't realize until much later that indeed they were Jewish, but looking back I think it is very interesting. It would be like me talking about a hick, or a bleached blond with mall hair, or a country club Baptist, as a way of declaring myself not that. Drawing another of those imaginary lines. As far as I can tell we all do it. *Yes, I belong to the group that has some of these weird members, but I myself am not weird, trust me.*

Jews were never off limits to me—they were simply in very short supply. I married at age nineteen. My husband's family was from Tuscaloosa, Alabama, where there was a larger Jewish population than I had been aware of in Tallahassee. One of his best friends, Ralph, was Jewish. My father-in-law, who liked Ralph quite a lot, often described him as a "Jew-boy." Ralph's father was prominent and well-to-do. Everybody knew and liked him. He had been a war hero and had written a book about his experiences, which it seemed everybody in Tuscaloosa had read. He was highly respected for his heroism.

I was amazed to learn that when my ex-husband was a boy growing up he was not allowed to spend the night at Ralph's house because Ralph was Jewish. His very nervous Christian mother didn't feel comfortable having her boy spend the night with people—no matter how nice or heroic or rich—who didn't love Jesus. (Never mind love Jesus, who didn't even believe in him.) My ex-husband told stories of the awkwardness of the spend-the-night question. "Naw, man, not tonight. I got baseball practice early tomorrow. Naw, man. I'm not feeling so good. Naw, man, I told my mother I'd be home by ten." Et cetera. Eating meals at one another's houses was fine. But it stopped there.

However, my ex-husband and his brothers often dated Jewish girls. This seemed not to present problems since, as my mother-in-law once said, "They were too young to be thinking about marriage." She would have been opposed to one of her sons marrying a Jewish girl, although I always felt (as her sons did) that if they ever were to marry one she would have been the first to get over it and adjust. She was never put to the test.

One of my ex-brothers-in-law in particular dated several Jewish girls seriously. When he went to college at the University of Alabama in the early 1960s he was frequently mistaken for a Jew, based on his looks and his choice of girlfriends. The story goes that he always got into all the Jewish fraternity parties because he "looked Jewish" and made the most of it. The Jewish fraternity parties at Alabama were a big deal because the members were thought to be rich boys who could always afford the best bands, food, and liquor for their parties. To this day my sister-in-law tells of going to parties at the Jewish fraternity with her then boyfriend, now husband, as if it were one of his more thrilling accomplishments.

Ironically, this same sister-in-law said to me once that she thought maybe our mother-in-law was Jewish—and either she didn't know it or hadn't been allowed to admit it. She said this because people so often commented on Don looking Jewish, and he looked exactly like his mother. This was an intriguing thought. We did think this might be possible. For one thing, our mother-in-law knew so little about her family history, which is highly unusual for the average Southerner. She didn't like to be asked questions. It was as though the family just suddenly appeared in the world and didn't go back much further than a generation. We also thought, based on our sketchy knowledge, that she looked Jewish: A small woman with dark features, not unlike Jewish women in pictures we had seen. As a young woman she looked very much like Anne Frank—which was almost all the evidence we needed to begin speculating. And she worried about everything all the time. Worrying was her full-time job and her hobby too. And we knew chronic worrying was a stereotype of the Jewish mother. (Or maybe all mothers!) We scanned family pictures for clues to her history, to the family origin, but discovered nothing. The irony that she might be a displaced Jewish woman who refused to allow her Christian sons to spend the night in Jewish homes was a beguiling idea.

Years later, when we lived in Tuscaloosa, my daughter, Leigh, had several Jewish friends. One of her best friends was Karen, who lived down the street. Karen's mother was Jewish and her father was Christian. Karen spoke often of the social dilemma her Jewishness presented. She was both proud to be Jewish and highly inconvenienced by it. Christmas was always an awkward time. Her family celebrated both Christmas and Chanukah, so, as she explained, she got "twice as many presents."

I remember her telling Leigh about the abuse she had taken in elementary school when other children taunted her by saying, "You murdered Jesus." Karen was a popular and assertive girl, and it was odd to think of her as having been mistreated—although we didn't doubt it.

The thing I remember most was Karen's great lamentation about not getting the opportunity to pledge for sororities when she got to the University of Alabama, where most Tuscaloosa children aim to go. In

Tuscaloosa little girls begin thinking in terms of college sororities around the age of ten. They discuss which sororities are best, which have the most homecoming queens and cheerleaders, who pledged which sorority, and who might be willing to write letters of recommendation for them. College is that mythical place where your social life gets even better, even wilder, than it was in high school. This makes it a good source of fantasy projections. And the networking starts early. Young girls know early whose mother pledged which sorority and whose good will they should cultivate in hopes of being sponsored. Such sorority discussions always upset Karen. She insisted she had no choice about sororities. The only one she could be a member of was the Jewish sorority. All the others, she said, required that you be Christian. (I have no idea if this is true, but I didn't find it hard to believe.) Karen feared a sharp decline in her popularity if she wasn't allowed to pledge one of what she considered to be "the best sororities on campus." I had actually seen her come close to tears when talking about this. "I'll have to be in the same sorority my mother was in," she said. "It's the only one for Jewish girls."

A more recent story: Morris Dees, contemporary freedom fighter extraordinaire, is a friend of mine and, according to his mother, may even be a distant cousin, which I choose to believe. We love so many of the same things that I think our gene pools must overlap at least a little. We love the state of Alabama—the people, the land, good barbecue, cotton fields both planted and plowed, muddy red riverbanks, fried fish, real talk, heavy accents, homegrown vegatables, storytelling, reading and writing, rereading and rewriting, country music, our families— and we have a shared vision of a brave new world. I talk about it, I dream about it—but Morris works toward it daily with a vigor and courage that is really beautiful.

Once when we were heading out to Waugh, Alabama, for some good food and good talk in Morris's beat-up, bulletproof car he mentioned that the white supremacist groups he had devoted his life to eliminating frequently called him a Jew. He told me he gets hate mail addressed to "Morris Dees, nigger-loving Jew," and more like that. I remember taking note of this and storing it away to think about later. It was a reminder that the same energy and fear that fuels white racism fuels anti-Semitism. I think the difference in the South is that because of numbers alone, one has been (and is being) played out right before our very eyes on the stage of our daily lives, and the other is largely confined to scripted rhetoric in darkened closets behind the lit stage.

I personally think for Morris Dees to be mistaken for a Jew should please Jews everywhere—just the way it pleases me to claim him as some sort of kindred spirit or distant cousin.

Recently when I was in New York I said to two Jewish friends, "I didn't grow up understanding that anti-Semitism was a major social issue." They told me that was a very anti-Semitic thing to say. Then I made it worse by saying, "I didn't even come to know the word *Holocaust* until I went to college." (I don't know why I have this compulsion to confess my ignorance. I guess it's because I'm afraid people will discover it for themselves in time, and this confessional route seems like the least painful shortcut to the ugly truth.) My confession about my ignorance of anti-Semitism made one of my friends furious. He was already some-what suspicious of the fact that I was Southern. I felt my confession had proven to him some awful truth about Southerners that he had long suspected—that we white Southerners were so busy oppressing blacks that we had developed a total insensitivity to oppression and conse-quently had failed almost totally to recognize the oppression of Jews.

In some ways this seemed true.

The fact is the South, even after World War II, still seemed more focused on the Civil War than on anything that had happened since. As a child I heard the Civil War mentioned one thousand times for every time I heard World War II mentioned—and one million times for every time I heard the word *Holocaust*.

In the sixties, when the Civil Rights movement took hold of the South, it took hold of me too and to this day has never let go. In some ways it seems that all social issues of my life are inspired by or connected to issues of integration. I was then and am now alert to everything black and white. I exhaust myself and everybody else around me by being this way. I think of the black-white conflict as the most crucial issue in American life—because in my American life that was/is true.

I don't think as a Southerner (or even as an American) I was alone in my focus on race in America. In the sixties it was *the* news. It was the constant drama playing itself out in our lives, our neighborhoods, our schools, our houses, and if I ever took a minute to forget that (which I didn't) the media reminded me nightly on the six o'clock news. While

I am not licensed to speak for all Southerners I think I speak for many in saying that we were so absorbed in the transformation of our own region and the issues of our own people that as a group, a huge group, black and white, we were barely aware of anti-Semitism, except as a distant concept. I did not walk out my door and look anti-Semitism square in the eye every day the way I did the oppression of black Americans. In fact, I didn't even have to walk out the door: there were oppressed black women right inside my house with me.

I know people outside the South find this lack of a larger awareness unbelievable. I've had lots of discussions about this in recent years in which Jewish friends have explained their own parts in the civil rights struggle in the South and talked about the numbers of Jews who volunteered and came South to fight for the cause. I've read accounts in books and newspapers about the role of liberal Jews in the Civil Rights movement—so factually, I understand that this was happening while I was watching. But did I know it in any personal way? No. All I really knew was that Jews were white people. And my world at that time seemed neatly and artificially divided in half.

A couple of years ago I went to Emory University on my way to visit my mother. The Jewish student organization had invited Henry Louis Gates to speak on campus—his subject: the Jewish-Black conflict. This was intriguing to me because I had no idea there was such a conflict.

I sat in the audience that night and listened to the discourse between Gates, members of the Nation of Islam who had come in full regalia, and Jews, young and old, from the campus and the community. A lot of these folks were angry. Some offered personal versions of the voice of reason. It was heated, animated, volatile—the dialogue building to emotional outbursts again and again. It was an incredible thing to witness—a conflict in which I had no direct part. A rare moment of blamelessness.

At the basest level the evening seemed to be—at least to one only recently inducted into the issue—a competition between the two groups for the title of "most oppressed." There were endless comparisons between slavery and the Holocaust and why one was worse than the other. Numbers were bandied about, getting higher on both sides as the dialogue continued, the bidding war almost like an auction where validation could be had for the right price. Numbers killed, numbers tortured, numbers destroyed in the aftermath, numbers still suffering today. I was silent. Numb. The anger was palpable, the pain real, the frustration contagious, both the desire to heal and the difficulty in forgiving apparent, the issue more potent than I could have imagined.

I sat in fear that someone would point to me and say, "You, whose side are you on?" It didn't seem like the sort of issue about which one should be allowed to be neutral. I sat amid the passionate outpouring and tried to muster an official statement of my own—if only in my head. It was like trying to decide what sort of torture was the worst torture, what sort of death the worst death. And motives? I barely knew my own motives for being there, barely understood my own attraction to the subject.

Was racism worse than anti-Semitism? Was anti-Semitism worse than racism? Was the expression of one more overt than the expression of the other and therefore more damaging? Was one group more economically empowered to battle their enemies than the other and therefore less deserving of assistance? Was one group soaking up sympathy that rightfully belonged to the other?

Why had I been allowed into the auditorium? Why hadn't they turned me away at the door? While they were fighting about which of them suffered the greatest victimization, they had let one of the enemy into their midst. One Southern, Euro, Anglo, Post-Methodist, Pseudo-Intellectual, Lipstick Feminist. Didn't I come from the people that all of this uproar was really about?

My friend, Kathleen Cleaver, who later turned out to be a Bunting fellow with me, was there that night, but I didn't know her then, didn't see her. I realized this though—all my life I'd been empathizing with black women the best way I could—as much as I understood how, as much as they would allow it. But it had never really occurred to me to empathize with Jewish women—I guess I never knew they wanted or needed any empathy. And maybe they don't. But I'd never thought of their lives as being particularly difficult. Not until this night when I saw the raw emotion, listened to the moving personal testimony, and witnessed the political outrage.

I met Sheila at a writer's conference. She told me she was a journalist for a major Southern newspaper, and I told her I was a fiction writer who didn't know whether or not I had the right to call myself a fiction writer. She was Jewish. I was lukewarm Christian, of the backslider persuasion. We hit it off in the magical way that sometimes happens when you're really lucky, when you're drawn to somebody who is drawn to you and neither of you knows exactly why.

Sheila had recently moved South with her family. She was suffering cultural shock. I was experiencing a cultural revival. It was a natural combination.

Sheila was a married woman, mother of two, who by my standards had been nearly everywhere and done nearly everything. Her doctor husband had recently taken a job in Mississippi and had moved the family down from New York City. Sheila was approaching the experience of life in the South the way a missionary might approach those who hadn't heard THE WORD. I loved listening to her talk about it. She was the scientist, and I was the specimen.

"Church," she said. "People's lives revolve around church down here. It's all they do. It's all they talk about. That and food. It's scary."

"You mean they think you're strange—since you don't love Jesus?"

"Are you kidding? They think I killed Jesus."

"Somebody from up North told me once," I said, "that the Southern church is theater. It's drama. You know, like improvisational art or something. Everybody is an actor. Try to think of it like that."

"Were you raised in the church?"

"Is there tea in China?"

"So are you sitting around here waiting to die so you can go to heaven?"

"Sometimes it seems like it."

"No offense, you know. But this Christian heaven thing is freaking me out. I don't get it."

"You don't believe in heaven?"

"Jews don't have that luxury," she said. "Thank God."

"So you think this life is it? This is the whole thing? What do you think happens when you die?"

"I don't count on sitting around on the clouds strumming my harp for the rest of eternity, if that's what you mean. I think death is death. Death is not just another word for a new and improved life. At least I don't think so. It seems like Christians are so busy trying not to do anything wrong—and failing miserably if you don't mind me saying so—so that maybe they can get to heaven, that they waste this whole life, you know, worrying about the next life, playing it too safe."

"And what about Jews?"

"We are raised to think that this life is our chance, our opportunity.

We are under great pressure to make the most of it. We are all born with certain gifts, you know. I show my appreciation to God—or whatever—I honor my parents, by making the most of my life, my gifts, here and now, on earth, during this life. I am supposed to show love for God by making something good out of myself. I don't think in terms of a second chance. I want to—have to—make as much of this life as I can. Accomplish as much as I can. Live full, you know, because as far as I know this is all there is. I can't take a chance on wasting it. I refuse to waste it. I mean, I think that's why so many Jews are so highly accomplished—and why so many Christians resent that, you know."

"I thought Christians resented you for killing Jesus."

"Well, that too," she smiled. "But this other thing. This *meek shall inherit the earth thing* down here has gotten a little carried away, don't you think? Am I offending you?"

I was imagining how I might live my life differently if I didn't have the buffer zone of heaven where everything was going to be right and perfect and fair if I could just hold my breath and hang on long enough down here on this lopsided earth. What if Sheila turned out to be right? What if I died and then they told me, *Ha! We tricked you. There is no heaven. You have to make your life on earth into heaven, dummy.* Was I buying heaven the way somebody in Arkansas would buy oceanfront property? Christians were the saved people. Suddenly that seemed very different from being the chosen people. I decided to try to aim toward being both chosen and saved. I decided to try to live my life like Sheila lived hers—full (just in case). That way, if when I died there turned out to be a heaven paved in gold where people finally acted right, then that would be a bonus. A nice surprise. But I would try not to spend this life getting ready for that one.

I told Sheila my plan and she thought it was a good one.

All of Sheila's mother's family had been killed in the Holocaust. Sheila talked about that. I listened. Her mother's pain had been passed on to her, she said. The umbilical cord was her direct line to the past. Although she was born after the war it seemed that she was born during it. She grew up terrified by the stories she heard. She slept with a light on. She saw all the ghosts of her mother's family appear one at a time in her mother's face, along with stories too terrible for one woman, stories that a daughter had to help a mother, a lone survivor, to bear.

Her father had not been as affected. Over time he had grown tired of her mother's sadness and pain. He had wanted her to put the past behind her. He took her on trips and bought her nice things and tried to help her forget. But she never forgot. She taught Sheila Hebrew. She sent Sheila to Israel when she was sixteen, and Sheila had visited once a year since. Sheila's plan was to siphon off as much of her mother's pain as she could, to take it with her, in her backpack maybe like so many heavy rocks, and when she and her husband traveled the world, to find some place where it was safe to unload this pain, get rid of the burden that was weighing them down, let go of it in some remote region, deposit it in some distant, desolate spot. She was looking for the right place. She would know it when she found it.

I had no story to offer Sheila. My own story was coiled tight inside me. I remember the day I was born, opening my eyes, looking around and knowing first thing that something was terribly wrong—that I was born on the wrong side of something, as if a person could put in a birth request choosing who to be in this life and expect that it would be honored. I tell myself that I would have chosen to be born on the side of things where people suffer—not the side that caused the suffering. But I was just lucky, and that was too flimsy a thing to offer up for discussion.

I never saw or heard from Sheila after that last night of the conference. I had come to hear Eudora Welty read about a rapist, and had cried through the whole thing. I left thinking of Sheila, the way her words had unlocked a door for me. Shown me where the door was first—and then unlocked it.

In 1989 I got my first fellowship to an arts colony and spent three weeks there working on a novel. What I remember most were the women I met. I had already learned from the six years I spent in Wyoming that a Southern woman could rub people the wrong way just by walking into a room. (Our stereotype it seems is almost in direct contrast to the stereotype of the Jewish woman, an idea that fascinates me and bears exploration.) A Southern woman doesn't even have to say anything to set people off. We can just be our smiling, overly made-up selves with our overly arranged hair sprayed into place and our natural affinity for accessorizing ourselves a bit too much and wearing bright, cheerful colors so that collectively we might look like a bowl of ripe fruit, but individually—especially in the Northeast where black is the color of choice and on rare occasions a woman might break out into neutrals, a little gray, a little tan, a little taupe—Southern women can feel like a tacky flashing neon light in a dark and stormy world.

We Southern women who are not born with smiles on our faces learn very quickly to put them there if we want to navigate the Southern terrain with anything akin to success. So I'm sure I came downstairs to breakfast my first morning at the artists' colony with a toothy grin on my face, dressed in bright orange looking like a too-happy tangerine, my hair curled, my half pound of makeup carefully applied. At the time I had no idea there was an invisible sign around my neck that read, YES, HONEY, I AM SOUTHERN WOMAN, HEAR ME DRAWL.

I sat at a table of women dressed in their casual, everyday funereal attire. They told me they were all from New York City. I could have guessed that. I told them I was from Alabama. They had already guessed that. I knew they were probably thinking about me, *Why don't you go upstairs and wash all that makeup off your face and try to be a real person. And isn't it time you started shopping in the adult department?* What they didn't know was that I was thinking, *Why don't you all go upstairs and fix up a little bit? A little pride in appearance never hurt anybody. Black is not even a real color, you know.* And so began an unlikely and amazing series of conversations that led us to become fast friends.

Of course, I had no idea that the four women were all Jewish. That was slowly revealed to me in the course of our conversations. They thought it was very funny that I had asked one woman if she was Catholic. She said she had been asked a lot of things in her life, but never that. She said it was like somebody asking me if I was from New Jersey.

My own frame of reference was more geographical than ethnic. I thought I could distinguish between a New Yorker and a midwesterner. Or a New Englander and a Southerner. Or maybe a Northwesterner and a Northeasterner. But I could not distinguish between a Jew and an Italian, for example. Or an Irish Catholic and a Polish Jew.

Eleanor, Janice, Joan, and Ann, my newfound New York friends, gave me a crash course in Jewish womanhood—more or less. We had a wonderful time comparing stories and analyzing each other. I understand that knowing just four Jewish women does not equate knowing all Jewish women—and certainly knowing me did not equate their knowing Southern women—but we had a good time dissecting and projecting. Afterward I felt very much changed, my view of the world permanently altered.

One thing I particularly remember was their telling me, more or less in unison, that I had the lowest expectations of men they had ever witnessed in a woman. I was shocked. Were they suggesting that it was possible to have high expectations of men? This was a revolutionary concept.

Through the weeks of watching them negotiate their private lives— one of them shakily married, like me, the others divorced or unmarried—I was appalled at the way they interacted with men. They were appalled at the way *I* interacted with men. For one thing I smiled at men no matter what. They didn't. I operated in a constant state of pity for the testosterone laden. I thought of myself as a one-woman volunteer rescue squad. I detected no pity on their parts. It seemed to me they had men jumping hurdles when there didn't need to be hurdles. And it seemed to them I was too busy clearing out all the hurdles from the paths of men so that they didn't accidently trip over anything difficult and hurt themselves.

Less than a week into my stay a male poet, bless his heart, had the poor judgment to join our table at breakfast one morning. "Nothing like starting the morning at a table full of beautiful women," he said, pulling out a chair and taking a seat with his mug of sugared coffee in his hand.

The other women bristled. Then Janice said, "We are not here to help get your day off to a good start. We are here to do work just like you." He looked for a moment like he had misheard her. "If you want us to take you seriously," she said, "then you need to start by taking us seriously."

I was paralyzed by her rudeness. I personally thought a mere "thank you" would have been sufficient.

The poet was almost as dumbfounded as I was. He mumbled something and moved to another table where he was more neutrally received. "That really makes me furious," Janice said, "for him to act like we're here for his entertainment."

"He didn't mean any harm," I said. "He was trying to be friendly. That's all."

They stared at me. I sat there in the harsh glare—the hot spotlight— of unenlightenment. "What are ya'll so mad about?" I asked. I had never known that being called beautiful could secretly be an insult. Who knew?

"Where I come from that was just good manners," I said.

They stared at me like they found my proclamation as profoundly sad as it was true.

Another evening after dinner when a group of colonists were sitting around with our shoes off in the afterglow of a good day's work at the computer or piano or easel, drinking wine or sparkling water, mellowing out in that end-of-the-day down time, Joan said to me, "You really touch men a lot."

"What?" I said.

"Men. You're always touching them."

"You've lost your mind," I said.

"At dinner. You touched John twenty times if you touched him once."

"John? I wasn't *touching* John!"

"Yes, you were," she said. "Wasn't she?"

The other women agreed that I was. "Maybe you're not aware of it," they said.

"What do you mean by touching? Do you mean *touching* like this," I touched Eleanor's arm, "or do you mean *touching-touching*?"

"Just touching," they said. "Touching."

"Well, of course I touch him. I touch everybody I like. I touch all of you, don't I? I touch nearly everybody like that. It's normal."

"I never touch anybody I don't know well," Joan said. "Especially men. In New York if you touch a man he thinks it means something. And of course, it does."

"It's a come-on," Eleanor said.

"Well, where I come from touching someone is not a come-on. It just means, here-we-are-two-people-in-a-nice-moment."

"Bullshit."

"I patted his arm!" I shrieked. (I was getting a little hysterically defensive.) "I was not groping for his crotch."

"Yes, you were," Janice said. "Figuratively."

"You are sick," I said. "You've gone crazy. When I was growing up my mother hugged every single person who stepped foot in our house— that included the mailman delivering a package and the guy who came to fix the TV. It meant *welcome to our humble home* and *thank you*. It didn't mean I want you for my love slave. Give me a break! People touch where

I come from. They hug hello, they hug goodbye, they pat each other on the back, they touch fingers when they pass the butter or put the owed money in the person's hand. It's the way you make yourself safe—touching. It's not sexual. It's just human. That's all."

"Well, maybe you can get away with it down there. Maybe you can even get away with it up here by pretending you don't understand what you're doing. But I guarantee you people in New York will interpret it differently."

Just then John—the living proof—walked through the room and we all stared at him.

"What?" he said.

"Will you please tell them that I was not fondling your genitals at dinner. They think I was pawing you. Tell them it was nothing. I didn't even know I was touching you at all—hardly."

"What the hell are you talking about?"

"See?" I said. "See?"

"We're talking about the connotations of touch," Janice said. "The regional differences in what touching members of the opposite sex means. How people interpret it."

"Oh," he said. "You were touching me? I didn't really notice. No offense."

"Thank you," I said.

I was careful afterward to try to think before touching. I didn't touch any of the men from that point on. I only touched Eleanor, Janice, Joan, and Ann if the moment absolutely demanded it and I could not help myself.

Several nights after this conversation John, our occasional dinner companion, asked me to drive into town with him for a cup of coffee. He said he was depressed because his work was going badly. We sat at a cafe and sipped decaf. "So," he said, "do you want to have an affair?"

"Is this a joke?" I said.

"No," he said.

"Did they put you up to this?"

"Who?" he said.

"You know who."

"Nobody put me up to this. I swear." He was silent a minute, then said, "Should I interpret your response as a definitive 'no'?"

I told no one about John's tragic overture. Partly because I didn't want to humiliate him. Partly because I didn't want to humiliate myself.

Until then I had not known the amazing power of my incidental touch—
like having ten magic wands for fingers.

It would be my last night at the colony before Joan and Janice both
confessed to having had the very same conversation with John over coffee. I guess he was more or less going down the roster until he found
someone who would say yes.

It was a relief to know that.

One day, as we were all at lunch in Lynchburg, Virginia, original home
of the moral majority, Janice asked me a profound question. "Why," she
said, "do Southern women prefer the Rhett Butler type to the Ashley
Wilkes type?"

I thought she must be kidding.

Janice went on to talk about Ashley's sensitive, intellectual, gentle
side and Rhett's obnoxious, selfish, arrogant side. I was dumbfounded.
I had never heard a woman speak ill of Rhett before. (Of course, I
could not think fast enough to mention the fact that Scarlett did in fact
prefer Ashley Wilkes, which, as far as vast numbers of other Southern
women and I were concerned, was part of her flawed character.)

Janice's question led to one of the most memorable gender conversations of my life. I have never looked at the issue of men and women in
quite the same way since, and in fact, think that conversation, at least in
part, led me to want to write the novel *Balls*—which explores Southern
gender issues in the microcosm of college football—just to see what I
might discover.

It seemed that my companions, these women from New York City,
writers all, Jewish all, whom I considered highly sophisticated, preferred
intellectual men. This amazed me. I mostly tolerated intellectual men—
considered them neutered or overly feminized or something. I only
liked smart men if they did not act too smart. In the world I came from
it was okay to *be* smart but it was not okay to *act* smart. The distinction
was subtle, but significant.

Coming from the anti-intellectual terrain of the Deep South, I fa-
vored physical men, you know, guys who could lift heavy furniture, fix
broken plumbing, run fast carrying balls under their arms. My colony
friends found this appalling and funny and extremely sad. Bookish men
just weren't appealing to me at that time. Ballish men weren't appealing
to them. It was a wonderful contrast and caused me to venture into the

swamp of my culture/myself in search of evolutionary clues. Some days I can still be found in there, waist high in the muck.

I left the colony that summer with a round of emotional goodbyes and plans for a reunion in New York City. Later that year I took my daughter to visit New York University, where she was thinking of attending college. We had a wonderful reunion there at Eleanor's apartment on the upper East Side and continued our exploration of life and love and the pursuit of meaningful existence. My daughter was as dazzled by these women and the conversation as I had been the first time—and was again.

The conversation ignited when my daughter, in a context that I can't remember, commented on Ann's referring to herself as "a Jew." It was a revelatory moment—not a particularly pleasant one—all around. "Why shouldn't I call myself a Jew?" Ann asked.

"It's not that you shouldn't," my daughter said. "It's just that I've never heard that. I would be afraid to refer to you as 'a Jew.' I would say you are 'Jewish.' I don't know why."

For a moment it felt like all six of us had spilled hot soup in our laps. Then a debate began between Ann and Janice—Ann declaring "I am a *Jew*," and Janice saying, "I am not a Jew. I am a Jewish woman, a Jewish writer." The debate expanded to include all four women, who discussed the extent to which they felt defined by their Jewishness. Ann felt she was a Jew first and everything else she was emanated from that. For Eleanor, her Jewishness was only one of the many ways she defined herself. Janice minimized her Jewishness, was married to a non-Jew, and accepted—but did not celebrate—her Jewishness. The conversation was passionate and animated.

My daughter and I listened in amazement. My daughter had the expression of the camper who had dropped the cigarette that had set the forest ablaze. She was upset and apologetic. I just kept thinking how such a conversation might go, not among Christian women (I was pretty sure how it would go), but among Southern women. It seemed this discussion was about identity—how much of it is imposed on you by your birth, your culture, circumstances that preceded you by generations and will impact you for a lifetime. How lucky or burdened does one feel about the identity that comes with birth? How much or how little will one embrace that identity, expand that identity, rejoice in that identity? I know some form of those questions too. I found the whole evening sobering and exciting and important.

Over the years Janice, Eleanor, Joan, Ann, and I gradually lost touch with each other. Geography can do that sometimes, outlast the letters and phone calls, but I have not lost touch with the part of them that they shared with me or the part of myself that they helped me discover.

I don't dress like ripe fruit now as often as I used to, although I still have my fruit moments—especially in the hot summers here. I am still makeshift blond, I still don't leave the house without my mask of dime-store makeup, I still sometimes forget to be offended by compliments from men, I still smile more than good sense allows, so outwardly I'm not that much changed. But inwardly I like to think that some drowsy, sleeping-beauty-like part of me has been awakened—and not by the kiss of a prince either, but by conversations with a group of remarkable Jewish women, all of them fine writers, all of them wise women. I like to think their Jewishness was an important part of what transpired between us. I choose to believe that. Just as I believe my Southernness was.

One of the all-time soul mates of my life I met recently—just two years ago. She is Jewish, raised in New York City, living in the Berkshires now. Our histories could not be less alike, our opportunities, our choices, our educations, our families, our means—but there is something that is more powerful than any of that—something that made all the other interesting but secondary. And writing this, I think, is the first time I've spoken or thought of her as a "Jewish woman." I don't think she thinks of me as a "Southern woman"—although, lord knows, she realizes I am one.

Most of the life she has led is "other" to me, but she is not "other." She is "same"—as in mirror of the soul, as in real friend, chosen sister. We talk about our mothers, our fathers, our grandparents, our children, our lovers, our husbands, our darkest moments, our moments of unimaginable light—and the details of the stories never match—but the essence always does. What I hear her say about her life echoes into mine with such familiarity that I feel totally revealed—set free—by her story. And I think my stories have loosened the reins on her too. I have seen her look at me and find herself there. I've found myself in her face, her stories a thousand times. Our friends who see us together or spend time with us will eventually comment on our oppositeness—looks mostly (she's dark, I'm fair)—but also the oppositeness of the places we come from, the paths we took, the history that backs us up, that lets us down, that we are working toward now. Each time someone tries to discuss how opposite we are I think it shocks us—I know it does me. Because inside all the opposite is a sameness that is so rare and wonderful that I'm amazed not everyone is able to see it instantly. It is large and real—and yes, really beautiful. I believe in it in a way I have rarely believed in anything.

At first I thought I wouldn't put my friend in this essay because it sounded like "some of my best friends are Jewish. . . ." But the more I wrote this mess of an essay, jumping all around, grabbing up moments and incidents and memories to substantiate a rather questionable expertise, the more I thought that the most important contribution I had to make to this subject could not be confined to the page—and shouldn't be. I am no expert. I guess that's obvious. Here is where I say something corny about the shared humanity of women—about finding the best of ourselves in each other and all that. That difference is magnificent—exciting, frightening, amazing. But once you sort through it, over and over again, you keep finding a basic sameness. And that's the real thrill.

Jewishness fascinates me—I like to hear about it, to watch it, to listen to it, to guess the parts I don't understand. I am chronically afflicted with the compare-and-contrast syndrome—I can't help it. I look for matching pieces—and for rare one of a kind pieces that only fit here but could never fit there. My interest in Jewishness has gone too far on occasion—annoyed certain of my Jewish friends who were less interested in it than I was—or who were suspicious of my motives. What can I say. So shoot me.

Oy vey.

Hannah's Teshuvah
(Hannah's Turning/Conversion)

ANN OLGA KOLOSKI-OSTROW

RABBI AL invited me to talk about my conversion to Judaism at Erev
Yom Kippur. The address, by one faculty member each year, is
considered the centerpiece of the evening service at Brandeis University. He suggested that I tie it in with the concept of *"teshuvah"*—
turning, answering, repentance—a fitting theme for the High Holidays.
It seemed an easy enough assignment in the abstract. As I confronted
my audience with my carefully crafted lecture, however, I was surprised
to find myself not just explaining *teshuvah* as an intellectual concept,
but actually experiencing it on that very night through the power of
words and memories. My Jewish self was changing as I spoke. I was coming closer to understanding what it is to be Jewish.

I've lectured in Brandeis classrooms for ten years now, but I was
trembling when I approached the lectern at Kol Nidre. "I've only been
a Jew for a little over thirteen years now," I began. I knew that Rabbi Al
would soon argue that it was getting high time for me to plan my own
bat mitzvah. I also supposed that my worry and preparation for this Kol
Nidre talk gave me at least a hint of the emotional roller coaster that
might precede a bat mitzvah! "So," I went on, "it's a great honor and
personal obligation, at my tender Jewish age, to be able to address you
on this ninth day of Tishrei, in the year fifty-seven fifty-six, the evening
before our Day of Atonement."

That's as far as I got before my eyes fell on Professor Aaron Slovonsky
sitting about three rows back. Oh my God, he's here, I thought. When it
was announced this past summer that Brandeis would add Professor
Slovonsky, a renowned expert on the destruction of European Jewry—
in particular Polish Jewry—to our faculty in Near Eastern and Judaic Studies, I remember shivering in a cold sweat. I'd been putting off meeting
him—even avoiding him on campus. I'm a second-generation American,
half-Polish Koloski, and I was raised as a strict Roman Catholic until

about age thirteen. I've always been sure that someone with the learning and the insight of Professor Slovonsky would know just by looking at
me that in second grade I was the kid who told Nora Pinsky that she killed
Christ. (In fact, she didn't even know who Christ was.) And wouldn't he
also be able to tell that there are anti-Semites in my family, the Polish
half of it in particular? I know it's illogical, but I live with considerable
guilt about that childhood episode and about those anti-Semites. It's
unfortunate. It's my nature. It's probably also very Jewish of me.

"I know you'll find it hard to believe by looking at me," I continued
ironically, with my eyes fixed on Professor Slovonsky, "but I was not always the 'serious' Jew you see before you, who, at this stage of my life,
even has the privilege of teaching Latin and Greek and Roman archaeology in the Department of Classical Studies here at Brandeis University. I first set foot on this campus in the summer of nineteen seventy-
three (I was twenty-three years old, by the way) because I was looking
for a rabbi who would perform an intermarriage—between me and
Steven Ostrow, my Jewish husband. We've now been married for twenty-
two very happy (and very challenging) years. We are also fortunate to
have two dear, not-so-little sons, Aaron and Benjamin."

I was greatly relieved to see that Professor Slovonsky was smiling at
me. I had felt a strong connection to Judaism back then, and not just
because of Steven and his remarkably complex and loving family. Rabbi
Al himself had no small role, like many other Jewish friends, teachers,
students, and colleagues. I just didn't know enough at the time of my
marriage to understand what it meant to be Jewish, or to understand
what I actually might have had in common with those who were.

Jews were so puzzling to me. Steven's father John, for example, has
always been committed to Jewish causes. Almost single-handedly he built
the Jewish Home for the Aged in Worcester. He would never deny being
Jewish, yet he claims he's an atheist. His god, he says, is the classical
music he loves so much. Steven's mother Zöe, among other things, the
master Jewish chef, who hardly knows what a commercial bakery is because she's always baked everything from scratch, always lights *yahrzeit*
candles for her mother, father, sister, and brother. She also fasts on Yom
Kippur. Jewish? Through and through. But she knows almost no Hebrew and never attends synagogue, except for bar and bat mitzvahs,
weddings, and funerals.

Steven himself, my very own Jewish sage, didn't know the essence of
our joint connection to Judaism. Shortly before Steven and I were mar-

ried, as an effort to collect some spirituality for our lifelong union, we had gone, along with Steven's parents, to greet his old bar mitzvah rabbi, Rabbi Kleinman. He *never* would have agreed to perform our intermarriage. And we had no intention of asking him. Mom and Dad sat quietly through the interview. It was clear that they felt as uncomfortable as we did.

After some neutral reminiscing, the encounter became surprisingly tense. Rabbi Kleinman suddenly raised his voice. "It's people like you," he said with his finger unmistakably pointing at me, "who are destroying Judaism." I stood up, took Steven's hand, and said softly, "No, Rabbi Kleinman, it's people like you." Steven's dad said he'd never forget it. Steven's mom assured me that Rabbi Kleinman types keep her away from synagogue. I was truly bonded to the Ostrows.

We told our own Rabbi Al about our outrage at Rabbi Kleinman's accusation. What is a Jew anyway? we challenged. Little did we know then that the very act of questioning was part of the answer.

"That's a good question," Rabbi Al calmly responded, and then he turned around and asked us if we had read any good Jewish books lately, Elie Wiesel, Isaac Bashevis Singer, or that "good book" the Torah? We were a bit frustrated to receive another reading list, since what we wanted was some kind of common denominator. How could we have anything in common with Rabbi Kleinman and be Jewish? The fact that Steven was willing to marry me was proof enough of that, it seemed. Rabbi Al smiled and slowly responded, "We are now and you were then all sitting together trying to figure out how to be good Jews. Isn't that a common denominator?"

Rabbi Al's only request of me was that I make a commitment—not an elaborate and impossible vow of some sort—just a commitment to *learn* something about Judaism, to promise never to turn away from it without *learning*. He hoped that Steven would help me with that commitment. He has, and we both have tried to keep that promise ever since.

I thought my Brandeis audience would appreciate hearing about that early *teshuvah*. "I was really lucky," I told them. "Rabbi Al had agreed to perform my marriage ceremony—a ceremony between a blond, partly Polish *shiksa* and a Russian Jew. I had long ago given up Catholicism. But it still took me eight years of married life—a decision to have children— and two and a half years of study with my rabbi in Hanover, New Hampshire, Rabbi Larry, before I was ready to be 'officially' Jewish, before I was ready 'to turn.' Finally, in nineteen eighty-one, I seriously began

preparing for my conversion. I was ready to become Jewish with conviction and, I thought, some understanding—to know that my Jewishness
was more than eating bagels and more than viewing Woody Allen
movies."

At this point in my talk, Professor Slovonsky seemed to be listening
very intensely. Then I noticed Dora and Nathan Abelman giving me a
gentle wave from one of the back rows of the Levin Ballroom. You could
always find Dora in a crowd—even this crowd of more than six hundred
people. She was habitually radiant, in her youth a beautiful redhead.
Nathan and Dora had come all the way down from Concord, New
Hampshire, just to hear me. Dora is a survivor of Auschwitz—the only
survivor I have ever known personally. She usually hides the tiny blue
numbers on her left arm beneath long-sleeve shirts. I'd known her and
Nathan for more than ten years, from days when I worked for the New
Hampshire Council for the Humanities. Nathan, a political journalist
now in his sixties, had many times given me teachings about what it was
to be Jewish on Yom Kippur and on all the other days of the year, just by
telling me about his life and his marriage to Dora. I had even heard him
speak in his own temple about "being Jewish." To him, and now to me,
being Jewish is being self-conscious. It is to be in a nearly constant state
of forgiveness. It is to be ambivalent, to be suspicious and watchful. It is
to be proud of surviving and sick and tired of being a survivor. It is to
contribute to and be compassionate toward society, and often to puzzle
over why you are sometimes hated for it. It is even to wonder what it
would be like to be a Christian or to wonder how it would feel to be in
the majority. I was spiritually buoyed to see Nathan there beside Dora in
my audience.

But Dora and I have an even closer tie than the "Jewishness" that I
share with Nathan. We both have Polish blood too. I know that I am to
her like the daughter she was never able to have. She could not have
any children of her own after her sufferings in the camps. In fact, she
lost everyone in her family while she was in Auschwitz—everyone she
ever knew from Rodom, Poland, except her brother Issie, who escaped
and survived by eating potato peels for several months. My own family
came to America in 1910 from Warsaw. That my closest relatives were
gone from Poland when Issie was eating potato peels and when Dora
was at Auschwitz is small comfort to me. I'm sure Professor Slovonsky
could tell me where my more distant relatives were in those same years
and what they were (or were not) doing. But I've not asked him. Dora

has always told me that she knew girls with long blond hair and green eyes, just like me, back in those days. Now she was sitting at Yom Kippur services to hear me talk about my conversion. And she too was smiling proudly at me.

I really wanted to interrupt my sermon and speak directly to Professor Slovonsky, Dora, and Nathan and tell them that I am frequently haunted by those days in my life when I was not encouraged to study and question—days in my non-Jewish youth—days when ambivalence and self-consciousness were not very much a part of me. Between the ages of six and thirteen (in the late 1950s and early 1960s), I attended weekly Roman Catholic catechism classes. We had much to memorize— prayers, songs, and in particular, we had to repeat what became known as "The Questions" and their accompanying "correct" answers in our catechism books.

"Who made you?" read the text. "God made me."

"Why did God make you?" the text asked. "To know, love, and serve Him in this world and be happy with Him in the next," the text assured.

There were many pages of such questions and answers. At home I was always expected and allowed to ask new questions, so I found it troubling that I was not given the same freedom in my religious training. But I quickly saw that when we recited, no one was supposed to "read between the lines" or "try to improve" on the questions or the answers. Our instructors, the priests and nuns, did not teach us children "from a corrected scroll," as the Talmud encourages the rabbis.

Professor Slovonsky, Dora, and Nathan would feel very sad for me if they could read my memory, but one spring day in my regular weekly Roman Catholic catechism class (in fact, my father had recently died of some unknown heart condition at age forty-seven so I was particularly vulnerable and trying to be particularly pious), I asked my parish priest, "Father, if all of us who have been good are going to sit at the right hand of God when we die, how will all of us 'good people' fit there?" I thought of myself as not just good, but excellent, and I certainly wanted to have a guaranteed space there beside God when I died. I suppose I also wanted to sit beside my own recently dead father as well. But the serious urgency of my question was quite misunderstood. Unfortunately, I was slapped hard across my cheek. I can still hear that crack. It still burns there sometimes. Now I realize that this situation is extreme, and not all catechisms are to be measured by what happened to me on that day in Great Barrington, Massachusetts, in May of 1962. But I'm sure it wouldn't surprise Professor Slovonsky, Dora, or Nathan that a whole era of my life had ended with that slap.

My mind was still wandering, now to those rote memorizations from my catechism book. It's amazing, given how much else I've forgotten or blocked out from those early lessons, that I have such a vivid recollection of those first two questions and their answers. It seemed that what God the Father had in mind when he created us, according to this catechism, was that we should get to *know, love, and serve* while we are here in this world and to *be happy* with God only in the next world. I think I noticed this split—knowing, loving, and serving are separated from being happy about it—but I surely didn't see the implications back then. The remarriage of the grammar in that catechism played no small part in drawing me to Judaism. And tonight as I was speaking on this Erev Yom Kippur, I was feeling like knowing, loving, and serving God with great happiness because I was ALIVE.

"Yom Kippur," I continued with my speech, "is a great time for questions because we spend almost the whole day praying and focusing our minds on the task of repentance and atonement. I find I get more orthodox about Yom Kippur every year. In addition to the prohibition of work, as on the Sabbath, there are five other prohibitions, as many of you in this audience know very well. We cannot eat or drink, use perfumes or lotions, have sexual relations, wash for pleasure, or, last but certainly not least, wear leather shoes. In my 'early' Jewish period—and I suspect it was so for those of you who have been in the business for a lot longer than I have—I knew the prohibitions well enough, but I didn't necessarily follow every one to the letter. But as I got into my 'middle' and 'later' periods, I found myself becoming more and more committed to the prohibitions and more and more curious about the messages of Yom Kippur, this time of great introspection and community prayer. Sometimes it's hard for 'outsiders' to understand why Yom Kippur has such an appeal for us Jews. Yet, despite all the prohibitions, none of us wanted 'to be left out' tonight. Certainly not me. And as I prepared for the holidays this year, I wondered a lot about why that is—why is Yom Kippur so appealing? I had once thought that my actual conversion to Judaism, including the ritualistic plunge in the *mikvah* after my interview by a panel of rabbis—would be my most memorable *teshuvah*, my most memorable 'turning or repentance,' that I would ever experience. But, in fact, *teshuvah* is unending and comes when you might least expect it.

And as Jews, we must be watchful, alert, ready to accept it at all times, ready to experience it."

I could hear myself explaining the preparation and rituals of my conversion to my audience. Suddenly, as I spoke, I felt my half-Polish and Jewish sides were at peace—not warring in a century of guilt, not guilty from the wars of the century. Professor Slovonsky, Dora, and Nathan were still listening contentedly and nodding at me from within the crowd. While I dutifully delivered my prepared text, which outlined the experience of my conversion, I remembered something even more powerful. I remembered the "prelude" to my dip in the *mikvah*.

"Why you hafta see? It's bath. Nothing to see," Mrs. Lundberg had hollered at me as she struggled to move her large frame down the narrow staircase from her second-story apartment. Her steps were percussive. About sixty years old, with gray-streaked hair, she was brushing flour from her apron as she slipped the key into the door of the *mikvah*, the ritual bath chamber.

Everything was already arranged, but not for today. Two days later my Jewish husband Steven and I were scheduled to drive three hours from New Hampshire, where we lived, so that I could be immersed in this Orthodox *mikvah* in Boston for my conversion to Judaism. On that day, the second of Sivan, 5741 (June 4, 1981) four rabbis would certify that I, Ann Olga, "came before a duly constituted *Beth Din* [a religious court] to declare my desire to enter into the covenant of the People of Israel as a righteous proselyte." I was confident that the rabbis would find me "sincere in my intention and adequately conversant with the doctrines and practices of Judaism."

How well I knew the language of the Certificate of Ritual Immersion. Even though I did not find myself really believing I was "dirty" beforehand, as a classical archaeologist I wanted to experience the actual ritual of *t'veelah* (dipping, immersing), whereby I would bathe in the *mikvah*, be freed from all "dirt," physical and psychological, and become Hannah. Since converts must take a Jewish name, I chose Hannah, which is my own name, Ann, in Hebrew. Secular or religious, the idea of renaissance has a lot of appeal.

Mrs. Lundberg was, of course, right. What did I think I would find inside the *mikvah* today? Would the ghosts of ancient Romans be floating on the surface of the bath waters? I know about their bathing rituals. I know that much of a Roman's afternoon was spent exercising, eating, socializing, and sometimes washing in the barrel-vaulted echo chambers of the public baths. Your slave guarded your clothes tucked in stuccoed niches in the changing room while you maneuvered from warm room (steam circulating inside walls, floors, and ceilings), to hot room, to ice cold room, not necessarily in that order. Each space was crowded, noisy, and brightly painted. The Roman writer Seneca (in the first century B.C.E.) tells us about hair-pluckers, sausage-sellers, ball-players, pickpockets, and mad splashers who added to the general confusion. The experience must have been chaotic, colorful, somewhat dangerous, and fun. Is that what I was looking for? I felt embarrassed. No one had tried to discourage me from coming, no one had the time or inclination to accompany me for this "prelude" to the Boston *mikvah*, and no one could have prepared me for my encounter with Mrs. Lundberg, the keeper of the *mikvah*.

I knew from my rabbi that she worked as the head pastry chef at a fancy cafe in Boston. Her body told her history of sampling many buttery goods over the years. Operating the *mikvah*—especially keeping it clean—was in itself a *mitzvah* for her, and therefore serious business. When I arrived in the city these two days early and asked for a brief tour, she abruptly let me know she didn't have time to talk and she didn't understand what I had come to see. The rest of what she said was lost to me in her heavy Yiddish accent.

She met me as planned at 2:00 P.M. I wanted to impress her with my knowledge of Judaism. I wanted to tell her that until we decided to have a baby, it didn't matter to Steve and me that I wasn't "officially" Jewish. It was enough to feel Jewish, to identify with Judaism. But now I wanted to say I am Jewish and know it as more than an emotional claim.

Perhaps I should quote some Bible to her, I mused. Yes, she should hear some Ezekiel from me: "With pure water will I cleanse you, and you shall be clean; from all your impurities will I cleanse you. A new heart will I give you, and a new spirit will I put within you. I will cause you to follow My teachings, and you shall keep My statutes. You shall be My people, and I will be your God" (Ezek. 36. 25–29). No, I am a classical archaeologist, I thought, whose head is filled with the theories and practices of ancient Roman bath ritual. That's what I'll talk about. Instead I nervously stood before her, and she heard no theories.

The key rattled in the door of the *mikvah*. I still couldn't say a thing. The press of the hot June air pounded at my head. The heat reminded me of Jordan ten years ago where I excavated an ancient Roman bath. My mind's eye reviewed my hands slowly brushing the dirt away—sandy soil that powdered quickly under the scorching Arab sun. I studied that bath. My Arab workmen and I found it after two thousand years buried in the dirt. Baths have defined my scholarly research for almost ten years since then. Seeing them in all their detail, describing them, pondering them has been my work. Perhaps I should tell this to Mrs. Lundberg. Wouldn't she appreciate these memories of ancient history? Archaeologists must always be aware of the fragility of the images we find. Mrs. Lundberg would understand that. But she was terse, she was in a hurry, she was busy opening the door to the *mikvah*. I remained silent.

I suppose it was unfair of me, but I had hoped for a real welcome. I wanted a little encouragement, a Jewish mother to smile at me, and maybe a touch of Yiddish humor. I thought this early visit to the *mikvah* would make my conversion somehow more thorough. The word *t'veelah* itself, with its metaphor of total immersion, appealed to my scholarly persona. I guess I slipped into the comfortable mode of researching an archaeological project. Maybe I'd be able to say the Hebrew prayers more authentically after I had this preview. But how could I explain my nervousness to Mrs. Lundberg in her impatient bewilderment? It seemed best to let it go for now. I'd get through the tour first. Instead of great learning about Judaism or archaeology, what fell from my mouth was small talk.

"How long have you lived in Boston?" I ventured.

She looked stern and annoyed. "About forty year. I was from ghetto in Warsaw." With that the door to the *mikvah* slammed shut after my peek of three seconds. I had stared into a small tiled pool filled with water, narrow tiled steps leading to it. Everything was very light brown, a muted beige trying to be white. That was it. Where was my leisure to absorb this space? How could Mrs. Lundberg be leading me out already? I felt stifled by the sultry urban air. This is not how an archaeologist studies a bath.

I did not protest as I followed her out. I was too defeated by my long drive, by the heat, by her manner to say anything more. As we approached the main exit, she suddenly turned and faced me. She looked as if she recognized someone she knew long ago.

"Your name, Koloski. That's Polish, no?"

"Yes." I answered, hesitating until I saw what I thought was approval mixed with memories of ancient history. "Yes, it is."

She paused while she studied my face. "You know what they'll call you now? You know? After the bath?"

They? Call me? After the bath? No, I don't, I thought. But her eyes, now moist and glistening, her eyes from which not one tear dropped, assured me she would tell before I could ask.

"A dirty Jew," she said. "They'll call you a dirty Jew. Your people."

There were three feet between us when she started this strange conversation. After these last words we moved our arms toward each other, and our embrace seemed at last to close the painful gap that had separated our histories until now.

The daydream of my "prelude" to the *mikvah* had come to an end, and I was glad suddenly to reconnect with the participants of the service, to realize that I was not alone, and to see my audience so visibly engaged by my description of my actual conversion ceremony. I had lost myself in wandering thoughts, but fortunately I had not lost this attentive crowd. I finished my speech, "Let me remind you that on Yom Kippur, we Jews are told to afflict our bodies through fasting and other forms of abstinence because we are meant to feel that the natural course of our existence is suspended on this day while our lives, or at least the quality of our lives, hang in the balance. We are to face what a permanent suspension of existence, death itself, would be like, and thus to learn how better to embrace life. Though these Days of Awe are solemn days, they are not sad days. A big part of the beauty of Yom Kippur for me, in fact, is that it is one of the happiest days of the year. How beautiful to get the gift of forgiveness, an expression of eternal and unconditional love."

At the moment I wished my audience all the blessings of Tishrei and a sweet and happy year ahead, I realized that as we fast and pray and ponder, it is very important to do so together, with one another, for each other, though we are closed within ourselves too, as I had been. While I suspect that this community action seemed a small thing to most of the Jews before me who had been Jews all their lives, it has very special meaning for me—even from my youthful Jewish perspective of thirteen years. For I never feel alone anymore. I am finally at-one-ment with the world of the living, the dead, and with my God.

Embracing Tikkun Olam
(Building a Better World)

Barbara W. Grossman

Unlike some of my contemporaries, I am not conflicted or ambivalent about my Jewishness and have never, ever wished that I belonged to a different ethnic or religious group. I do not find Judaism a source of angst, but am proud to be a Jew, deeply grateful to have an opportunity each day to affirm my Jewish identity. I derive particular strength from the knowledge that Judaism promulgates ethics, ideals, standing up for what is right, and striving toward social justice. As I recently explained in a television documentary called *The Jews of Boston*, "Wherever you are on the observant scale, when you commit to Judaism, you commit to a moral value system, which carries over into every aspect of your life." I love Judaism's emphasis on family, community, charity, and concern for others, and I cherish the rich tradition I am honored to uphold. Israeli poet Abba Kovner has written that it is important to remember the past, live the present, and trust the future. I sincerely believe that Judaism has empowered me to do just that. It has provided a historical, moral, and religious framework for my life, but it also has allowed me to find meaning and value in my unique experiences as an individual.

There is a saying in Hebrew, "*Kol Yisroayl aravim zeh boh zeh*," which means, "All Israel is responsible for one another." We *are* responsible for one another and for honoring the worth and dignity of every human being. As naively idealistic as it might sound, I have internalized that maxim as one of the guiding principles of my life. I am committed to Jewish activism, to doing my part each day to make the world better. That is an essential Jewish *mitzvah* (commandment or good deed) known as *tikkun olam*: the healing and repair of the world. I take it with the utmost seriousness, trying as best I can to have a positive impact on people's lives. I am involved in Jewish causes but also give my time to a wide variety of nonsectarian cultural, educational, philanthropic, political, and human service organizations. I am convinced that each of us can make a difference in our communities, our country, and on the fragile planet we inhabit. I have been blessed with a wonderful family, superb education, and resources I can allocate. Giving back a portion of what I have been fortunate enough to receive is both a duty and a privilege.

Although I have always been proudly Jewish, my commitment to Judaism has intensified over the past three decades. As I have matured as a woman and grown into the roles I have assumed as wife, mother, and professor, I have found that my Jewishness is an integral part of my sense of self and extends to everything I do. In my professional life as a theater historian and director, Jewish ethics and values affect my teaching, my relationships with students and colleagues, my respect for learning and scholarship. Making a Jewish home with my husband, Steven, and our three sons, David Maxwell, Benjamin Isaac, and Joshua Adam, has been immeasurably enriching for all of us. From the *hamotzi* (blessing over the bread) we say before dinner to the celebration of Jewish holidays and life-cycle events, we have tried to instill in our sons a deep appreciation of their heritage and of the connections that reach from generation to generation (*l'dor v'dor*). My passionate commitment to Judaism today has developed from several distinct, yet interrelated transforming life experiences: my years at Smith College and Camp Tevya in the late 1960s, marriage and motherhood, study trips to Israel, involvement in Holocaust-related projects, and dedication to social activism.

Anti-Semitism and Awakening: From Smith College to Camp Tevya

I had chosen Smith College over my parents' objections and had gone to Northampton in the fall of 1965 determined to prove them wrong. I arrived on campus looking forward to the happy whirl of freshman activities and was shocked at how alien I soon felt in my new environment. Part of it was the closetlike room I had in Laura Scales House. Spartanly furnished with desk, dresser, and undersized bed, it was in the dorm's old "Maids' Quarters." Many of its previous occupants had been the servants wealthy Smithies typically brought with them, an idea that struck me as ludicrous and somehow made me uncomfortable. Part of it was the absence of boys in my classes, an obvious consequence of selecting a single-sex school, but one for which I had not adequately prepared myself. Since most of the Ivy League and "Seven Sister" colleges were not coed in 1965, being in an all-girls or all-boys situation was a given. I had come from years of public school in which the male presence, though occasionally annoying, was always stimulating. I was used to having heated discussions with my male classmates, heady intellectual exchanges where verbal ripostes flew back and forth and challenging debates were the norm. I had enjoyed working with boys on the yearbook and student council, in clubs and class plays, and had counted them as my friends. I was startled at how bland the classes at Smith seemed in comparison, how slowly time passed when my fellow students either doodled or looked at the professor with bored, blank, uncomprehending faces and no one spoke. Except me. I was a one-person debating society but found it impossible to duplicate the spark and spirit of high school academics on my own.

Mostly, however, my feeling of alienation came from the realization that I was different. As a Jew on a predominantly Christian campus, for the first time in my life I felt like a member of a minority group. That may sound strange since Jews make up only a tiny fraction of America's population, and our country is one that has always emphasized its Christian roots and values. Nevertheless, in my everyday experience that was not evident. We lived in a Jewish neighborhood and celebrated Jewish holidays, my parents primarily had Jewish friends and belonged to a Jewish country club, my father worked at a Jewish hospital, and most of my classmates in the Newton, Massachusetts, public schools were Jewish. In fact, Newton South High School was so overwhelmingly Jewish that my friends and I irreverently labeled it the "Golden Ghetto." There were some non-Jews, of course, including most of the faculty. There were even a few students from the inner city, bused in on the METCO program. Nevertheless, the culture of the school, with its emphasis on academic achievement, clearly reflected the hopes and aspirations of its largely Jewish population. Study hard, get A's, go to Harvard, become a doctor—or, in the early 1960s, marry one—were the messages we all heard, the immigrant values we had internalized and by which we lived.

Smith was so white-bread Brahmin, it almost took my breath away. There were the obvious differences from Newton South, the emphasis on gracious living rather than academic achievement, the cloth napkins and silver napkin rings instead of plastic cafeteria trays. There were the more subtle ones, such as the requirement that members of the freshman choir, to which I briefly belonged, sing in chapel on Sunday mornings. Aside from my reluctance to get up early on the one day a week I could sleep late, I resented having to attend a Christian service and, much as I loved choral singing, soon dropped out of the group. There was also the anti-Semitism—covert, but ever present.

Had I arrived on campus with an obviously ethnic surname, I might have been more oblivious to the hostility. People who disliked Jews simply could have avoided me or, social masks in place, politely disguised their distaste. Veiled glances, arch looks, and cutting asides might have escaped my notice—for a time, at least. My last name, however, was Wallace. It provided no clue to my ethnic identity or religious affiliation, as I quickly discovered in a conversation with one of my dormmates. Mary lived two doors down the hall and, like me, was a freshman. Angular and athletic, she had come to Smith from rural Ohio. Smith had been her first choice, and she was delighted to be in Northampton. Standing in the corridor outside our tiny rooms, we spoke about many things and found we had several common interests. When I mentioned that I was Jewish, our talk abruptly stopped. Mary looked stunned. She peered at me quizzically as if she couldn't quite understand what I had just said and exclaimed, "You can't be!"

"But I am," I responded, puzzled by her reaction and eager for an explanation. To her credit, she answered honestly that she thought all Jews had dark brown hair, brown eyes, and large noses. Since mine were blond, blue, and relatively small, respectively, I defied the stereotype. I laughingly corrected her, but hadn't yet heard the punchline. After a brief pause, Mary admitted that there was something else. She had grown up hearing lurid stories about Jews and had even been told they had visible horns and tails. I was the first Jewish person she had ever met, and my obvious lack of horns was undermining all her assumptions. At first I thought she was joking. When I realized she was serious, I was incredulous, but I also appreciated her forthrightness. Her shocking statements precipitated an intense discussion about religion and prejudice, the first of many we would have over the next four years. From two totally different backgrounds, we learned to respect each other in our time together at Smith and actually became close friends. Religion never became a divisive issue in our relationship as we took pride in each other's growth and accomplishments.

With others, however, there was not the same learning curve. Take Nancy, a sophomore from California, as a representative example. Nancy was our dorm's self-appointed social director and guide to life at Smith. Delighted to help with our orientation as first-year students, she provided the information she considered essential about Laura Scales House and its residents. Taking me into her confidence one afternoon, she whispered that Ellen, one of the juniors with whom I had become friendly, was someone to be avoided. I wondered why. Snorting with laughter, she said it was because she was a "typical New York Jew" and I knew what that meant. I was furious, but looked at her with all the dignity I could summon and replied, "Yes, Nancy, since *I'm* Jewish, I *do* know what that means." Crimson with embarrassment, she sputtered a clichéd apology ("Some of my best friends are Jews. . . .") and attributed her confusion to my appearance (the blond hair and blue eyes again) and surname. Unlike Mary, however, it was obvious that Nancy had no interest in overcoming her prejudice or even in acknowledging it. The lines were drawn and she had no intention of crossing them again. Nor, frankly, did I. After several futile attempts to change her offensive views, I gave up. They were too ingrained, and it was clear she did not want a debate or a dialogue with me. Whereas Mary's quick wit and formidable intellect enabled her to move beyond the anti-Semitic stereotypes she had learned as a child, Nancy regarded them as legitimate criteria for social ostracism. Jews were not welcome in *her* California neighborhood, country club, or private school, and she accepted such misguided elitist proscriptions as perfectly appropriate. They were as natural to her as the sunshine she sorely missed on gray days in Northampton. Blinders affixed, remarkably impenetrable, she infuriated me, but she also made me sad.

The immediate result of that upsetting encounter was my decision to wear a necklace with a Jewish star. It would help eliminate some of the confusion which, fortunately, didn't extend to my own sense of identity. I had always been proud of being Jewish and never wanted to "pass" as a non-Jew. In fact, I disliked the name Wallace both because it was so misleading and because I associated it with one of my few unpleasant childhood memories. When I was ten, I was old enough to realize that our name originally must have been something else and asked my mother about it. She said my grandfather, my father's father Abraham, had changed it from Wishnik when he arrived in this country from Poland in the early years of this century. Thrilled with this information, I ran down to the playroom where my father was working to tell him I preferred the *real* family name. "I'm Barbara Wishnik, I'm Barbara Wishnik!" I gleefully informed him, enjoying the sound of that name on my tongue. I liked it better than Wallace already and thought he should change it back. My father did not share my enthusiasm. In fact, he erupted with a fury that astonished me. Shouting that I must never mention that name again, that it wasn't ours any longer, that Wallace was, he launched into a tirade that was as uncharacteristic as it was unexpected. Baffled by his response, I stared at the black-and-white tiles on the floor until they blurred. I didn't understand the anger. I didn't know that it was rooted in his experience as a first-generation American, that it went back to *his* childhood, to his encounters with stone-throwing Irish gangs on the way to Hebrew school, with bigoted teachers who told him his immigrant aspirations were inappropriate and who ridiculed his dreams of becoming a doctor. He belonged to an era when blending with the dominant culture was the goal, when ethnicity belonged to the "old country" and Americanized names helped accelerate the process of assimilation. As a ten-year-old girl in Newton, I had no sense of that history but knew in a way I couldn't yet articulate that Wishnik was a link to my heritage and my family's past in Eastern Europe. Ironically, it was my Grandpa Wallace, architect of the new family name, who gave me my first Star of David when I was six.

Clearly identified as a Jew, I had no more anti-Semitic encounters that year at Smith and thought far more about the lack of men on campus than about Judaism. I knew I was going to have to change my summer plans. I was supposed to teach swimming at the camp I had summered at for years and loved. It was an idyllic spot on a beautiful lake in Winthrop, Maine, and I had looked forward to returning. But it was Camp Kippewa for *Girls,* and, after Smith, I needed a different environment. Barry, a close high school friend who was then at Harvard University, suggested I join him at Camp Tevya in Brookline, New Hampshire. I was skeptical. Tevya was coed and that was good. It was also affiliated with a more traditional branch of Judaism, the Conservative movement, and that might be problematic. Although I was proud of my Jewishness, I was far from observant. Tevya was strictly kosher, combined classes about Judaism with athletic activities, and kept the Sabbath from sundown on Friday until sundown on Saturday with three religious services. As a Reform Jew, I thought that might be too extreme for me, and I didn't know if I could deal with that intense a summer. It wasn't the kind of Judaism with which I had grown up.

Still, a drastic change from Northampton and single-sex Smith was in order, and I decided to try it. I arrived at Tevya in late June and was relieved to see that it looked just like a camp should with tennis courts and ballfields, a lovely lake with sunfish, rowboats, and canoes, and small gray cabins lining the grounds. My fellow counselors were a lively crew, and it was wonderful to be in a coed environment again. My eleven-year-old charges were happily unspoiled, and I enjoyed teaching swimming. The best part, however, and one that I never anticipated, was the Jewish observance. I loved everything about it: the kosher food, the blessings we chanted before and after each meal, the Hebrew songs and folk dances. The services I had so dreaded were surprisingly accessible. Held outdoors in the glorious New Hampshire woods or down by the lake for *Havdalah* (the end of Shabbat) with fragrant spices and braided candles, they were joyous and inspiring. Full of the traditional prayers and rituals my synagogue had eliminated, they were profoundly moving. Even though I didn't understand much of the Hebrew, I loved the *sound* of it, and the haunting melodies touched me deeply. For the first time, I appreciated the richness of Judaism the *religion*. I realized it was not simply a question of historical obligation, tribal identity, or language and culture. It was a vibrant, complex, warm, intelligent, ethical tradition I had not understood or fully appreciated. In short, I had an epiphany, a true spiritual awakening I never imagined possible.

Family Ties: Orthodox Roots, Reform Affiliation, and Respect for Learning

My beloved parents had been raised in Orthodox households and rejected the rigidity of their religious upbringing. My mother's father, David Stern, was particularly observant. As a child, he had emigrated from Russia by himself and would never discuss either his life there or his rise to wealth here. He had made a fortune in real estate and had eight grown children when he married my grandmother, Minnie Aarons, following the death of his first wife. When my mother Bernice was born, one of three children in his second family, he was already in his sixties. He died in his eighties, just months after my birth in 1948. In the few pictures I have of him, he looks serenely at the camera. He wears a skullcap and is reading the Bible. He was so religious that he had a *mikvah* (ritual bath) in his home, but he was enlightened enough to let my mother attend Girls' Latin School (where she won the Latin Prize) and Radcliffe College.

My father Joseph, having overcome the negative expectations of his elementary school teachers in Mattapan, moved successfully through

Boston Latin School and on to Harvard. My parents were both science majors and, thanks to my mother's pink cashmere sweater, met in the library over some chemistry notes. My mother had accelerated on account of the war, finishing Radcliffe in three years instead of the usual four, so that she and my father graduated together and married in June 1943. Frustrated by an insidious quota system that threatened to derail his career plans, my father began to despair of studying medicine. On the day he planned to enlist in the air force as a navigator bombadier, however, he received his acceptance to Boston University Medical School. He subsequently graduated second in his class and became a highly successful obstetrician and gynecologist. My mother, like so many women of her generation, worked professionally (as a science editor at D.C. Heath Publishing Company) until she had me, then opted for full-time parenting and occasional, usually child-centered, volunteering.

My younger sister Ellen and I were raised in a Reform household, but there was no question about our identity. We knew we were solidly, unmistakably Jewish. Our home had a *mezuzah* on the front door and Sabbath candlesticks in the kitchen, even though we generally didn't light them on Friday nights. We always celebrated Chanukah, our favorite holiday, never Christmas. We went to synagogue on the High Holidays, first Rosh Hashanah, then Yom Kippur, when we did our best to fast. We observed Passover with my Wallace grandparents, since my mother's parents had both died, but it was never a particularly festive affair. Their Mattapan apartment was dark and unappealing, the seder more obligatory than celebratory, and my grandmother's cooking surprisingly unappetizing. Even in an era when women were known for their wonderful recipes, my Nanny Lily (Golinsky) opted for mixes and packaged food. Her indifference to meal preparation was less a feminist statement than an expression of her world-weariness. Decades of hardship had taken their toll on this sweet but curiously remote woman, who often seemed ambivalent about her family and whose expressionless blue eyes had lost their spark years before. Still, the table was always set with the best dishes, and my grandfather proudly produced silver dollars for us when we found the *afikomen* (a special piece of the Passover matzoh that is hidden). That became more difficult toward the end of his life when his immigrant success story soured. Having done extremely well in the pickle business he founded in Roxbury, he refused to sell it when he had the chance, ran it into bankruptcy, and spent his last years driving a truck when he should have been enjoying retirement. Nevertheless, his grandchildren brought him *nachas* (happiness), and he enjoyed watching his favorite television programs and reading his daily Yiddish newspaper.

No one ever tried to teach *us* Yiddish. In fact, our parents infuriated us by speaking it whenever they wanted to keep us from understanding them. It had been my father's first language, taught to him by his maternal grandmother Baba, for whom I am named. How I wish now that I had learned it then! (My father says the same thing about Russian, which his parents used for private communication when he was a boy.) We did not keep a kosher home and did not observe the dietary laws. We went to Sunday School at our synagogue, Temple Israel, but not to Hebrew School during the week. Some girls did, but Temple Israel in the 1950s discouraged bat mitzvahs. In fact, Temple Israel at that time had stripped the service of much of what I now find most memorable. There was no cantor, and a sizeable portion of the liturgy had disappeared in a misguided attempt to Americanize the service. (Thankfully, much of it has now been restored, and there has been a full-time cantor at Temple Israel since 1972.)

The most interesting part of my religious education took place in tenth grade, the confirmation year, when we dealt with ethics. Our curriculum centered on a book our rabbi had written called *Little Lower than the Angels,* and it was the first time I had thought about the human condition in any meaningful way. Rabbi Gittelsohn challenged us to grapple with complex issues (legal, moral, metaphysical) and helped us understand that ambiguities and uncertainties are part of life, that Judaism has never opted for easy answers or dogmatic proscriptions. Through intense discussions of topics ranging from Vietnam to valium, prejudice to premarital sex, I came to appreciate Judaism for its latitude, liberalism, and enlightened tolerance.

Finding a Life Partner

I recently heard a wonderful story attributed to the Baal Shem Tov (1700–1760), founder of the Hasidic movement. According to him, each human soul emits light, and its radiance reaches upward to heaven. When a couple falls in love and marries, the light emanating from both souls intertwines and produces far greater illumination than the two do by themselves. I responded immediately to the image of intensified light, because I honestly feel it accurately describes my relationship with Steve, my beloved husband of almost thirty years. I regard him as my other half, as he considers me his. I have helped him achieve some of his fondest hopes, dreams, and goals, as he has supported me in reaching mine. His strong commitment to Judaism has reinforced my own and has been an integral part of our life together. We have both worked hard to create a Jewish home full of warmth, light, and love and know that we have been able to accomplish far more as a couple than either of us could possibly have done alone.

Moving back through the decades to 1968, the year in which we met, I was a junior at Smith College and had just ended a significant relationship with a Dartmouth senior named John. A wonderful person, he was an Episcopalian, and I was uncomfortable with the religious difference, not that either one of us was contemplating marriage. He was about to join the navy, and I planned to apply to doctoral programs in English, but we liked each other too much to risk more serious involvement. My parents had long stressed the importance of marrying a Jewish man and, after my summers at Tevya, I agreed with them. Although marriage and children seemed as remote to me then as flying to Mars, I knew that I wanted both at the appropriate time. Much as I tried to consider the alternative, I simply could not imagine a future with a non-Jewish husband. I was determined to avoid the complications of intermarriage and the risks of creating a home in which my ability to carry on Jewish traditions and values might be compromised.

In 1968, as my class's newly elected representative to Smith's Judicial Board, I received an invitation to be a Junior Usher at graduation. It was an honor I almost declined in a fit of late adolescent cynicism, but I decided it would be a nice opportunity to say goodbye to my senior friends. In addition to carrying the ivy chain during the commencement exercises, we were expected to make life as pleasant as possible for the visiting alumnae. Since my ushering duties included helping the returning classes with their luggage, I reported to my station at the front desk of Laura Scales House to welcome members of the class of 1943, back for their twenty-fifth reunion.

It was an extremely humid day in Northampton, and I spent a good portion of it dragging suitcases up the stairs for a parade of surprisingly unfriendly alumnae. Just as my shift was about to end, a tall, attractive, athletic woman strode through the door and asked for her room assignment. She wouldn't let me carry her bags, but smiled warmly and bounded up the flights to her room. She was happy to compare our respective experiences as Smith undergraduates, and, in the course of that animated conversation, we discovered we were both from Newton.

I waited on her table that night at dinner in the dorm and, when she asked where she ought to go with friends afterward, I suggested a popular local tavern. I headed there later myself and, spotting her at an adjoining table, went over to say hello. From the nature of the pleasantries we exchanged, I could tell she was trying to figure out whether or not I was Jewish. Again, *Wallace* was no help. My strategic references to working at *Camp Tevya*, one of the *Eli and Bessie Cohen Foundation* camps, and to my father's being on the *Beth Israel Hospital* staff must have convinced her. She suddenly asked, "Are you engaged?" I answered the unexpected question with a firm no. "Are you pinned?" she shot back. Amused, I answered, "Definitely not." "Do you date?" she pointedly inquired. All too rarely, I thought, and boldly answered, "Of course."

Delighted with my responses, my amiable interrogator told me she had a son to whom she'd like to introduce me. A Princeton graduate and a first-year student at Harvard Business School, he was at home babysitting for his eleven-year-old sister, so she knew exactly where to reach him. As soon as I said I'd be willing to meet him, she phoned him and announced, "Do I have the girl for you!" I never expected him to call and actually was quite surprised when he did. Our first conversation was incredibly sophomoric as each of us tried to impress the other with our worldly sophistication, implying that neither of us *needed* to be fixed up, especially by his mother. When he arrived for our first date in a maroon Corvette, which convinced me he couldn't possibly be a serious person, I was sure we'd have nothing in common. How wrong I was! To say it was love at first sight would be hyperbolic, but it came close. That unforgettable member of the Class of 1943, Shirley Dane Grossman, became my mother-in-law. Her son, Steven, the reluctant target of her matchmaking efforts for years, became my husband in December 1969.

Since our marriage (when I was very happy to take the name Grossman and finally jettison Wallace), we truly have become life partners. We have been blessed with three wonderful sons, cherish the Jewish holidays we observe with our extended family, and value the Jewish traditions we proudly carry on. From our first meeting in 1968 to the present, Shirley and her dear husband Edgar have been marvelous role models. Their loving relationship and positive, energetic approach to life have helped inspire our own. Their annual celebrations of Rosh Hashanah, Yom Kippur, and Passover—complete with bountiful meals and such special dishes as Grammie Dane's Bulkies, the unforgettable cheese Danishes created by Shirley's late mother, Mollie (Levin) Dane, to break the Yom Kippur fast—have given us years of joyous family gatherings with, I hope, many more to come. The warmth and beauty I first found in Judaism at Camp Tevya have always been in abundant evidence around Shirley and Edgar's festive holiday table.

The Holocaust, Israel, and Social Activism

Steve and I attribute our active involvement in Jewish life, in large part, to trips we made to Israel in the late 1970s under the auspices of the Combined Jewish Philanthropies of Greater Boston (CJP), the oldest Jewish federation in the country. Steve went to Israel first. In October 1977, one year after our son David's birth, a friend asked Steve to join him on Acharai ("Follow Me"), an all-male "mission" designed to develop young leadership. When he returned after ten days, it was clear that the intense participatory group experience had had a dramatic impact on him. Struck by the importance of supporting the State of Israel and Jewish communal organizations both locally and nationally, he made a generous financial gift to the CJP campaign and began working tirelessly as a volunteer. Acharai marked the beginning of a lifelong commitment to Jewish activism and philanthropy, and Steve has generously donated his energy and resources to a variety of organizations ever since.

At the time, however, I was baffled. The cataclysmic mission was the first major event we hadn't shared since our marriage, and, much as Steve tried to explain what he had experienced, I couldn't understand it. I didn't resent it; I just felt left out. Fortunately, there was a women's mission scheduled in January that he encouraged me to join. Although I tried to find reasons not to participate—toddler son, too far, too much work—it was perfect for me. Only a six-day trip (four of them in Israel, two for air travel), it meant I wouldn't have to be away from David for too long. I had begun a Ph.D. program in drama and was in the midst of my coursework, but the mission would be back before the second semester began. Not knowing what to expect, I decided to seize the opportunity and go. I've always been thankful I made that choice.

Just as Steve's trip was a transforming experience for him, mine had a profound impact on my development as a Jewish woman. Traveling with twenty other women ranging in age from sixteen to eighty-four was meaningful in itself because it made me realize how irrelevant age is as a criterion for friendship. Shared values and zest for life do far more to forge ties between people than chronology, and I treasure the relationships that began on that special journey. We bonded as a group as we sped through a dizzying whirl of activities and programs. I remember some of them vividly. Visiting the Ghetto-Fighters' Kibbutz, as well as hospitals, schools, and military bases. Walking through Jerusalem's Old City and Arab Market. Spending time at Beit Hatfutsot (the Museum of the Jewish Diaspora), which traces Jewish history and achievements throughout the millennia, and at Yad Vashem (Israel's principal Holocaust memorial), commemorating the near annihilation of the Jewish people during this dark century. The latter was an emotionally wrenching experience, as confronting the horror of the Holocaust invariably is. It reaffirmed my strong sense of Jewish identity and unwavering commitment to a Jewish future.

We toured an impoverished neighborhood in Herzliya called Neve Yisrael, site of an urban renewal project with which Boston had been partnered, and met a number of its female residents. Mainly Sephardic Jews—immigrants from Iraq, Syria, and Yemen—they welcomed us warmly and took us into their simple homes for tea. I was struck by our ability to communicate, despite the difference in languages and backgrounds. We were still Jewish women relating to Jewish women, sharing food and smiles in apartments with *mezuzot* on the door frames and candlesticks on the shelves.

That night, over a kosher Chinese dinner, we met with a very different group—all high-powered female professionals, members of the country's academic, business, and military elite. I found myself drawn to one woman in particular, an officer in the Israeli Air Force named Dahlia. It turned out that we were almost exactly the same age, both born in May 1948, along with the State of Israel. Everyone commented on how much we resembled one another, with our short blond hair and blue eyes, similar features and physiques. Her English was as good as my Hebrew wasn't, and, as we spoke, we realized that her grandparents had emigrated from Eastern Europe to what was then Palestine at roughly the same time as mine had left for America. One of her grandfathers even came from Lumza, a small town in Poland obliterated by the Nazis, which was my Grandpa Abraham's original home.

There were certainly obvious differences in the personal and professional choices each of us had made. She was single and a military officer; I was a doctoral student with a husband and son. Yet the parallels were striking, the coincidences almost eerie. In Dahlia, it seemed as though I had found an Israeli double; she said it was as if I were her American twin. That encounter, meaningful on multiple levels, strengthened the bond I had immediately felt with this country—so foreign and yet so familiar. A Jewish homeland still torn by ancient rivalries, redolent with history and biblical significance, it remained a land of dramatic contrasts (the black-clad Bedouin on his camel in the desert near the sprawling new community development), challenges, and opportunities. I returned to Boston determined to make my own contribution to Jewish life through activism and philanthropy.

If Israel has played a formative role in my adult development, so has the Holocaust. I first learned of that incomprehensible horror by reading Anne Frank's moving diary. When I asked my parents if any of our relatives had died, they exchanged significant glances and nodded in sad acknowledgment. Evidently, my paternal grandparents had left a large extended family in small villages in Poland and Russia. They used to correspond with various aunts, uncles, and cousins, sending them letters and care packages from the United States. In the 1940s, the mail from Europe abruptly stopped. There were no more requests, only silence, as the villages were leveled and their inhabitants gassed. Haunted by these nameless, faceless ghosts, I would try to imagine what their lives had been like before the Nazi inferno, imagining my own fate had my grandparents not fled pogroms at the turn of the century and come to America. Grateful to them for their courage, I nevertheless felt a strong connection with those who had remained behind and perished, as well as with Jews throughout the millennia who had suffered and died for their faith. The painful history of Jewish martyrdom and persecution made me weep. It also made me terribly angry, as mindless brutality always does. Yet the resilience and tenacity of my forebears inspired a deep sense of awe. I was proud of my heritage, proud of the survival of the Jewish people, and acutely aware of my obligation to both past and future.

Deeply affected by our visits to Yad Vashem, Steve and I resolved to become active in Holocaust-related projects. For more than a decade, we have taken leadership positions in organizations that not only honor the memory of the millions slaughtered by the Nazis, but that also use the terrible lessons of the Holocaust to combat racism, anti-Semitism, and homophobia today. From co-chairing the first state dinner to raise money for the Holocaust Museum, now a splendid reality in Washington, D.C., to working with the award-winning educational foundation Facing History and Ourselves, to co-chairing the dedication of the New England Holocaust Memorial in October 1995, we have done our best to support projects that teach people about the corrosive effects of prejudice and the need for vigilant moral action.

Our lives have been enriched by our contact with survivors and their families, and we are proud of all we have been able to accomplish in partnership with them. There are so many whose moving stories truly are inspirational: Steve Ross, who spent his childhood in a series of concentration camps and lost his entire family (with the exception of one brother), was liberated by an American soldier, and, following his arrival in this country he lived for a time in a car, put himself through school, obtained a graduate degree in psychology, and has devoted his life to working with troubled youth in the city of Boston; Jacob and Mira Birnbaum, who met in a concentration camp, found each other after liberation, emigrated to America, and on their fiftieth wedding anniversary in April 1996, renewed their vows surrounded by their many children and grandchildren; Marianka May, member of a secret chorus at Terezin, who wears a delicate G-clef on a gold chain around her neck in acknowledgment of the music she believes sustained her in that hellish place.

After almost a decade of planning, the elegant and evocative New England Holocaust Memorial has become a powerful work of public art. As art always does, the memorial raises a number of questions. Are its six glass towers supposed to represent pillars? Are they chimneys, symbolizing the death camps' crematoria? Are they candles, illuminating the darkness, suggesting the triumph of good over evil? As a place of contemplative meditation and memory, it leads viewers to wonder in the broadest sense who we are and what our responsibility to our fellow human beings ultimately is. To the people who asked about the appropriateness of such a monument in Boston on a choice spot adjacent to the Freedom Trail and politely inquired if such a memorial *really* was necessary, the answer is a resounding yes! The New England Holocaust Memorial is not an ending, but an effort to rebut the lessons of this violent and bloody century. It will serve as a permanent reminder of the tragic consequences of bigotry, ignorance, and intolerance; of what can happen when people are stripped of every right, every liberty, every dignity; deprived of home, family, love, and life. As one of the Memorial's text panels puts it so eloquently, "The memory of the Holocaust is the legacy and the responsibility of all humanity." Here in Boston, it will stand as a beacon of light and hope for us, our children, and generations to come.

Looking toward the Future

In the documentary film *The Jews of Boston*, Steve observed that "as we've been deeply involved in community-building of all kinds over the years," he's become more religious—not in the sense of being more committed to Jewish religious practice, but in his recognition that "perfecting one-self and the community in the image of God is a driving force in [his] life." I related a story about visiting the White House in April 1995 when, struck by the dramatic contrast in settings, I suddenly flashed back to where I imagined my family must have been just a century before. As I put it in the taped interview, "I remember sitting in a lovely room look-ing out over the Truman Balcony thinking: here I am with the president of the United States, and one hundred years ago, my relatives were probably in *shtetls* in tiny houses with dirt floors. That's why I'm proud to be an American, but that's also why I'm proud to be a Jew!" I appreci-ate the enormity of the leap the Aaronses, Danes, Golinskys, Grossmans, Levinses, Sterns, Wishnik-Wallaces, and so many other Jewish immi-grants have made in a relatively short period of time. I'm grateful to my family members for their vision, courage, and commitment to Judaism over the generations, their emphasis on hard work, positive achieve-ment, *tsedakah* (charity), and contributions to community.

I wear a small gold *hamsa* (hand to ward off the "evil eye") now instead of a star. Like the positive values I received from my family, I inherited my share of "old country" superstitions as well. Even though I don't take them terribly seriously, I'm happy to know there's a recog-nizably Jewish totem working its magic as it rests securely around my neck. I have come to respect Smith College for empowering me as a woman. Judaism, family, feminism, and scholarship have been the most important forces in my life, and, in a sense, I discovered them all in Northampton. "Women's minds matter," a recent college publication noted, and I appreciate Smith for its longstanding commitment to women's education and its more recent emphasis on social activism. I truly am proud to be a Jewish woman and look forward to discovering more about Judaism's rich heritage in the coming years. I have not yet become a bat mitzvah, and that remains an important personal goal. I still have theological questions and unresolved metaphysical anxieties, being much less certain of God's existence than Steve is, but I find in Judaism a source of strength, satisfaction, serenity, and fulfillment.

There is so much I value in Jewish tradition and ritual, so much that is thoughtful and loving, fundamentally decent, and humane. Judaism celebrates life and harmony, marking special moments in what could easily be regarded as ordinary events. For example, friends of ours in Mobile, Alabama, recently made it possible for their temple to buy beautiful hand-painted covers for their Torahs (the Five Books of Moses), sacred and cherished objects in every synagogue. On a Saturday night after the *Havdalah* service, the temple held a special wedding ceremony in which the new Torah covers were married to the Torah, accompanied by festive singing and dancing. I see that as a quintessentially Jewish event: warm and joyous, celebrating renewal and continuity. In forging a relationship between the sacred books and their new covers, it is typical of Judaism as a whole, which is all about relationships. Judaism emphasizes the sacred bonds between each of us and our fellow human beings, our ties to our scholarly and humanistic traditions, our connection to God and the universe, our links with past and future. For me, being Jewish is a joy, a gift, and a blessing, as well as an awesome responsibility. It is my heritage, and it is also a choice I make with a strong sense of positive affirmation and personal gratification on a daily basis.

Confessions of a Shiksa

NANCY A. JONES

NOT LONG AGO I found myself seated with a jovial group of
women scholars at a conference banquet dinner. As sometimes
happens on such occasions, the conversation turned in a friendly manner away from professional matters to our own lives. During dinner, an
amazing coincidence emerged: somehow it was discovered that each
and every one of us was a partner in a mixed marriage between a Jew
and a non-Jew, with the majority of us non-Jewish women married to
Jewish men. In other words, it was a gathering of shiksas. There was some
chuckling about cultural differences and relations with in-laws, but the
general tone was happy.

I didn't think much more about the dinner encounter until quite
recently, when I read a few articles about the shrinking population of
American Jews due to intermarriage. I now found my own life identified
with a widespread social trend, one which many in the Jewish community find disturbing since it threatens the future of the Jewish religion
and traditions. When I consider my marriage in this light, and not in
purely personal terms, I can begin to understand the distress felt by
those who see an entire people and tradition about to dissolve into the
larger fabric of American society. At the same time, I resist the notion
that intermarriage itself is entirely a negative phenomenon, and I'm
bothered by a purely hereditary definition of Jewishness. But thinking
about my "intermarriage" from both personal and sociological perspectives leads me to examine my non-Jewishness and the ways in which
Jewish American culture has attracted me throughout my life.

The issue of my relationship to Jewish culture and religion has become more urgent since the birth of my daughter Cora in 1994. Both
my husband and I are secular people who do not practice any religion.
At the same time, we both hold on to some of the moral and spiritual
values from our respective upbringings (his by an Orthodox grandfather

and mine by devout Presbyterian parents) and by no means reject everything about those traditions. Curiously, it's me rather than my husband who feels most strongly about giving Cora some Jewish education. The challenge will come in a few years when we'll have to take concrete steps to help Cora learn about her Jewish heritage. Meanwhile, I've begun to educate myself about Judaism and Jewish culture. But the dilemma for secular parents like Charlie and me won't disappear: When neither of us really follows a faith or participates in a culture, what attitude do we take toward religious instruction? How do you rear a child to follow ambivalence? I'm glad I had some religious education, yet I don't regret leaving behind the formal practice of religion. I ask myself how I would react to a daughter who became religious, especially if she became Jewish. I'm not sure.

From the Other Side of the Mirror: A WASP Girlhood in Southern Indiana

During my 1950s and 1960s childhood in a small midwestern city, the social "other" was neither the Jew nor the African American, but the Catholic. I remember staring out my first-grade classroom window at the empty playground of St. Charles's parochial school across the field. Another day off for the Catholic kids, I would be thinking in envy—all those saints' days or something. I wasn't alone in holding the extra vacation days against the students of "St. Chuck's." We used to tease them on the school bus. Their separate school, their nun-teachers, their Church calendar, their duty to confess to a priest, their Friday fasts (until 1962 at least), and, above all, the Madonna statues on their lawns and the crucifixes in their houses gave me a greater sense of difference than my contact with Jewish kids ever did. Perhaps those statues provoked some vague form of iconoclasm within my Protestant sensibility; perhaps they represented the alien intrusion of religion into everyday life.

Listening to some of my Jewish Bunting sisters speak of the painful erasure of their culture in WASP institutions, I realize that the Jewish kids, as a much smaller minority in the community than the Catholics, must have had to endure a great deal of indirect pressure to assimilate. I sort of knew who was Jewish, but it didn't seem like a big deal to me. My school observed religious differences in a kind of naive token way— we would learn a little about Chanukah because of its proximity to

Christmas, and the same with Passover and Easter. But I also recall the entire class watching Christmas films about the manger story—films of an unabashedly Christian nature, in other words—as if this were universal culture. I wonder how Steve, a Jewish boy in my class, felt about all the angels and candy canes. Maybe he and his family were too oppressed or pained by their marginality in Bloomington to object. Raising a fuss over such issues wasn't very common in those mild years before 1963.

Similarly, I don't have a clear recollection of people discussing the Holocaust during my childhood. I do remember lots of anti-Nazi propaganda left over from the 1940s, which had filtered down to children's culture, such as the naughty ditty about Hitler and Mussolini and the Three Stooges' parody of Hitler. I grew up thinking that the Nazis were simply the dimwits we Americans trounced during the war. The general attitude toward the Nazi genocide could be summed up by the 1960s TV show *Hogan's Heroes*. In this series the Nazis appeared as benign comic bumblers and wimpy inept bureaucrats manipulated by their Allied prisoners of war. No mention was made of the *other* camps in which the bureaucrats were all too efficient. Were we to conclude that the unmentioned, unshown Jewish prisoners lacked sufficient intelligence and bravery to thwart their captors?

Not even Anne Frank's diary made much of an impact on me as a teenager, despite the fact that I was an avid reader. Like most other "serious" books of my youth, *The Diary of Anne Frank* was assigned in school as part of a set of "well-written books" about personal bravery in the face of danger that included the now-forgotten *Death Be Not Proud*. I recall the *Diary* solely in terms of individual heroism and literary expression, and not in terms of the horror of the Holocaust experience that produced it. It may be that no one during my childhood years was ready to come to grips with this historic catastrophe so soon after the event. Today I can't help feeling that this silence about the Holocaust was part of a larger national silence about the role of genocide within our own country's history that wasn't challenged until the Vietnam War era.

But do I recall overt anti-Semitism? It's painful to think of the warm and friendly community in which I grew up as being capable of the demeaning and hostile slurs and attacks some of the Fellows have experienced. As the seat of the major Indiana state liberal arts university, Bloomington has long been known as a relatively "enlightened" college town. My own recollections offer a mixed picture. During the 1950s and 1960s, one still felt the vigor of small-town midwestern institutions in

Bloomington—feed store, farm co-op, county fair, RCA factory, Pentecostal churches—alongside the cosmopolitan world of the university with its grand opera house, libraries, and stadiums. The social divide between town and gown cultures, simplistically portrayed in the popular 1970s film, *Breaking Away*, was much more acute during my childhood. I grew up associating racial and ethnic prejudice with what we laughingly called "red-neck" culture, unaware of the more subtle prejudices held by my own middle-class community. There were several layers of gentile society in the community. I associated ignorance and bigotry with rural and working-class people who had little or no contact with any nonwhite, non-WASP person. It seemed to me that prejudice grew out of sheer ignorance rather than out of a historical tension between groups. Overt racism was rare. To be sure, there was talk of Ku Klux Klan activity twenty miles up the road in the sleepy town of Martinsville, and the Klan once petitioned to march through downtown Bloomington (the city government quickly rebuffed them). But not until I came to politically Democratic, multi-ethnic New England did I personally witness the kind of naked racial and ethnic hatred commonly associated with backwoods America. The Midwest of my youth wanted people to forget their pasts and their ethnic particularities.

Evangelical Christianity was and is popular in southern Indiana. I'm not sure that it necessarily produces anti-Semitism. This is one lesson I learned from a woman named Betty, whom I met during the year I spent in Strasbourg, France, through Indiana University's Junior Year Abroad program. Betty was one of the Purdue students in the program, and at first this farm girl seemed to me like a fish out of water in France. Her broken French and thick Hoosier accent made her an embarrassment to all of us "serious" students. She was incredibly naive and ignorant about anything European and always introduced herself in terms of her born-again Christianity. She had come to France as a French and Religion double-major, and she soon set about studying Hebrew at the university so that she could read the Hebrew Bible in the original. She had requested lodging in a family, an arrangement that was difficult to come by in Strasbourg. The family that housed her turned out to be immigrant Orthodox Jews from Morocco. To our astonishment, Betty flourished that year and developed a very close relationship with her Jewish host family. In this case intense religious faith built bridges.

On the subject of anti-Semitism in Bloomington, however, my own memory and experience are obviously limited. I've read autobiographical accounts of life in Bloomington by Jewish women that confirm my sister Fellows' experiences of racism, prejudice, and cultural isolation. One older woman paints a stark picture of the links between anti-Semitism and racism in 1940s Bloomington, and another writes of the loneliness of being Jewish in a southern Indiana town where none of her kids' teachers knew anything about Chanukah or Yom Kippur. During my childhood there was no real synagogue in Bloomington. The Jewish community worshipped in the spartan-looking Hillel building on campus. Most of the town's Jews were affiliated with the university. The campus itself must have seemed like a small island in a vast sea of *goyische* faces.

I do remember some institutionalized attempts to liberalize racial and social attitudes during the 1960s. During the Civil Rights era, my elementary school adopted a "progressive curriculum" that preached color blindness. My family's church made similar gestures through its youth programs. My formal introduction to religious difference came during the years when I was active in the First Presbyterian Church youth group. We traveled to visit churches and a synagogue in other parts of the state, presumably to learn tolerance. (This coincided with the era of liberal Protestant ecumenism.) On one trip we traveled up to Indianapolis, where we shyly listened to a gospel choir at a black church, and on another occasion we visited a synagogue in an Indianapolis suburb. I remember not understanding much of the service and being amazed by the bar mitzvah reception held in a large banquet room afterward. The opulence of the feast, complete with silver candelabras, made a great impression on me. I couldn't figure out why they had invited us strangers for such a special occasion. Surely a group of twelve-year-old Presbyterians from out of town must have seemed out of place. I have since come to know how important hospitality is to Jewish people. In our church, we had no such elaborate rituals even for weddings. Confirmation as a member in the church was the official rite of passage for teenagers, but the study involved was minimal, and the ceremony was brief and modest. The emphasis was on personal "readiness."

My first realization that there was such a thing as a Jewish world within American culture came through a fifth-grade friendship with a Jewish girl who moved to my neighborhood. Her family, like most of the Jewish families in Bloomington, had recently come to the area for professional reasons. I can't remember how we became friends, but I vividly remember my friend's mother. She was much more interested in talking to me than any of the other mothers I knew. She spoke frequently about their family background and the large Jewish community she had grown up in in Fort Wayne. They, however, had become Unitarians—a fairly common practice, I've noticed. My friend's grandmother was the great bearer of Jewish tradition in that family. This lady brought with her the aura of a distinct matronly culture I had never known before. She would give us canasta lessons whenever she came down from Fort Wayne. I remember her heavy bracelets and her assertive, spirited manner of speaking—again very different from my mother and the grown women I knew. Looking back, I wonder if she was the kind of willful, well-heeled dowager who so alienated my mother when she and my father visited Miami Beach one year. Such women were the subject of the only anti-Semitic remarks I ever heard my mother make. She resented what she saw as their ostentatious wealth, their loud voices, and their insularity. I'm embarrassed and shamed by this memory.

Although my relationship with my friend eventually deteriorated, I always enjoyed a sense of personal validation within her family. With them it was okay to be smart, opinionated, and talkative. Girls, I sensed, were considered to be as interesting as boys. Looking back, this experience led me to associate Jewishness with an intense family life that became all the more intense because of my own personal sense of isolation within Middle America's anti-intellectual and anti-feminist culture. Not surprisingly, the pattern of quasi-adoption by a vibrant Jewish family would repeat itself during my post-college years in Boston. Once again, I would grow closer to the friend's family than to the friend.

Coming of Age in Boston: I Discover I Am a Shiksa, Not a Yankee

During my senior year in college, I decided to head east after graduation from my hometown alma mater, Indiana University, and seek a job in publishing. I had spent my college years immersed in the worlds of French and English literature and the new field of women's studies. A year in France enabled me to participate in a vibrant foreign culture, and I fervently admired the combination of *savoir vivre* and intellectualism in French life. I became quite fluent in French and felt the strange charm of the hybrid persona that comes with fluency in a foreign language. Living in France also helped me to discover my identity as an American feminist, for I chafed against the sexism in French culture. By senior year, a certain restlessness set in, and I felt the need to break free of the European university world for a while. Something told me that I needed wider horizons. Literature, I felt, was my calling, and I wanted to be around people who liked books. So, as luck would have it, I came to Boston with some meager savings, a few friends, and youthful optimism.

With a little pluck and lots of luck, I landed an editorial position at a prestigious Boston publishing company. At first it seemed like a great opportunity: didn't every literature major aspire to land a job with a venerable press and to have contact with serious (and sometimes famous) writers? It was all happening to a person who had no publishing experience and who had never worked in a city. But despite my good fortune, I was terribly lonely and insecure within the company's Boston Brahmin atmosphere. I was the only member of the editorial department without a prep school background or Harvard degree. Needless to say, I had little sense of Boston mores and social hierarchies. Many people sounded British to my Midwestern ears! The company wasn't exactly a meritocracy. My miserable salary meant living in one of Boston's ugly student ghettos. I couldn't figure out how the other assistants could afford apartments on Beacon Hill or in Cambridge, having never heard the term *trust fund*. My duties as editorial assistant were excruciatingly boring. A typical day was spent reading the dreary slush pile of unsolicited manuscripts, typing correspondence, answering my boss's phone, and proofing jacket copy.

Alienation on the job was only one part of my life in Boston, however. At the same time I was exploring the city and meeting lots of interesting men. Not long after finding my job, I began dating a Jewish MIT graduate student whom I'll call "Tim." Tim came from a world in which everyone was smart, well-educated, and ambitious. I had never known any men like him before. He represented a new model of masculinity; somewhat nerdy and a bit fretful, perhaps, but refreshingly open, nonsexist, and, yes, talkative! What fun to have a smart boyfriend! Tim awed me with his involvement in the abstruse world of physics. When I decided to leave publishing and apply to graduate school, he was very supportive, and I was touched by his efforts to try to understand my literary studies. We were intellectual opposites, and for a while this was very exciting. We were also discovering each other's cultural backgrounds. For the first time in my life I felt "exotic," for he saw me as an inhabitant of the foreign universe of WASP America. Tim had grown up in a suburban Boston community where it was possible to go through one's youth without ever having known anyone who put up a Christmas tree. He was, in other words, the product of a Jewish upbringing very different from that of anyone I'd known.

We were soon going steady, and eventually we began living together in an apartment in Cambridge. It wasn't very long before I was drawn into the family circle, and for five years or so I felt like a member of the family, even though Tim and I never became formally engaged. The warmth, personal interest, and generosity showered on me by Tim's family was a precious gift during those years when I was struggling to find my life's path, first in publishing and then in graduate school. I'm sure that my relationship with Tim lasted a lot longer than it would have otherwise because I loved being a part of his family.

Acceptance wasn't immediate, however, largely because I wasn't Jewish. Tim's parents, especially his mother, were very proud of their heritage. They had always dreamed that their kids would marry highly educated, successful Jewish people, preferably from their town or some-place like it. Not long after I met his family, however, their daughter revealed that she was divorcing her Jewish husband (an MIT M.D.-Ph.D., no less!) because she was in love with an Italian American psychotherapist from a working-class background. This was a bombshell. They loved their son-in-law and thought of him and their daughter as a fairy-tale couple. But before long the desire for closeness with their children prevented Tim's parents from rejecting them, and so they came to accept their daughter's choice, and eventually they accepted me too. Or sort of.

Jewishness and non-Jewishness remained a theme in my life because Tim's family was so open about it. We often went over to his parents' house for meals, family occasions, and holidays. I got lots of instruction in Jewish family life because they were interested in sharing it with me. I couldn't imagine similar conversations in my family about WASP life. There was lots of humor and critical self-awareness, too, much of it expressed in psychological terms since Tim's mother and sister were both practicing psychologists and loved to analyze people's behavior. It was impossible to remain aloof in this family circle. Talk was very direct—often disconcertingly direct for me. I wasn't used to being asked about my parents' sexuality, for instance, or how much I weighed, or what I ate for breakfast every day. All of it well-meaning, but a bit intrusive by my family's standards. Compare my mother's furtive and anxious inquiry to me when I first brought Tim home to Indiana to visit my family: did Tim eat only kosher food? My mother seemed to assume that all

Jews followed kosher laws. She didn't want to offend him, and, of course, she wouldn't dream of asking him herself.

At the same time, while I basked in Tim's family's warm interest in *me,* I felt their lack of interest in my background as if I were a kind of blank slate. While they cared a lot about me and my personal growth, my heritage was to them as bland as my name. I remember vividly how my "outsider" status became clear—one day at a family gathering, I heard someone use the German/Yiddish word *Schul* in conversation. I asked what it meant, and then Tim's mother turned theatrically to the other people in the room and said, "Oh my God, she doesn't know what *Schul* means!" implying the horror of having me, an ignorant *shiksa,* for a daughter-in-law. I was too embarrassed to speak.

My initiation into the family's ways also involved beauty lessons— Tim's mother and sister kept giving me gifts of gold jewelry and makeup. My fashion consciousness had been formed during the antifashion years of the mid-1970s, altered somewhat by the plain Talbot's look I wore to the office. I suppose they wanted me to conform to their idea of femininity. Unfortunately, I kept losing or breaking all those gold chains: surely a sign from my unconscious that this was *not* my style! *They* indeed looked fabulous while I probably looked unconvincing. These feminine attentions were motivated out of affection, and I'm rather amused by these memories. By the same token, I confess to viewing Tim's older sister as a bit of a Jewish American Princess because her love of shopping and her petulant moods (indulgently tolerated by her family) all seemed excessive to me. But this same woman was also a workhorse in her professional life and very devoted to her patients, students, and family. More than once she proved a caring and insightful friend. She also surprised me with her angry outbursts about the anti-Semitism she had encountered as a student at Wellesley College, then my idea of a liberal institution. As usual, I was too embarrassed (or afraid) to ask her precisely what the anti-Semitism consisted of, fearing that I might be unconsciously guilty of the attitudes she so resented.

The cultural contrasts between our respective families may seem like something out of *Annie Hall.* Most significant for me then was the contrast in family attitudes toward sexuality. My parents never voiced opposition to my living with a Jewish man. The issue for my father was my living with a man I wasn't married to. The sexual revolution affronted him, and he was hard-pressed to deal with the turbulent lives of my older siblings. They were struggling with out-of-wedlock pregnancies, early marriages and parenthood, underemployment, and later, divorce. The sexual liberalism of my boyfriend's parents (contrasted with their strong desire for their kids to *marry* Jews) felt rather enlightened by comparison. During the stormy period when my father and I weren't on speaking terms because of my "immoral" living arrangement, Tim's family was my bulwark.

An Academic Love Story in which I Settle Down with the Ideal Husband (Yes, He's Jewish!) and Reflect on Judaism's Appeal to Me as Wife and Mother

Toward the end of graduate school, Tim and I grew apart and decided to go our separate ways. I wanted to live and study in France; he was headed for a career as a corporate scientist. We parted amicably, if sadly. I missed his family and, as in many actual divorce cases, felt that I had left them too. It was a period of emotional numbness. I spent an interesting but lonely year in Paris researching my dissertation. The following year I returned to finish my Ph.D. in comparative literature at Brown University and accepted a teaching job in Upstate New York for the following year. During this period, I became friendly with my future husband, a Brown classics professor who had just lost his beloved partner to cancer. I had previously known Charlie only distantly as a brilliant faculty member in another field. During that period of his grief, we slowly became acquainted and found ourselves meeting occasionally for coffee or lunch. I was drawn to his intellectual nature, his love of literature and Europe, but equally to his generous, sympathetic nature, expressed so vividly by his love for Alison, whom he had nursed so tenderly during her last months. We were both struggling with loss and uncertainty about the future. At the end of the year he left for a sabbatical in Greece and Rome and was I believed on his way out of my life. So it was a delightful surprise on my first day in my new job to find my campus mailbox stuffed with letters from Greece. After several months of correspondence, he returned to the States, and we began exchanging visits. Eventually I changed jobs and joined him in Princeton, New Jersey.

During the first two years of our relationship prior to our marriage, I gave little thought to Charlie's Jewishness. Other forms of difference—he is twenty years older, has two sons by a previous marriage, and has achieved an eminent standing in his field—seemed much more significant. Our personal compatibility and enjoyment of each other's company was so complete that the differences in background were interesting rather than troublesome. We were married in my hometown by a university chaplain in a simple, nonsectarian ceremony. Gathered around us and our family members were the friends and neighbors from my childhood, who seemed genuinely moved by our modest wedding. No one had ever expected me to marry locally, if at all (given my antimale feminist attitudes), and no one seemed surprised by my choice of spouse. My mother, who was initially awed by Charlie, soon became very fond of him. She has had the joy of seeing her daughter married to a man who enjoys cooking and small children and who has absolutely no interest in sports. My father was relieved to see me finally marry the man I was living with.

In many ways, I married a man who had left his Jewish identity behind. Charlie grew up in Dorchester and Mattapan, once the Jewish neighborhoods of Boston. His family, like many Jewish families in that era, were blue-collar second-generation Americans. My knowledge of his childhood is sketchy. Charlie's father was always struggling financially, and his frustration and anger created a lot of tension in the household. My husband doesn't like to talk about his childhood very much. It's clear he has a lot of painful memories. I got a glimpse of Charlie's early life when we went to see Woody Allen's *Radio Days*. The loud family arguments and the evocation of the old Jewish working-class neighborhood in Coney Island made him laugh and reminisce. What's missing is a living family tie to Jewish culture and Judaism. All of his serious relationships have been with non-Jewish women. None of his siblings has any formal ties to a Jewish community. One brother has become a Unitarian with his non-Jewish wife. We gravitate toward my side of the family, traveling to Bloomington for Christmas. (He's happy to sing Christmas carols, and, yes, we usually put up a Christmas tree!)

Charlie says that he rejected Judaism for its chauvinism, but at the same time he is very proud of his Jewish heritage and of the Jewish community. His Jewish identity also emerges in his professional life in one striking way: he won't travel to Germany, although he has been invited by many German universities and has friendly relations with many German classicists. He talks freely about the anti-Semitism he experienced in his student days at Harvard, and I know that his relatively recent decision to return to Harvard as a faculty member was a difficult one for him because of his earlier experiences.

But if asked about his deepest identity, I would have to say that he is a

Hellenist at heart—the landscape and civilizations of Greece and Rome are his spiritual home. Charlie's classical education, begun at Boston Latin School, fulfilled him in ways that his Hebrew education never did. His years in Athens and Rome distanced him from both his American and Jewish roots. I sense in him an affinity for European culture stronger than my own, for he lived happily in Catholic Italy for years. We make a curious pair, my Jewish husband and I. He, a Boston-born Jew, relishes a Mass in one of the vast Baroque churches of Rome, while I, a born-and-bred Presbyterian, squirm amid the gilded opulence of the Counter-Reformation!

Neither of us wishes to fully reembrace the creeds of our youth. We have lived happily and comfortably in the relatively cosmopolitan world of academia where such mixed marriages are fairly common. As parents of a small child, however, we have experienced longings for the respective certainties of our childhood worlds. The warm cohesiveness of Jewish Dorchester and small-town Bloomington are precisely what we can't give our daughter in 1990s Cambridge. More important, we ask ourselves how we can nurture spiritual values in our daughter without participating in some form of organized religion. We both feel that our own identities are grounded in childhoods spent in families and communities with distinct beliefs and values. As we push ourselves to examine our common beliefs and values, we feel ourselves increasingly drawn to Judaism. I find myself attracted to the wisdom and poetry of the Jewish liturgy with its evocation of the seasons and the life cycle and its emphasis on ethical living. I'm intrigued by the intellectual community of Jewish feminists I've seen at Brandeis University, where I am a resident scholar in women's studies. While I sense much common ground between Christianity and Judaism, I find it difficult to accept Christian theology with its stress on professing a specific creed. At the same time, I want to meditate further on the commitment to civic consciousness and political justice that I gained from a Protestant upbringing and to get beyond the negative and simplistic images I too have internalized about my background.

It's hardly a finished story. We have much exploring to do as a family. The cultural, religious, and personal spheres will overlap and conflict at times: I like the family rituals of Rosh Hashanah, Chanukah, and Passover, but I also love the festivities of Christmas and Easter. As we seek points of entry into Judaism and Jewish culture, I expect that there will be times when we will feel unwelcome or suspect, and perhaps wary

ourselves. Our daughter is after all not Jewish except in the Reform tradition, and perhaps I'll always remain a *shiksa*. But as a partner in a marriage in which both of us honor our distinct heritages, I'm not merely a
shiksa. Charlie and I will have to decide on the depth and degree of our
commitment to Jewish institutions and observances in working out our
family spiritual identity. At the same time, I hope to give Cora the blessings of our "mixed" marriage—the appreciation and curiosity we have
felt for each other's heritage, the critical self-awareness our differences
have given both of us, and the sense that we have consciously striven to
pass along the best of both heritages to her.

Half-Breed or Hybrid

Helena Meyer-Knapp

MINE WAS A mixed marriage. I sometimes see it as the fourth link in a chain of mixed marriages. It is probably more accurate, though, to see it as the addition of yet another color and motif to a family tapestry that is now quite complex in its juxtaposition of distinctly different ethnic and religious backgrounds. Others might see in our blended rituals the weakness of knotted threads and garishness of clashing colors; they might see in the wide variety of the images we treasure only insufficient purity. To me, our tapestry is both strong and beautiful. I see six pointed stars, the star over Bethlehem, and American stars. They are connected by swirling multicolored lines, and the whole creates an experience of adventure and openness.

The first of the knots was tied in an international marriage between Paula Rindscopp, a Dutch woman and a Jew, and Meyer Cohn, a German banker from Berlin and a Jew. They were my great-grandparents.

The next motif blended cultural and religious patterns and came with the marriage of their daughter Maria Meyer-Cohn, a German and a Jew, to August Weber, a German Protestant.

A new strand of color was added in London by the marriage of their daughter Paula Weber, both German and half-Jewish, to Roger Quirk, an Englishman. He was the descendant of two generations of Anglican clerics. I am the youngest daughter of this union and was raised in England.

My marriage to an American, Rob Knapp, is the fourth in the series; our children represent the fifth generation to live in a multicultural household.

Each new family found its blended, multicultural status a mixed blessing. With hindsight I am most aware of those strengths in each generation that a geneticist would associate with "hybrid vigor." None of the problems of inbreeding here! Yet I know from personal experience and from family stories that each of us has also suffered hostility and pressure because we set aside local cultural standards of purity, because our children were "half-breeds." American Jews, given a heritage of ambivalence about intermarriage, clearly recognize both the benefits of connections outside the culture and the harm of such connections to the integrity of the Jewish community: do the imperatives for Jewish cultural survival and individual fulfillment depend on assimilation or on ethnic and religious purity?

While I was growing up in England in the 1950s I expected to get married to someone from one of the four corners of the British Isles. Comparable assumptions about straightforward religious and cultural continuity are evident among American Jews today. Often a parent's deepest wish is that his or her child will marry another Jew, not necessarily an American, but please God, a Jew. Among deeply rooted English people, and in the Jewish American community, older generations look on with pride when the young are born: a specific history and tradition is alive and well in the cries of a squalling infant. The continuation of that tradition—its memories, values, and riches—almost seems to depend on English people marrying English and Jewish people marrying Jews. The story embodied in my family is testimony to the value of something else: survival, strength, and spiritual growth in a complex cultural context.

The varied strands of color in my family tapestry are now intriguing and beautiful to me. Although I have no instinct to be family "archivist" and I don't yearn to be trustee of family "treasures" handed down the generations, still the stories of the making of our family are integral to my identity. A description of my identity includes painful memories of my lack of cultural "purity" and admiration for the resilience of the "hybrid." Ultimately I am glad my children know intimately a multicultural way of life.

Berlin: The 1930s

My family survived because, during the Nazi period, my Jewish grandmother and my Aryan grandfather offered each other strength and practical assistance amidst the horrors of rising anti-Semitism. They drew their survival skills and strength from the very fact that they came from different parts of the German cultural milieu.

The Nazis categorized Jews as a separate race, distinct from pure

Aryans. They chose, right up until they actually began the extermination program in 1941, to officially classify the children of such interracial relationships and both of their parents as Aryans. So my grandmother, with her small, dark, classic Semitic features, was "Aryan."

My grandfather August Weber (we called him "Opa") had enormous eyebrows—vast, gray, bushy eyebrows. He had a public reputation for integrity well before the Nazi challenge became serious, and as a child I was always convinced Opa's eyebrows were central to his power. In Germany he monitored the impending ascendancy of the Nazis with horror, and he never wondered what the implications of a Nazi victory might be. The evidence was not hard for the family to find.

Hitler was elected in 1933. My mother was in her first year at University. She was the daughter of an active opponent of the Nazis, and as the second semester began she learned there would not be space for her in the chemistry lab. My grandfather understood the threat implicit in that announcement and he lost no time. The younger children were sent to Switzerland to continue their schooling. My mother, the oldest, went to work in Geneva. Her siblings were in Lausanne, living ultimately with their grandmother, and together this unusual family began constructing a new life. Though they went back to Germany for vacations for a year or two, they were exiles from 1933 onward. The irony is that the children's exile in 1933 was a product not of their Jewish blood, but of my grandfather's political action.

My grandfather was motivated by more than concern about the fate of the Jews. He abhorred all aspects of fascism, but I am convinced that he worked all the harder because of his own intimate relationship with a particular Jew. And he was arrested repeatedly. Seven times in all. Usually he went to jail in Berlin. He was often sent to concentration camps, and it was up to Granny to keep finding him, engineering yet another release.

It's such an ironic story. While the Reichstag was passing anti-Jewish legislation, while the Brownshirts were breaking windows, while so many German Jews were either in denial or in flight, my intellectual Jewish grandmother was getting her banker husband out of jail, over and over again. Granny and Opa managed to stay in Berlin until 1938. She was safe, safe because in the eyes of the Nazis she was not a Jew. He was safe because she prevented him from becoming one of the "disappeared."

In 1938 even they, who tried so hard to combat fascism, knew they must flee. My mother had reached London by then. She got word to

Frank Foley in the British Consulate in Berlin (a man now being called the British Schindler), who gave to my grandparents two of the priceless exit/entry visas he was giving away as fast as he dared to everyone at risk under the Nazis.

Links can still be added to the family chain, the family tapestry can get larger and more complex, because these people did good work and survived. They survived because together they had the cultural resources and the independence to resist the Nazi juggernaut, and they lived to tell the tale.

I now realize that my entire working life has been shaped by this part of my heritage. I learned about courage in the face of devastating information from the real-life experiences of my grandparents. Their work demanded a day-to-day willingness to risk their lives (though not the lives of their children). My work on war, conflict, and cease-fire requires that I remain willing to be ever mindful of and concerned about suffering. My family heritage has been part of the inspiration that keeps me concentrated on the task in hand.

Family Patterns

In each generation the women were the ones to take the adventurous steps in the marriage. We each left the security of family of origin and plunged into new worlds and lives. We each left the foods, the houses, the physical realities of our childhoods and did our best to settle comfortably in a foreign environment. As we began weaving new sections of the family tapestry, the disconcerting awkwardness that was part of our cross-cultural existence was evident to each of us in our daily lives. We felt physically, politically, and spiritually different from the men and women surrounding us in our new culture.

All four generations of women lived under domestic regimes that were dominated by their husbands to an unusual degree. I know only a little about the first generation. I have seen a photo of the Berlin building that contained the Meyer-Cohn bank and my great-grandparents' apartment: it is stone, has only two stories, and has a wide continental elegance, not at all like the typical Dutch red-brick, tall and narrow, canal-side house, in which my grandmother would have grown up.

In the next generation, my grandparents lived and raised their children in the manner of the prosperous Protestant corporate executive, my grandfather, not in the manner of my grandmother's Berlin Jewish community. My mother's stories of her youth are largely rural, the subjects her family's country house, dogs, and horses. The children were sent to a rugged, though progressive, Christian boarding school in south Germany, which they loved. There they were taught tolerance, love of learning, and the virtues of physical as well as mental action.

All that ended in 1933. For nearly a decade my mother was a refugee, braced always for the next crisis. Finally in 1941 she married. Some relatives in my father's family were ambivalent at best. How could a loyal Englishman marry an "enemy alien"? New weavings appeared on the family tapestry with the birth of their oldest daughter two years later.

London: The 1960s

Attributing positive benefits to cultural pluralism is commonplace in the United States in the 1990s. It would almost certainly be more suspect among people in Britain, even now. When I was a child, thirty years ago, the cultural pluralism of our family seemed to lead us to live a double life: the visible English and the shadow foreign. The shadow foreign was an inspiration, and I now see it as the source of my ability to develop a spiritual life.

As a child I was embarrassed again and again by the flaws in our English facade: my mother made strange foods, we never ate English puddings, and we drove unconventional cars. When we went on picnics with friends our sandwiches were salami on dark bread from loaves that were round and flat. All the others had neat square sandwiches— cucumber, say, or cheddar cheese on white. My children were equally embarrassed by me: they minded that I failed to stock the house with cans of soda and took years to understand why I refused to let them watch Saturday morning cartoons on TV.

Minor domestic issues had deeper implications. It seems pretty clear that my father worried that my mother's social demeanor, her vibrant clothes, faintly irregular English language usage, and forthright energy might be an impediment to his professional rise in British government service. I know that in the United States, my English accent is often taken as evidence of arrogance and cultural elitism. Regardless of such difficulties, I saw our family tapestry as bright and beautiful. None of us doubted the deep love my parents felt for each other, which underlay all the cross-cultural tensions. At times my father, and my husband also, have enthusiastically joined in as the women were casting aspersions on the manners, the educational system, or the politics of their adopted countries. For the most part, however, each generation struggled with the day-to-day dynamics of family life without much regard for whether the culture supported or undermined us.

It was harder for my mother and me to look at our bodies as beautiful. In my case I know that as a child I linked the difficulties specifically to being part Jewish, not "purely" English. Two portraits hang in my house, one of my great-grandmother Paula, the Dutch woman who moved to Berlin, and the other of the Paula who is my mother, the war refugee who has now lived in England since the mid-1930s. Both portraits show strong-featured women with dark auburn hair. Neither bears any resemblance to that classic "peaches-and-cream" complexion so common in the British Isles. Furthermore, my mother wears vividly colored clothes and flamboyant jewelry, hardly the Anglo ideal of womanhood.

As a young teenager I was also afflicted, if that is the proper word, by my own bodily characteristics so in line with the English stereotypes of Jews: early menstruation, larger breasts, and early development. My social setting valued a pink, slim, tall, rather straight physique. I found my evident Jewishness uncomfortable and worried about whether it harmed my chances for success and popularity. At school I watched as others who were openly Jewish "left," and thus were left out of, the daily morning prayers, the only time when the school acted as a single community. I now know that this was the action of a hospitable school, but then it seemed that if I acknowledged my Jewish heritage I too was inviting linkage with "un-English" qualities: too interested in money, too serious, too suburban. The school rarely selected Jews as captains for sports, or student body president, though many were successful as musicians. That I might be both Jewish and not Jewish never occurred to me when I was a teenager.

But in fact I was leading a double life, Jewish and non-Jewish simultaneously. That double life was rarely reconciled, and in public, under the pressures of my childhood, I tended to ally myself with English definitions of happiness, goodness, success, and aspiration. In private I loved Granny Weber. Granny seemed free of the intellectual, class, and social ambitions that drove all my friends at school. And yet she was also an intellectual, and adventurous. She'd travel to Egypt and bring photos back of herself on the back of a camel. She had a Ph.D., and for her, study was energized by love of learning and not merely by the prestige of getting into Oxford. I loved her visits. I loved walking over to her apartment for yet another meal of overcooked boiled carrots, boiled rice, and boiled chicken.

My English life included country houses, tall blond men, strawberries, traditional ties to famous boarding schools, King's College Carols on Christmas Eve, the Athenaeum Club, wonderful theater, Oxford and Cambridge. My father's ambitions as a senior government official were enmeshed with these traditions, and in public we rarely strayed beyond these structures. We spent vacations walking and sailing in the Lake District, surrounded by other families with similar origins and ambitions.

Our other life was quite different. Almost all the events took place inside our London house. The people were short and dark and they had strong accents. We were hosts for successive generations of refugees. Refugees from the 1930s Spanish Civil War lived in the apartment at the top of the house for several years. My nanny fled East Germany during the Berlin blockade in 1948. I lent my violin to a Hungarian refugee in 1956 so he could look for an orchestral job. Relatives arrived for visits from all over the world. Lili W. came from Israel. George came from America. Gertrude from Australia. My mother's sisters came from Los Angeles.

These visitors were intriguing, exotic. And we never talked about their Jewishness. I have difficulties giving an honest explanation for the silence. I could say it was because neither of my parents were actively involved in religion, which is true. In fact, I suspect that it was because it was easier for my father to be hospitable to foreigners and to refugees than to Jews. The English part of my background was careful never to be or even feel openly anti-Semitic, but England, after all, is a country with a State religion. The Queen is the head of the Anglican Church. My father was the son and grandson of Anglican clergymen, one a canon of Salisbury Cathedral, the other bishop of Sheffield and Jarrow. My father despised bigotry, but I imagine what I saw at home was evidence that some kinds of difference were easier to live with openly than others.

My parents avoided any serious encounters with most spiritual questions by maintaining a kind of progressive agnosticism toward all faiths: they professed that religious belief was more likely to lead to war and fanaticism than to health or salvation. Thus I was unable to probe spiritual matters with depth from any perspective in England. Our participation in the Anglican Church was strictly seasonal. Our parents never claimed for us any affiliation with England's Jewish community. I certainly never saw myself as Jewish. I doubt my sisters, still based in England, see themselves as Jewish to this day. My mother says, though, that she always knew I was "different." I now realize that the Jewish part of our double life was one reason I believed that different was possible.

Those visiting Jews reminded *me* that adventure, achievement, and meaningful ethics consisted of more than the bland Sundays and impressive ceremonial rituals of the Anglican Church. In later years I recognized that I drew encouragement from the ambient Jews in my life, much more than from the mandatory daily Anglican assemblies at school, to look beyond my parents' agnosticism, to integrate an active spiritual life into my identity.

America, 1990s

I came to the United States in 1969 to go to graduate school, lured by the incredible openness of the place, the times, the energy. Neither Nixon nor the Vietnam War were enough to put me off. Eldridge and Kathleen Cleaver were American. So were Berkeley and free speech, Martin Luther King Jr. and civil rights, and Woodstock. The FBI snooping in my Philadelphia neighborhood made everyday life an adventure. Above all this was a life that opened up all the once-fixed categories, providing me with the opportunity to truly become aware of and engaged with the Jewish images in my family tapestry.

Much time has passed since I came to the United States. The Jewish half of my double identity, buried when I first arrived, has "come out." I have become able to integrate and make whole the hybrid identity.

What made such a change possible? By comparison with England, Jews in America represent a highly visible religious group. Religious and/or spiritual life is valued in the States, rather than dismissed as the opiate of the masses or the basis for dogmatism and conflict. Many people here hyphenate the name "American," pairing it with other national, cultural, or religious markers. I have joined an interfaith community, and my children, unlike their English cousins, are well aware of the Jewish parts of their history and identity.

And yet there are still difficulties in that mixed heritage.

Even now, among many Jews, among most of my Jewish friends, the phrase "Jewish parts" is an oxymoron. One is entirely Jewish, or not Jewish. Our local temple is not enthusiastic that the interfaith community I belong to celebrates Jewish festivals. A long-standing joke, but a joke with an edge, runs between my family and our closest Jewish friends: In their family only the father was born Jewish. They attend the synagogue regularly, and yet by Jewish matrilineal traditions my children are more purely Jewish than are his.

Which takes me back around the circle. Is being Jewish a matter of racial, or at least spiritual, purity? Can I and my children, descendants of four generations of mixing, ever meet anyone's criteria for purity? We seem to live, still, in a world that measures ancestry by percentage ratios of ancestral blood: Native Americans seeking to be added to the tribal role, immigrants to Germany seeking government resettlement funds, and Jews wanting to move to Israel all have to demonstrate their blood lineage and the purity of their claims.

I know that my family's survival, my strength as a working professional, and my spiritual practice are all a product of racial, national, and religious mixing. My children participate with their friends at bat and bar mitzvahs at the temple, and they recognize the blessings as ones we also sing regularly. I love the Sufi dances, the confluence of Easter and Pessach, and the attentive waiting during Advent that all shape the weekly celebrations of our interfaith community. The tapestry is beautiful, and the bonds are strong.

But I still wonder how my sister contributors to this book and others will see my story, how those who are writing about their discovery of flaws in American Jewish attempts to assimilate will see it. Am I a Jew, or not? If my daughter, growing up in America today, wants to marry a Jewish man, will his parents find her Jewish enough? I wonder, how can the word *enough* ever be used to characterize an identity?

What Kind of Name Is Wyche?

Karen Fraser Wyche

The Early Years

AS A CHILD I always knew I was not white. For a little while I thought
it would be "cool" to be Native American. Obviously, I had no
understanding of the history of native people in the United States. Perhaps we were studying something in my elementary school class that
made me think that being Native American would be a romantic identity for a girl. I have a memory of mentioning this to my mother who set
me straight. I was a Negro. The term *black* was derogatory then and the
term *African American* nonexistent. My mother gave me the "race talk."
It is the talk about being proud of yourself and your heritage. It is the
talk of cautions. Parents tell you that there will be people who will not
respect you, who will not treat you as they do others. It is the talk that
socializes you to the realities of life, so that when racism and discrimination slap you in the face, you are prepared. It is the talk that helps you
understand that white people will try to categorize you in ways you
never dreamt about because people in your family have different skin
colors or hair types. For example, if, like me, you have light skin, they
will try to say that you are "mixed" and should not call yourself "black."
It is the talk that gives you guidance to deal with this situation and to
state proudly that we come in all colors, sizes, and shapes. It is the talk
that I gave many years later to my own children. I never thought I was
white and never wanted to be white, and no one ever thought I was. I
was happy with myself. Race pride was important in my family.

We lived in Harlem where people's skin was a rainbow of colors—the
same rainbow of colors found in my family. Harlem in those days was
a tightly knit community. From ages two to four I lived with my parents
in the Riverton apartments. These apartments were bordered by 135th
Street and the Franklin D. Roosevelt (FDR) Drive, which winds along the
East River in Manhattan in the neighborhood of Harlem Hospital. My

father's sister and her family also lived there. The apartments were built by the Metropolitan Life Insurance Company for "colored" people in the 1940s. We were one of the first families to move in. It was not until I was much older that my mother told me that this company also built Peter Stuyvesant Village, which is downtown and also along the FDR Drive. Although the floor plan was the same, the apartments differed in two ways: The Peter Stuyvesant apartments were larger than those in Riverton, and only white people could live there. Both of these apartment complexes are still standing today and look alike to the observer. However, Peter Stuyvesant Village is integrated, and Riverton continues to be inhabited primarily by African American families.

When my father lost his job as a liquor salesman we moved to my grandmother's brownstone house on 137th Street. I was about five. What a great time that was—four generations in the same house. Grandma and Grandpop, my great-grandmother, my uncle, my parents, and my brother and me. There were also the three tenants who rented rooms on the third floor. They were almost always men. Grandma's rules were that no overnight visitors were allowed. The only woman I remember was a lady we called "Petticoat Junction." She was a Pentecostal Christian, attended church all the time (which made her acceptable to Grandma), and wore very long skirts to cover her legs.

For me there was little interaction with Jewish people in Harlem. My family attended St. Martin's Episcopal Church on Lenox Avenue and 122nd Street. The congregation came primarily from the various islands of the English-speaking Caribbean. I remember the church ladies very well. They dressed in bright colors with big fancy hats. Their voices were lyrical. My cousins went to a parochial school in Harlem where all the kids were African American. On my block all of the merchants were African American.

Some Jewish merchants owned businesses on 125th Street, which was a big shopping area. There were butcher shops, pharmacies, small grocery stores, and other businesses, including Blumstein's department store. All the employees were white. The women in my family did not shop in this district because prices were higher than they were downtown and the quality of the merchandise not as good. For example, the meats, fish, and vegetables were not as fresh as those in other neighborhoods in Manhattan, even those on the lower East Side, which was also a neighborhood of poor people. So we went downtown, a round-trip bus ride of over two hours, to shop. As I think about stereotyping and prejudice, it is this kind of situation that breeds hatred and contempt. I was taught not to generalize to all Jewish merchants because of the situation on 125th Street. I was taught that if we as African Americans stereotype other groups of people who differ from us by race, ethnicity, or religion based on contact with a few people from these groups, then we only repeat what happens to us. However, it was difficult for those who shopped there not to have negative feelings about those merchants who were engaged in overcharging for substandard merchandise. People who feel powerless do not protest, so we did not boycott. Mainly we were scared that merchants would leave and stores would close if protests began. In recent years the older generations' messages of nonviolence have been replaced with violence committed by youths who rob some of the existing stores. Many of those stores are now owned by merchants from Asia and the Middle East and the work force includes more African Americans. But the victimization of the community continues. While the variety and quality of products are better, the prices are still higher than in white Manhattan neighborhoods.

I remember clearly the day in 1987 when I took my Uncle Charlie to fill a prescription at a drugstore on 125th Street. I had taken him to his clinic appointment at Harlem Hospital, and when we got the prescription we were told that this was the only drugstore in the area that could fill it. At the time he still lived in my grandmother's house in Harlem, but I lived in Teaneck, New Jersey, with my husband and three sons. Since he needed the medicine right away, I could not go to Teaneck to get the prescription filled. So we went to the recommended drug store. The pharmacist owner was a Jewish man and the clerk a West Indian man. When I went to pay for the medicine and other items, I was not given a receipt by the clerk. I asked for one and was told that they didn't give receipts. Why did I want one anyway? I insisted that I get a receipt with the cost of each item and the amount of New York State tax. The clerk looked sadly at me and said he was instructed not to give receipts. I was outraged. I knew this was the way customers were cheated. But, at the same time, I felt caught in this web of a race dynamic between employee and employer. My uncle was embarrassed. I was acting too assertively. He had learned to accept this situation, and he told me to leave it alone. I insisted that the price of every item be listed on the outside of the bag along with the tax. Later that night, I wondered if I had jeopardized the job of the clerk. The pharmacist was the one who had developed a policy that was both unethical and racist. I struggled with my own historical knowledge of the relationships that existed between Jewish merchants and the African American community during my childhood. How easy it was to label the pharmacist as another Jewish man perpetuating the same thing. How hard it was to see that this was a man whose business practices represented his own individual values about his customers. I have not thought about this incident for years, and writing about it still upsets me. It seems to me that it is this type of situation that fuels the fire of discrimination of all types. No ethnic group can escape from this.

Living in a homogeneous neighborhood did not raise issues of racial or ethnic identity for me until I ventured out of that environment to go to school. School experiences brought me in contact with Jewish people on an everyday and personal level. From kindergarten until fifth grade I attended the Ethical Culture School. I was a scholarship student. The school was comprised of children whose parents were upper-middle- to upper-class liberal, professional Jews. Some children came to school in chauffeured cars. I remember only one white child who was not Jewish. His father was an Episcopal priest. He and the African American children were the minorities. There were no Latino children. Each grade had three classes, with one African American child in each class.

As I think about it now, most of the white people I knew as an elementary schoolchild were Jewish. I knew there were whites who were not Jewish, but I didn't know them; I mainly saw them on television. For example, Bishop Sheen of New York City had a television show, but except for my cousins I did not know the Roman Catholic people to whom he spoke.

It was no big deal to me that my classmates were Jewish. The parents of this school prided themselves on being progressive, which translated to a curriculum that included the teaching of the Holocaust as well as slavery. I have no memories about how either was presented, which makes me wonder if these terrible historical events were presented in a matter-of-fact fashion so that elementary school children would not feel personally vulnerable. Jewish holidays were celebrated as well as Christian ones—Christmas carols and Chanukah songs were given equal time.

In school I was the "other." Protective parenting had to prepare my brother and me to withstand rejections and other kinds of threats to our sense of self. We could not hide. Because my family was working class, money was not available to protect us from a hostile white world. Class issues were as salient as race. All the African American children were on scholarship. We all knew each other because we all lived in Harlem. We all rode the Eighth Avenue bus that went up Central Park West to Harlem. The bus, filled with whites and African American cleaning ladies during the hours that schoolchildren got on, would empty of whites before crossing into Harlem. This still happens today.

Because the school had both full-pay students and scholarship students, the administration encouraged a policy of having birthday parties at school rather than at home. Although equality was the aim, these parties became lavish affairs. One child's parents owned a toy company. What wonderful gifts we got—dolls for girls and trucks for boys.

Sometimes I was invited to have a "date" with some of the other girls, all of whom were Jewish. These dates were just little girls getting together to play—nothing unusual. Often my grandmother would take me to their apartments, and we were usually told by the doorman that we needed to go around to the back servant's entrance. I remember how shyly my grandmother would say that we should be announced. After a while, Aunt Lorraine, a much braver woman, took me. We would walk up to the doorman, and, before he could speak, she would say that we should be announced.

It was the economic differences that were so difficult for me to understand. I remember that some of these girls lived in large, prewar apartments, the size of some modest houses, on Central Park West. Their families had servants. Lunch was served by African American women dressed in maids' uniforms—black dresses, starched white aprons, and white caps. This made me uncomfortable, having ladies who were of my people and like my female relatives wait on me. It was also confusing. Now I wonder what these women felt when this little black girl came for lunch. Today I am still uncomfortable when African American people are the waiters or waitresses at private parties where my husband and I are often the only African Americans. We smile at each other. I am polite. I feel uncomfortable.

When it was my turn to repay all the "dates" from school, my mother said we couldn't invite kids to come to my grandmother's house because no one would come to Harlem. So we went to Van Cortlandt Park in the Bronx for a picnic. This was a very long time ago, but I wonder if she was right, that parents would not bring their children to Harlem. They did come to the park. It is this kind of interaction between race and class that shaped my identity and still influences me today. Even though I am a middle-class professional woman, live in a big house, have an academic position, and seem to "have it all," it is difficult for me to sometimes take on these adult identities, so vivid are my childhood memories.

Journeys through Life in a Jewish World

In 1954 my parents moved to a small town on eastern Long Island to escape the decay starting in Harlem. The main employment in this town was from small factories or farms that grew Long Island potatoes. It was a predominantly Roman Catholic working-class community of people from Italian and Polish heritage, where the Italians felt superior to the Poles. It wasn't until I lived there that I realized Jewish people were discriminated against. Until that time I thought white people discriminated against blacks, not against each other.

There was a clear distinction between those people who were the permanent year-round residents and the summer people. The summer people had more money, were better educated, built houses that remained vacant for most of the year, were mainly from New York or New Jersey, and relied on the labor of the indigenous community to fulfill their needs. Summer people were viewed as a homogeneous group, regardless of religion, and were generally despised, although they were needed for the economic support of the town.

The only year-round Jewish residents I came to know were a dentist and his family. There was a tiny synagogue, so there must have been more Jewish people in the area, but I did not know them. Many residents of the community went to this dentist (there was only one other). I don't remember if there was much anti-Semitism. Naturally, a person can be a patient of a Jewish dentist and still be anti-Semitic, but I was naive about this since I was coming from the New York experience where there were mainly Jewish families. As a twelve-year-old I had a simple thought—the dentist's family was the Jewish family, and we were the African American family, all escaping New York. But as I think about this now I do remember feeling that my brother and I and the dentist's children were the "others" in the school system.

I attended Adelphi University, a college that had a predominantly Jewish student body. The reason for choosing this college was simple: Wellesley rejected me and Adelphi accepted me. I had wonderful friendships with the women in the dormitory where I lived for four years. There were only four dormitories because it was primarily a commuter college. We were a close-knit group of women students, many of whom were Jewish and from New York and New Jersey. I can't say that the Jewish women who became my friends and I "found" each other, for most of the women in the dorm were friendly. Perhaps it was just that the Jewish women who became my friends had a lot in common with me. We were freshmen together, were not cheerleader types or beauty queens, we liked music and having a good time, and we were not "party" girls. So it seemed natural we would become friends.

Among these women was the first Orthodox woman I had ever met. At the Ethical Culture School the families had not been Orthodox. She introduced me to kosher food and to the religious traditions her family followed. I visited her home and got to know her family. She was strong and confident, as were all of the Jewish women I befriended. Another friend's family owned a hotel in the Catskills, the resort area with hotels for the Jewish community. I have fond memories of visiting that hotel. Looking back on those days, the Jewish women I knew spoke with pride about their Judaism.

My husband and I started dating during my college years. He was one of the few African American men in a Jewish fraternity at Cornell University. At that time, Christian fraternities did not have African American or any other non-white members. A few Christian fraternities had Jewish members. One of my current neighbors, who was at Cornell University during the same time period as my husband, was one of the few Jewish members of a predominantly Christian fraternity. At Cornell, our social life revolved around my husband's fraternity. He was the social chairperson, so there were many opportunities for parties in the big fraternity houses along fraternity row. Some of his Jewish fraternity brothers dated African American women. It was the 1960s—a time when African Americans and Jews came together in the civil rights arena on college campuses. After college those fraternity bonds did not hold, and my husband says he maintained little contact with his fraternity brothers. He states that some of the Jewish fraternity brothers kept in touch with one another—something he knew from reading the alumni newsletters.

As a married couple with children, we moved to California and then to a college town in the Midwest. I met Jews who seemed so different from those whom I had known in the earlier times of my life. They did not seem ethnic, but rather vanilla. They were so different—no accent, not funny, more uptight, less self-assured. Their lives did not revolve around the Jewish community or Jewish friends. As I think back on this, perhaps I confused being ethnically Jewish with being a New Yorker.

My life continues to have intersections with the Jewish community. When my husband and I taught at Hunter College we lived in Teaneck, New Jersey. Across the street was a synagogue. My children delivered the newspaper to several Orthodox families and were aware of the religious holidays. This meant that at sundown they could not ring doorbells to collect money for the paper delivery service. We sold our house to an Orthodox family. When we moved to Rhode Island my children asked us why people were not walking to temple on Saturdays. In Rhode Island I took aerobics classes at the Jewish Community Center in Providence. I also assumed that there would be no traffic in Boston on Yom Kippur and that I could easily drive to downtown shopping areas. My friend who accompanied me, another African American woman, kept asking me how I knew this. My reply was that everyone would be heading home before sundown. How shocked I was to see all of the traffic on the main artery into Boston. I had a cultural knowledge for the wrong city. Catholic Boston is not the same as Jewish New York.

I am now a faculty member at New York University, which has always been strongly affiliated with the Jewish community. There are many Jewish women and men on the faculty. This has also been true in all of the universities that I have been associated with. These Jewish women and men seem so confident and strong. How surprised I was to hear about ambivalence regarding Jewish identity among some of the Fellows participating in this project.

Identity: Reflections and Loss

Identity can be shaped by historical influences. I became acutely aware of this during the past semester when teaching a course. All of the first-year masters students in the social work program were given an assignment in an ethnocultural class to trace their family's immigration history back for three generations. Although my section of this class was ethnically diverse, most of the white students were Jewish, and the students of color were African American.

The immigration patterns for the two groups were different. African American people were the only ethnic group to come to this country involuntarily. Our history from slavery through the present time has been marked by the continued presence of racism from the dominant society and by our attempts to fight this. Power in this country comes from money, and there are still great income disparities between whites and African Americans. We have been denied access to school and jobs both historically and at the present time. It is a long and depressing litany of discrimination and racism. This is the story the African American students wrote of their families. It is my story as well.

Discrimination and racism continue in many ways. My sons, my husband, and I have all experienced discrimination. Both of my sons have been asked by college teachers if they had someone else write their term papers because they were written so well. They have all experienced racist statements and treatment in the classroom. Both of my sons have been followed in clothing stores by security people who assumed they would steal. My husband, my sons, and I, both together and alone, have been pulled over for "routine" traffic stops, asked where we work, why we are in a particular neighborhood, and other such indignities. I have been asked too many times what kind of a name is "Wyche" and how did I get blue eyes? My response when in a hostile mood is that Wyche is a slave owner's name, and my blue eyes are slave owner's eyes. When in an educative mood, I explain that African American people are of different shades, heights, eye colors, sizes, and so on. We have normally distributed physiognomic characteristics. We are not deviant.

The Jewish students in the class all wrote of their families coming to this country to escape the horror of persecution in Europe or Russia before, during, or after World War II. There were clear themes to their families' migration patterns. First, every student wrote of their family members arriving in New York and going to live with other family members who provided shelter and a job. This important social support network embraced the family and cushioned the shock of immigration. It provided cultural continuity. No one was alone. Another theme was that most of those who came to the United States were either literate and/or possessed a marketable skill. So these women and men entered a job market where their skills could be translated into jobs. In the second generation students wrote of an increasingly affluent and educated group of relatives who moved away from the lower East Side of New York to the suburbs, where depending on which suburb, they found either a welcome or discrimination. The third generation maintained the educational advancement and acquired more economic power, which while not stopping anti-Semitism provided some protection.

Parenting and Identity

Child rearing and ethnic socialization shape our identities. It is difficult to be a parent of African American children. There are multiple challenges. How can we inculcate our children with a sense of self-esteem and pride about who they are while at the same time socializing them to the reality of the race-focused society in which they live? This means providing protective messages about survival. It goes beyond the messages of "Be a good person," "Work hard," "Get good grades," "Be kind to those who are less fortunate than you," and other kinds of prosocial and altruistic parental interactions. It means that you prepare them for being followed in stores, for police harassment, for teachers who will devalue their work, for the employer who will not include them in the networking sessions, and for being passed over for promotion. It means telling them that their racial group membership is salient and race is what people see. If they date outside their group, they risk the chance of becoming targets of hate. As African American men, you tell them to be careful because they are seen as a threat. My sons have experienced this. They have been harassed and viewed as the enemy. The people who have this type of mentality do not care that they are good people or who their parents or grandparents are. Those who victimize or even murder African Americans do not see them as individuals and as fellow humans struggling to live their lives. When my sons were younger, they used to say that my husband and I were racist to make all these statements about the ways in which society would see them. However, with age and with the experiences I have described, they now see it as a reality of their lives.

There are other aspects of identity that I have not addressed. Identity is passed on to us through our families, our parents, and our grandparents. Since beginning work on this essay I have experienced the death of both my mother and my maternal grandmother. These great losses have forced me to face the reality of my new status in my family and the issues of identity that are a part of this process. Because of the death of these women, I am the "older" woman in the family, the matriarch. Although my great-aunt is still alive at age 101, I am her caregiver and the manager of her life. "Matriarch" is a very uncomfortable label for me. Someone wise was always that person—Grandma or Mom. I do not want to be the oldest person in my family. I do not know how to act.

I want someone to be there for me to look up to, so that I can find so-
lace from them.

My grandmother and mother shaped my ethnic and racial identity.
Because I could observe both women for more than fifty years I have very
clear memories of them. Getting an education, being self-sufficient,
caring for family, both kin and extended kin, are some of the values
they emphasized. These values are not unique to African Americans as
compared to other ethnic groups, but the feminist agenda of women's
self-sufficiency may have been unique. It was seen in all of the family
women, from both my maternal and paternal sides. Their message was
clear—you must learn to take care of yourself. The women all worked.
There was no choice if the bills were to be paid. Their jobs as civil servant clerical workers were often dead end and boring. But the necessity
of their work quieted complaints. This socialization was shaped by protective messages that said you will be discriminated against not because
of who you are as a person, but because of the group to which you belong. The message that was passed along was that your racial group
membership was obvious and could not be changed. The message was
to stand tall and be proud. The message was to uplift the race by doing
better than they had done. The message was always that the group advancement was to be prized over individual advancement. This message,
which was passed along to me, I have passed on to my own children.

Identity searches are each unique. Some of the Jewish Fellows have
discussed an ongoing identity search. Some share the experience of a
childhood where silence surrounded issues of Jewish identity. Their
ethnic identity search in adulthood seems to be shaped by parenthood.
By that I mean that as parents they have the opportunity to examine
how issues of Jewish identity were discussed in their families and then to
compare their memories to what kinds of parents they would like to be.
This is an ongoing process because even when their children are older
they can continue to educate them about their identity.

My experience as a parent, remembering how I was raised, is different: Racial group membership was always salient in the child rearing
that my brother and I experienced. Protective parenting meant that we
had to know who we were and be able to withstand racial slurs, rejections, and other aspects of threats to ourselves from very early on. We
could not hide. Class issues also shaped us. Because we were not middle
or upper class, money could not protect us from hostility in the white
world, nor create a protective world for us.

Some of the Jewish Fellows have stopped searching for their identity. Who they are as Jewish women is very clear to them. They have stories to tell, often conveying strong intergenerational messages that have been handed down to them about never forgetting. They are in the process of transmitting their ethnic values to others, especially children born or imagined. Perhaps I am closest to those in this group. My feeling is that our clearly focused identities, theirs of being Jewish women and mine of being an African American woman, will face challenges from our children. Our children may choose different paths from ours and find partners who have different religions or races, thus creating bicultural or interfaith unions. I cannot argue whose pain or rejection from the larger society would be greater. I only wish to point out that current societal prohibitions are greater for biracial relationships than for interfaith ones. With these threats to our identities we as parents will be forced to leave the comfort of our ethnic selves and begin to examine what all this means.

Will I have the Chanukah discussion and you the one about the Christmas tree?

The Other Side

LOIS ISENMAN

GIENEK, a Polish graduate student whom I knew just slightly, said, "When you get to Warsaw call my parents. I'll give you letters to bring to them. When they hear you have letters, they'll say come and stay with us. Don't hesitate—do it. It will make your visit a lot more pleasant, and they'll enjoy it too. And when you get to Israel, would you be willing to deliver this little gift to my aunt?" At first I doubted I had heard him correctly, but as we struggled to locate his aunt's kibbutz on my map of Israel, I realized it was probably true. Gienek was Jewish, and there were still Jews left in Poland!

I needed a change of pace, an adventure to mark the completion of the first draft of my thesis. The idea of a trip to Poland followed by a visit to Israel captured my imagination and became real as I struggled to get a visa and a reasonably priced ticket on short notice. I didn't know what I would do once I got to Poland. Perhaps I would visit the small town near Warsaw where my mother's father was born. Somewhere in the back of my mind I knew I would go to Auschwitz, however, I couldn't yet admit it to myself. But with my visit to Gienek, the trip seemed to take on a life of its own.

From my current vantage point many years later, I wonder why I chose this journey to mark the end of my doctoral studies in biology. I suspect I needed to balance my scientific worldview with a closer look at both the savagery unleashed on European Jewry in the recent past and what it means to me to be a Jew. Presently I am at the end of another important passage in my life, a year as a Bunting Fellow. During the year a new area of interest opened for me: I began to explore the process of intuition and the role it plays in how we know and understand the world. Writing about the experience of being Jewish provides me with an opportunity to revisit this pivotal trip during which I first recognized the intuitive as well as the spiritual side to life.

On the plane to Warsaw, I toyed with the idea of settling into a hotel on my own and then calling Gienek's parents. But my fatigue and the emptiness of the airport on Sunday afternoon helped dissuade me from trying to manage on my own. I called and soon found myself knocking on the door of Gienek's parents' apartment in a lovely old building close to the center of Warsaw.

Max was a handsome, slender man with a thick shock of white hair and a manner both gentle and intense. Now retired, he spent his days queuing up to buy meat and babysitting for his grandson. Hannah, his wife, was a somewhat plump and pleasant maternal-looking woman with a soft yet bemused and knowing quality. She worked in an office. Struggling to communicate half in English and half in French, we quickly formed a bond. Since I had lived away from home for many years, I was amazed to find myself in Warsaw sharing daily life with a Jewish family similar in many ways to my own. Indeed Max and Hannah had all my parents' best qualities: warmth, humor, good taste, and limited pretensions. No doubt my sense of kinship with Hannah and Max was intensified by the fact that they lived as nearly solitary Jews in an almost completely Christian world, as I had during my high school years.

Approximately three and a half million Jews lived in Poland at the outbreak of the Second World War. About two hundred and fifty thousand returned at its end. By the time of my visit the postwar Jewish community had further dwindled to only several thousand, and Hannah and Max were part of this remnant.

We spoke often about Jewish issues. Newly married before the war, they had survived by going close to the Asiatic border of the Soviet Union and working in mines. I told Max, "How forward thinking of you to leave Warsaw when you did." He gave me a long, searching and unbelieving look, as if he couldn't comprehend what I had said. Finally, he responded quietly but with great feeling, "No, if you had eyes to see, it was perfectly clear. Hitler wrote it all in his book."

Over the intervening years, I have reflected on the implication of Max's response many times. Were those who knew of *Mein Kampf* and chose to stay when they might have left blinded by attachment or lacking in survival instincts? Others have said, quite to the contrary, that at the time it was quite reasonable to assume that Hitler would not be foolish enough to reveal plans as sinister as these if he were really serious about bringing them to pass. Just recently I understood that Max was unusually intuitive and saw more clearly than most. And indeed, like most unusually intuitive people, he did not realize that his lucid vision was a special gift.

Thomasz, their other son, took me to see the parts of Warsaw of interest to younger people. "What has happened to the postwar Jewish community?" I asked. "Why has it just about disappeared? Did everyone go to Israel?" "No," he told me. "Those who left after nineteen forty-eight went to Israel, but in the more recent exodus most went to Sweden. The Jews were blamed for the student riots in nineteen sixty-eight, and the authorities not only allowed Jews to leave the country, but actually put pressure on them to go. Many people lost their jobs. My parents stayed because they felt too old to start again. Also, they are deeply committed Socialists, although they have little use for the Russians."

My initial thought was that in blaming the remnant Jewish community, the Polish authorities had engaged in the time-honored tradition of scapegoating Jews. However, with distance, I realized that the implied assumption that Jews represented a disproportionate number of the leaders of the riots might have been true. Indeed Jews as a group do tend to focus more intensely on issues of social justice than do many other groups. Nonetheless, the authorities' efforts to rid the country of its remaining Jews, even if many were happy to leave, serves as a disheartening epilogue to the tragedy of Polish Jewry in World War II.

Hannah and Max insisted on accompanying me to see the memorial commemorating the Warsaw Ghetto, although they were obviously reluctant to reconnect with this part of Warsaw and the past. The night before the trip Hannah warned me of the power of the monument and added in an uncharacteristically cranky way, "It's always Jewish, Jewish; sometimes I wish we could just be people."

The monument recounted in an acutely disturbing way the crowding, turmoil, and anguish of the ghetto and its final destruction. The density of detail and suffering conveyed by the large convex bronze relief clashed in an eerie sort of way with the quiet, grassy, sunlit field on which it sat. I had difficulty focusing on the monument; my thoughts instead were pulled to this empty field, which once had been the Warsaw ghetto, and to Max and Hannah.

Just beyond the field, much of the old Jewish quarter, where the Jews had lived before they were restricted to the Ghetto, still stands. Hannah and Max had both grown up there. As they stood by the monument looking over to the Jewish quarter, crying quietly, they told me for the first time about their parents and other close relatives they had lost to the Nazis. Both Hannah and Max, generally so upright, slumped noticeably on our quiet trip back to the center of Warsaw.

Max and Hannah tried to talk me out of my plan to visit Auschwitz, as I'm sure my own parents would have done. With time, they became resigned. Max, however, did insist on going with me to meet Irena Wyrzykowska who, as the head of the Polish branch of an international reciprocal hosting organization for travelers, had offered to arrange my trip to Auschwitz and then Krakow. An English professor at Warsaw University, she happened to be working on the first translation of an Isaac Bashevis Singer novel from English into Polish. Singer was born in Poland and wrote in Yiddish about Jewish life in Poland.

When Irena heard Max speak fluent Polish and only very broken English, she assumed he was Israeli. We had to struggle to make her understand that there were still some Jews in Poland. When she finally accepted it, she confirmed that he also spoke Yiddish and quickly pressed him into service translating into Polish the common Yiddish words and expressions that appeared in the English edition of Singer's text. Before we left she made plans to consult with him further. It seemed fitting that Max should play a role in the symbolically charged act of bringing Singer's work back to Poland.

She also asked if I would send her a Yiddish-English dictionary when I got back to Berkeley, where I lived at the time. I was proud to have a further role in the project too. Indeed, according to one *Midrash*, a story that elaborates on a passage from the Torah, each person is really on this earth for only one purpose. Maybe this is my real purpose, I thought, as we left Irena's building in the late afternoon. Yet back in Berkeley on my way to the post office with wrapped dictionary in hand, my pride ran out and I felt only dizzy and strange. Having Singer's work available in Poland struck me then as such paltry and painfully ironic compensation for the needless destruction of the once so vigorous Polish-Jewish culture, the culture that his work so skillfully evokes.

I was born in late 1943, when the slaughter of Polish Jewry was moving into high gear. I cannot remember when I first became conscious of the Holocaust. Probably it was always there, but for a long time just dimly in the background. We lost only distant relatives to the Nazis. All four of my grandparents came to America as young adults around the turn of the century, and most of their extended families soon followed.

The object of fear, the enemy, when I came into awareness was the Japanese, and indeed for several early years I thought the word *Jap* meant enemy. In elementary school, the Russians were the enemy. The A-bomb drills, although terrifying, also conveyed a sense of excitement and awe at the potential force of nature. Both the Japanese and the Russians were national enemies, and my attendant fears were good American fears.

For my first three years my family lived in Dorchester, a Jewish neighborhood of triple-deckers in Boston. When my father's floor wax and chemical manufacturing business began to prosper, we moved to suburban Newton, where we were the first Jews on our street. People were not unfriendly, yet I felt the boundaries between our neighbors and us much more strongly than I had in Dorchester. Also, I knew it was considered much better to be "real Yankees," which was my mother's way of saying "WASP." Some of the other families on the street were not real Yankees either, but as Christians they were clearly closer to it than we were.

The tragedy of recent Jewish history directly entered my consciousness during the McCarthy era. Night after night, our dinner table conversation was dominated by my parents' agitation at the growing power of the senator from Wisconsin. A large number of the people investigated were Jewish, and my father insisted we get passports "in case the political climate in the United States became too uncomfortable for Jews." I remember the trip to the North Station area of Boston to get our passport pictures taken as an exciting special event in the general routine of life. My mother was unusually attentive to me. On the one hand, we were apparently happy, upwardly mobile, middle-class Americans, all dressed up for an afternoon "in town." On the other we were Jews planning for the possibility of persecution, flight, and exile.

I understood that my father's concern reflected the whole history of persecution of the Jewish people, as well as the recent savagery of the far, far right in Europe. Indeed, in the world in which he had grown up, the pogroms of the relatively recent past were the historical events that provided scripts for nightmares and evoked the terror of potential annihilation. When Hitler's atrocities against the Jews in Europe first became known, I suspect they were assimilated at a deeply personal level by many first- and second-generation American Jews as another chapter in a grim historical epic, rather than as events in a category of their own. Certainly for me as a child the activities of the Third Reich were too recent, too vague, and too threatening to focus on fully, or even very much. However, the Inquisition and the expulsion of the Jews from Spain, which I learned about in Sunday School, touched me in a deeply personal and stinging way. What would my father have done if we had lived then, I worried. To renounce Judaism was impossible. Even though we were primarily secular Jews, my sense of who we were had been so deeply formed by the experience of being Jewish that to give up being Jewish meant to give up being ourselves. Yet clearly my father could not choose that we burn at the stake.

From my current vantage point, I see that on a preconscious level, the Spanish Inquisition blended in my mind with both McCarthy's activities and what I had garnered of Hitler's persecution of the Jews. On that level, the question I thought the House Committee on Un-American Activities asked of its victims was, "Are you now, were you ever, or were your parents ever Jewish?"

One night my father brought home an underground phonograph recording that was funny enough to take some of the sting out of the McCarthy threat. It started with a convincing imitation of McCarthy, apparently in heaven, trying to interrogate Karl Marx. However, by mistake he first begins to interrogate Karl Marx, the tailor, a very humble-sounding man with a strong Yiddish accent. Nonetheless, just to be sure, to the accompaniment of dramatic musical annotation, he banishes the poor tailor from "up here" to "down there." On his next try, he gets Karl Marx, the piano tuner, who also speaks with a strong Yiddish accent and banishes him as well, and so on and so forth. In frustration at not being able to get to the "real" Karl Marx, he proceeds more and more aggressively against a number of other significant figures from the past such as Beethoven and Saint Peter, banishing them all. The record ends as McCarthy arrives at the top and in full voice banishes the Almighty from "up here" to "down there."

For high school, my parents sent me away from home. At Northfield School for Girls, a Christian school with a strong religious orientation, I learned a good deal more than I had learned in Newton about the social barriers between the Jewish and WASP world. For the first two years, I was the only Jew, and for the last two years, one of only a few at the school. I never thought of hiding the fact that I was Jewish, yet I would have done anything, except of course give up being Jewish, to be accepted in that world. The casual grace with which some of the other girls wore their kilts, Shetland sweaters, and camel hair coats, very often inherited from sisters or even mothers, or the way they called each other "de-ah" with a perfect blend of affection and distance, spoke so appealingly of belonging, tradition, and safety.

As soon as I could, I acquired a kilt and a few Shetland sweaters. But the sweaters I bought were not the right kind, and the kilt was an untraditional plaid. As the token Jew, I felt locked in the role of outsider and unseen for who I really was. There seemed no way to break through, and I was plagued by headaches for much of the year. To fill my spare time and assuage my loneliness, I read one girl's adventure book after another.

When choosing a dormitory for the second year, fortunately I chose the one where the unconventional girls, the ones with bohemian leanings, tended to go. There the currency of value was eccentricity and for many girls an unrestrained joie de vivre. Being Jewish was a ready-made eccentricity, and I had plenty of spirit. Several girls whom I admired sought to get to know me. The simple friendliness and sustained kindness of one in particular, a gentle, charismatic, and exceptionally intelligent girl named Gretel, dissolved my residual defenses, and I blossomed. At the end of second year, many girls asked me to room with them. While I still felt marginal in the school as a whole, from the safe base of the dormitory I was able to reach out to others with whom I felt an affinity. Eventually I even more or less mastered "preppy dress."

Oddly, my favorite part of the weekday at Northfield was midmorning Chapel. I felt relaxed and present to myself as I sat in my assigned seat in the comfortably rounded, high wooden pews in the old stone church. Singing a stirring Protestant hymn, listening or not to someone talk about some school matter, and filing out with my row after another hymn, invariably left me feeling refreshed.

Moreover, I found Religion one of the more pleasant required subjects. They approached the Old Testament of the Bible from a scholarly viewpoint, a new, more distanced perspective for me. I thought the New Testament interesting, although enigmatic, and I resonated strongly with much of what we read of C. S. Lewis. But partly I felt so at home in Religion class because the words *Jew* and *Jewish* came frequently and in a very matter of fact way. This was certainly not true of most other situations at the school.

Mandatory Sunday church was a different matter. Here I was in dangerous territory, and lapses of attention left me in a dim, unpleasant state. I felt I had to stay vigilant or else I might be extinguished in the deeply unfamiliar cadence of the Christian worship service. No doubt the intermittent historical record of Church enmity toward Jews also played a role in my discomfort.

To avoid church and ease the stifling formality of Sunday at Northfield, for my last two years I joined the Northfield Rural Work project and taught Sunday school to preschoolers in a nearby Unitarian Church. Northfield placed me at a Unitarian church because Unitarians focus less on Jesus than do other Christian denominations. However, the only teaching materials were a few storybooks about Baby Jesus, borrowed from a nearby Baptist group. Even though as a Jew I didn't believe in Jesus, I was fixated by the pictures of the infant, his stillness, and especially his large, pale yellow halo. I stared and stared at that halo.

I dutifully read these stories to the children and from time to time tried to talk to them about the theme. But invariably I ended up simply repeating the lines from the story I had just read because nothing else came to mind. I had no experience of this gentle, always present, worldly yet otherworldly love and had no ready store of platitudes to call on instead. I felt earnestly frustrated at my inability to come up with anything else to say. However, this was overlaid by humorous appreciation of the situation. Here I was, a Jew, frustrated with my inability to reach Unitarian preschoolers about Jesus.

The real payoff for doing "rural work" came on the way back to school. The bus stopped at a nearby country store, and we bought ice cream cones. The ice cream was exceptionally good and brought with it a moment of full-bodied gratification that was a surprisingly powerful antidote to Sunday at Northfield.

For part of each vacation I traveled around the Northeast visiting with various friends from Northfield. The night before I was to set off on one such jaunt, my father asked to speak with me and said in a strangely formal voice, "I think you should know that there will come a time when you will not be accepted in the homes of these people."

I was dumbfounded. I knew this was true of the world he had grown up in, but I felt things were changing. My dormmates, if anything, thought being Jewish was not only interesting, but also fun and kind of cool. For example, the refrain to a favorite song we sang in the dining room to express our longing for the freedom of vacation went:

> Bagels and cigarettes,
> bagels and cigarettes,
> bagels and cigarettes,
> and brown bread too.

At some level I experienced my friends' openness to Jewish culture as a harbinger of a more open world. And yet I knew the weight of evidence from the past was on my father's side; Jews and Gentiles did not mix much socially. Since many of my friends came from unconventional families, I told him that I felt certain I would not be excluded from the homes of these people. Yet even as I was saying this I had to acknowledge to myself that I could not really be absolutely sure. And then I found myself shouting at my father, alas only in my head, "Well then why in the world did you send me to this school?" I did not say this out loud because the feeling was too intense, and I never shouted at my father. Besides, I identified so much with my new role of bridging the Jewish and Gentile worlds that I could not say anything that might put this at risk.

I was elected to the student council in my senior year and became responsible for everyone on my floor. I saw this as tangible proof that I had made it in the WASP world, and I was very proud. During the year the headmaster had groups of seniors over for dinner and chatted a bit with each girl about some school matter. I was particularly looking forward to my turn. I envisioned the approval and congratulations he was sure to express at my achievement, the official seal on my acceptance. When he came over to me, he wore a bright, perhaps even conspiratorial, old-boy smile that far surpassed even my fondest hope. But then to my horror, he started to talk about my father's business.

I could not believe what was happening. Not only had he not mentioned my accomplishments, but I tried never to talk about my father's business at school or anywhere else. And perhaps most disturbing of all, I felt he was singling me out because I was Jewish. When he saw I was conflicted about talking about my father's business, he moved on.

When I got back to my room, I cried for hours in a way that I never had before and could not stop long after I wanted to. I tried to explain to the two friends trying to console me why I was so upset. He made me feel, I told them, that no matter what honors I earned, he could think of me only as a Jew, and the only reason they had even let me, a Jew, into the school was my father's business success.

My friends didn't understand what I was saying, and indeed with distance I see that several alternative analyses of the pain he triggered might fit as well. However, I suspect my feeling of being completely shattered came from an even more essential place. I think I glimpsed the fact that the feeling of safety and the sense of well-being that I longed for would never come from what I wore, or did, or what honors I achieved.

At home on vacations from school, I would often look at my father's growing collection of books about the Holocaust. My family seldom spoke about the Holocaust; my mother could not face it, and my father felt the pain and shock too deeply to express in words. I was both attracted to and repelled by the subject, but my attraction was much stronger. I looked at every picture and read here and there in many of the books.

I found the photographs utterly compelling and did not know why. I knew these images were records of historical events, yet I could not assimilate them as such. The brutality and suffering the pictures captured found only slight resonance in my conscious experience, yet my fascination indicated that they spoke strongly to more hidden layers of my psyche.

On an intellectual level, I never doubted that the Holocaust had happened; however, on an emotional level, it did not seem real to me. Indeed these events played little apparent role in my life except from time to time when I was at the mercy of generalized fear and anxiety from my unconscious. Only then would I think about the Holocaust.

A subdued sense of this fear was with me constantly, just below the surface, on the journey to Auschwitz. Irena Wyrzykowska had arranged for me to travel by car with a Flemish couple about my age, whom she promised I would like especially well. When she told me they were not Jewish, I experienced a moment of overwhelming threat at the prospect of visiting Auschwitz in the company of non-Jews and felt an unspoken urge to cancel the trip. But the wise and lightly bemused smile on Irena's face as she watched me helped me trust her decision and my fate.

Indeed, they turned out to be excellent companions for this grim pilgrimage. They were sensitive, thoughtful, and unusually calm people, and we had much in common. They told me right away that the Flemish history of persecution, first at the hands of the Belgians and then at the hands of the Germans, had sensitized them acutely to the persecution of ethnic groups and was the reason for their trip. They also mentioned that ongoing anti-Flemish discrimination had limited certain choices in their lives. When I heard this, I relaxed my guard completely.

The trip, with many stops, took two and a half days. Although not unpleasant, it was somber; we laughed some, but rather quietly. Our desire to reach our destination was balanced by our dread of what we would confront there.

As we entered Auschwitz through its wrought iron gate, I was surprised to see a large series of orderly, long, brick buildings. I found their clear physical outlines and their feel of modernity grounding, and even comforting. Many schools and hospitals in New England, as well as my father's old factory, all shared this simple brick functionality. I had not expected this. This was the world that I had grown up in, the world that had shaped me.

My relief on walking through the gate of the camp and confronting the neat rows of brick barracks was short-lived. The simple brick barracks, stripped of their horror, planted the Holocaust in historical space and time. The very ordinariness of the buildings forged a separation between my unconscious terror and the atrocities of the Third Reich. As I focused on the physical details of the barracks, such as the color of the brick and the spacing of the windows, I let in fully that Hitler's Final Solution had been both real and recent.

Signs before the entrance to the barracks requested silence. The respectful quiet all around us as we walked through the display barracks was resonant with feeling. Most visitors had tears in their eyes and some were crying quietly. The sense of shared pain was comforting and made the experience more possible to bear.

Pictures of Polish political inmates lined the corridor walls, some decorated with flowers. The displays as I remember them were few and rather simple: the striped pajamas the inmates wore, the pallets they slept on, and the bowls they ate from. We went to the gas chambers where the clean, gray-painted walls gave no evidence of, and indeed appeared to mock, what had really happened there.

A large warehouselike space in another building housed two enormous glass display cases, each almost the size of a room. One was entirely filled with suitcases belonging to the deportees, the other with shoes. Some of the suitcases still had the owner's name and address legible in chalk, presumably written on the night before deportation. I made out several common Jewish names before I started to feel sick. This collection of suitcases from the early 1940s, some of fine leather, others of inexpensive cardboard, some barely used, others falling apart, all too clearly evoked the experience of the deportees in their last hours at home, their common forced journey to Auschwitz, and their well-organized and efficient death.

As I turned away distraught from the mountain of suitcases, I sensed an almost tangible substance coming up through the floor from the ground under the building. My mental image was a crowd of dim, translucent people among a complicated maze of shadowy train tracks. Then an inner voice different from any of those that make up my usual consciousness said in a terse, tense way, "This is not the end. This is only a point of transfer."

I did not reflect on this strange voice. It felt emotionally congruent and was no more extraordinary than anything else I had witnessed that afternoon. I just accepted it and its enigmatic message as the psychic culmination of my visit to the camp.

A museum housed Holocaust-related exhibitions from a variety of countries. By the time I reached the final exhibition, a separate Jewish one, I could absorb no more testimony to the Nazis' inhumanity and sadism. My attention wandered quickly over the displayed photos until I came to a blowup of a handsome, imposing Parisian woman, stopped by the Gestapo at a road block. Her sense of presence, the contemporariness of her appearance, and the air of urban sophistication with which she wore her trench coat and sunglasses were completely riveting. This picture reminded me once again, with a jolt, that the events to which the other pictures bore witness happened neither in dream space nor in some distant time, but in the very same world into which I was born.

Close to the end of the exhibition, the photos gave way to canvases depicting contemporary Jewish life. I scanned quickly until my eye came to rest on a tableau of a bar mitzvah boy reading from the Torah, flanked on one side by his father and on the other by the rabbi. Again I was entirely engrossed. In its treatment of the figures and the light the picture revealed to me a sense of the sustained upward impulse of Judaism into spirit. In it I recognized the basic religious urge that is at the core of the Jewish experience. The gentle streams of light filling the sanctuary above the absorbed figures evoked feelings of both profound yearning and fulfillment. The loving light gave both new and renewed meaning to the familiar images of Torah reading and religious coming of age; in that moment I realized how thoroughly Jewish I am.

I let myself momentarily merge with the light and felt it assuage and transform my pain. As I continued to look at the picture, I remembered experiencing similar, yet much less dramatic, moments of gentle emotional elevation within the context of Jewish practice from childhood on. These moments had certainly felt good, but I had no idea what they were. As I stood there, I realized that even as a Reform Jew, the least religious of the three Jewish denominations, I had been strongly influenced by the subtle reach of my community upward toward spirit. Before I had found it comforting to participate in the sacred unconsciously from time to time. Here at Auschwitz I saw what it was, realized how much it had shaped me, and caught a glimpse of its sustaining power.

The final display was a sculpture in sand; my Flemish friends and I stood together transfixed. Pieces of lightly charred driftwood resembling bones had been arranged in a pattern evoking human remains in a low, long rectangular box filled with sand. The sculpture, with its strong compositional and emotional import, so powerfully suggested the movement of human energy into spirit that its far side appeared to me to be both elevated and bathed in light. The horizontal constraints of the sculpture and the earthly suffering it so starkly portrayed, resonated in my vision with the equally strong suggestion of the vertical passage of the material into spirit. This sculpture clearly spoke of the terror of Auschwitz. But its unresolved tension between the earthbound and the sacred spoke clearly of the human condition in general as well as much of the Jewish historical experience.

My trip to the death camp helped convince me that there is more to existence than what science can hope to describe. Nonetheless, the skeptic in me sometimes wonders if I am just protecting myself against even greater despair than I already feel at the carnage of so many Jews that occurred around the time of my birth. I do not know what happens to the soul after life. However, as something within me seems to have sensed as I turned away from the mountain of suitcases at Auschwitz, I generally feel that the spirit of so many souls cannot be destroyed in that chillingly efficient way.

In the years since I returned from my trip, I have become more involved in the life of the spirit and in Judaism. I seek and cherish those moments of opening that I experience within the context of Jewish practice. However, I have not found a real home there yet. Jewish spirituality and study are not at the center of my life, as I often wish them to be. Rather, I try this and that in the hope that something will allow these moments of approach to the sacred, of elevated being, to be integrated more fully into my life.

I sense that to some extent the indirect pain of past Jewish persecution prevents me from turning more fully toward Jewish spirituality. And yet, paradoxically, I first recognized its loving light and healing power amidst all the death at Auschwitz. It may be that only this light can give me the feeling of safety and belonging that I long for.

Looking Back

Deirdre Chetham

I GREW UP in a family that celebrated Christmas and Halloween and relied on fortune tellers and astrologers for spiritual guidance. My father came from an English and German family that first came to New England in 1634 and spent most of the next 350 years as swamp Yankees, with an occasional rise in fortune. My mother's family was Irish, with some English and Norwegian thrown in, and emigrated to the United States in the mid- to late-nineteenth century. Despite the fact that neither practiced either religion, the gap between my parents' Episcopalian and Catholic backgrounds was too much to bridge, and I was brought up without any particular religious training or sense of ethnic or religious identity beyond being firmly rooted in Massachusetts. In this essay, I have attempted to recapture childhood sensibilities and expectations regarding ethnicity without imposing an adult interpretation.

One day, back in college one of my suitemates was telling me about her troubles with a friend. "The worst of it," she exploded, "is that she called me a 'JAP.'" My roommate then launched into a complicated story that seemed to me to have no connection to what she had just said. I finally interrupted. "First of all," I said, "why would anyone think you were Japanese?" My roommate, a Jewish girl from New York, looked at me as if I had lost my mind.

Thinking back, trying to recall what meant what about whom and when, I remember that I was not oblivious to generalizations or stereotypes about Jews and other people. Nonetheless, I was relatively unaware that these stereotypes had a particularly negative connotation. I knew that Jews had Jewish traits; Armenians, Armenian traits; or Irish Catholics, Irish Catholic traits—it was just one of those things in life, partly true, partly false, sometimes a problem, sometimes not. As I remember childhood, eventually everyone was singled out for something— any distinguishing characteristic would do—and being Jewish or Catholic or fat were just a few of the many possibilities for persecution. Also *not* being Jewish or Catholic, being Italian, having parents who didn't get along, not having brothers or sisters, having too many brothers or sisters, or being too dumb were some of the others. Everybody was fair game.

In the late 1950s, little boys still scrawled, "Kilroy was here," on walls and shouted out, "Kill the Huns," in neighborhood games. Like everyone else I knew as a small child, I was always aware of World War II and in some way of the concentration and death camps, but the war was just out of reach for me, just barely beyond memory, like the hurricanes of 1938 and 1952. I wasn't there, but I knew what everyone else was doing. My father was a graduate student at Harvard University when I was a young child, and it was not uncommon to meet people who had been in concentration camps. I remember asking a family friend (in the direct way of three-year-olds) why she had numbers on her arms. She answered equally directly that she had been in a camp in Europe during the war and that the Nazis had branded numbers on the inmates to keep track of them. Though it hadn't seemed to me that she minded the question, my parents later told me that it was not polite to ask personal questions and confirmed her explanation that she was Jewish and had been in a concentration camp. Neither she nor my parents offered any further commentary, as is generally assumed to be necessary in discussions with children these days, nor did I expect one. The facts seemed clear enough. I do not know exactly what I knew of Nazis or Jews then, and I assume it was not much. I do remember that while I had to ask what branding meant, I had a pretty well-formed concept of a concentration camp, a faraway place where bad things happened for unknown reasons.

We moved to Amsterdam in the middle of 1958 when I was three and a half. I noticed that there were more men missing legs or arms in Europe than in Boston and overheard conversations about people who had spent the war in cellars, camps, and forests. These were interesting and mysterious stories, but my attention was on other things, such as seeing every doll house in Europe and wondering why the milk in France tasted so bad. Odd, mutated versions of wartime life affected me more directly. On December 7, Saint Nicholas rides through the streets of Amsterdam on an enormous white horse surrounded by "Black Peters," boys in blackface carrying huge sacks, roughly the Dutch equivalent of Santa's helpers. Good children later get their wooden shoes filled with candy and small gifts. Bad children are taken away in the sacks. I have forgotten the traditional account of what happens to these children, but the version I absorbed was more sinister and modern. Once a Black Peter got hold of me, I was destined for a work camp on the Russian border.

After returning to America, while my father finished his graduate work, we lived in Somerville, Massachusetts, a working-class city bordering Cambridge where a mixture of nationalities and religions were jammed in close proximity. By the age of five, after two months on the block, I knew exactly what everyone was, who was Armenian, Irish Catholic, Greek, Episcopalian, Italian, or Jewish. Distinctions were explicit. Next door was an Irish Catholic family who kept a boarder named Barney. He was daft, everyone said, and it was neighborhood sport to search for him when he disappeared, which he often did. Eventually his mind went altogether and he was shipped away. The people referred to as the slovenly Italians, as opposed to the regular (and neat) Italians, lived down the street. Their six children were allowed to throw garbage off the front porch and run wild in the streets, often getting hit by cars. Sam, who was Jewish, owned the drugstore at the top of the street, which sold hand-packed coffee ice cream for twenty-nine cents a quart, and Charlie, who was Italian, ran the corner store where you got Fudgsicles and Wonder bread. Down at the bottom of the hill was another Jewish pharmacist, but it was hard to cross that street, so I never got to know him well. To the right was a WASP family; above us, Greeks. There were no blacks.

I had a vague idea of how everyone got there—that someone slaughtered the Armenians, and the Nazis went after the Jews, and the Irish starved to death, maybe because they wouldn't fish. Of course, you couldn't help but hear what a shame it was when a Protestant married a Catholic, or when both sets of parents were enraged if a Greek married an Italian. For the most part, knowing that someone was Italian or Protestant was like knowing his or her name. It was a fact, neither good nor bad.

Concrete and brutal images of the war began to take shape about this time. I remember listening to a friend of my parents talk, half-jokingly, about how his relatives had been made into lampshades, and I tried to puzzle that one out before asking my parents what he was talking about. (I had learned to be more tactful.) Thirty years later, looking at objects made of human skin on display at the medical clinic at Auschwitz, I found myself remembering that conversation.

In my own family, my grandmothers were the only ones who had much to say about Jews, or any other group, for that matter. My father's mother, an Episcopalian, had put herself through the New England Conservatory during World War I partly by teaching piano to Jewish children in Boston's South End, an almost entirely Jewish neighborhood at that time. As the metronome ticked and she grumbled with despair as I played on, she often reminisced about the many Jewish families who had been kind and encouraged her, a respectable young woman, in the then almost unheard of position of living alone and paying for her own education.

My other grandmother was a Catholic and a rather fanatical one at times. When I was three, she taught me the Hail Mary, making me promise not to tell my parents. Later, when my sisters were born, she spent many hours telling me what was going to happen to their unbaptized souls should they die in a year or two, something she presented as a likely possibility. She often said that had she not had the good fortune to be born a Catholic, she would have chosen to be Jewish because Jesus was. And not only because of this—Jews were educated and took care of their families.

Eventually my family left the city streets where children shouted to one another from the front stoops to come out and play and tossed jacks in the gutters. We arrived on the campus of Smith College, our next home, in midsummer when the college was closed and there was not a human being anywhere, only empty dormitories, noiseless streets, and the oppressive humid heat. Sometime in August I met another child and trudged to her house, knocked at her door, and asked if she could come out and play. Her mother looked at me for a while, then said, "She has a friend over. You should have telephoned first," and shut the door. I retreated, baffled by these unfamiliar customs, having never met anyone my age who had received a phone call.

Soon thereafter I became a fixture at the freshman dorm next door. I spent hours listening to the lovelorn lives of my eighteen-year-old neighbors, many of them from New York, many of them Jewish, almost all of them bored out of their minds in Northampton. I went to tea at the French house, spent afternoons with the college gardeners, and hung about at the student center waiting for the counter ladies to give me the almost empty vats of ice cream to finish off. When it started,

school was a world far different from what I had known. Like the
schools I had left, here there was also (entirely unintentionally) a fairly
diverse mixture of students. My class had about nineteen kids, which included one half-Indian, half-black girl; one Italian; two Jews; one Polish
Catholic; and various others of mixed backgrounds and nationalities
who came and went. Along the way, there were two long-tormented
scapegoats—one boy, one girl, both WASPs.

As in the places I had lived before, students knew quite a bit about
one another, but, a little older now, the knowledge seemed more subtle
and adult and correspondingly less benevolent. In earlier neighborhoods, teasing was directly confrontational and usually short-lived.
Here, in a school where children were delivered from the surrounding
towns by car every morning, there was no neighborhood. Children were
almost always polite, no matter how venomous the information trans-
mitted over telephone calls and in car pools. Good order began to break
down slightly and inevitably at about age eleven or twelve when the boys
began to beat each other up, a trend that coincided with increasingly
more barbed observations about one another by both sexes. Classmates
began to speculate on the reason why Italians became Congregationalists
or Jews became Quakers, and the student who was half-black began to
mention that certain people's parents much preferred to think of her
as an exotic Indian from India rather than an American black.

I cannot remember anyone ever commenting one way or the other
on the fact that one kid in the class went to Hebrew School, but certainly, among the brawls between boys, there were vaguely articulated
accusations of bigotry and anti-Semitism. Once or twice I remember a
group of girls playing Holy Communion in the English room in the
sixth grade, but exactly why escapes me. And then there was the daily
message, GOD IS DEAD left on the blackboard each morning for the
history teacher, who as a supporter of the Vietnam War seemed fair
game on any grounds. And there was the day a friend and I spent our
lunch hour lighting every candle in the basement chapel of the Catholic
church, unaware that you were supposed to pay for the illumination. If
there was bigotry, it was the well-brought up kind, the not-necessary-to-
express kind of mutual understandings about other people.

From grade school on, history always stopped somewhere around
1915 when time suddenly ran out and the semester ended, while on a
day-to-day basis, the Vietnam War dominated current events and recent
history. Still, we knew about World War II somehow. There were books

and Saturday afternoon movies. For a quarter a copy, you could get paperback books like *Ten and Twenty*, about ten Jewish children hidden in a French convent school with Gentile children, or *Escape from Warsaw*, about three children whose parents were arrested for opposing the Nazis, from the mail-order Arrow Book Club.

We did not learn much about religion in school, at least not formally, and this never caused much controversy, pro or con. Back in Somerville, we had to pray before snack time, but since we also got hit with rulers, were allocated one pencil per semester, and had a teacher who tied bad students to their seats, prayer was the least of anyone's problems. In about the fifth or sixth grade we read stories from the Old Testament along with Greek and Roman mythology. In music class, we sang Christmas carols, which no one in the school questioned in those days. The words of "I have a little dredl, I made it out of clay" and "Havah Nagileh" and other such songs were also drilled into our heads.

In high school in Vermont, my roommates my first year were both Jewish, a fact that did not seem particularly noteworthy. If I think back, there were probably dozens of kids who were Jewish, a few kids who were Catholic, and some who were of any other noticeable religious affiliation, which may have meant they were Episcopalians. It was not something to which anyone paid much attention. Other differences were far more noticeable—black versus white, drug users versus non–drug users, those who summered in Europe versus those who spent their holidays in the kitchen of a local restaurant.

In the school's midmorning assembly, we saw film clips of concentration camps and were taught by faculty members whose lives had been turned upside down by the war, people who would never have ended up on a hilltop in Vermont under normal circumstances. In first-year German, we struggled through Max Frisch's *Andorra*, a play about fascism and individual responsibility, and then spent the next two years reading tortured postwar German stories of war, sorrow, and guilt.

As time went on, new shades of complexity and differentiation emerged. I remember talking to a slightly older girl, I don't know about what, and her sudden irritated exclamation, "Now you're thinking that I'm Jewish!", and my own sudden confusion because I had been thinking precisely that. She was giving it a significance that I had not, yet somehow it seemed I was at fault. What was wrong with thinking that she was Jewish? She was. Would someone else be as likely to snap at me, "Now I can tell that you think I'm a Baptist"?

By then, the easy disorder of childhood streets was already far away, and the simplicity of obvious divisions was gone. Distinctions that had seemed straightforward and part of the natural order of things at age six or seven no doubt had their less benign side. Looking back, I re-member how little girls played Chinese jump rope on uneven sidewalks while the boys tied one another to traffic signs in overheated games of Cowboys and Indians. In the background, on summer nights, you could hear the voices of relatives on front porches and back verandahs. Bits of conversation in Greek and Armenian, Italian and Yiddish were inter-spersed with louder shouts in English as adults greeted one another across clotheslines or shouted at their children. In that time and place when differences and the reasons for them were taken for granted, identification with a group rarely seemed self-conscious or imposed, perhaps because there was no choice. Everyone knew who or what everyone else was, and for the most part, accepted the unspoken rules of contact and interaction. This neighborhood and most like it have long since disappeared, but memories linger on of a childhood time when everyone was something different but still belonged, by choice or by fate, to the same place.

Reflections

RUTH-ARLENE W. HOWE

I AM THE only child of African American Christian parents who did not teach hate. My personal upbringing, combined with my May 1, 1995, visit to the Slave House Museum of Gorée-Island provide the grounding for my reflections on the similarities and differences between anti-Semitism and racial prejudice and discrimination. My visit to the Slave House Museum made me aware of many feelings that before had only simmered in my subconscious.

Prior to participating in this exchange with my Bunting sisters, my perceptions and feelings about Jews were based primarily on contacts and relationships with individual Jews I have known. Although I realize the dangers in making generalizations about all members of a group based on limited contact with just a few individuals, this is, in fact, the reality of how my perceptions developed.

A Family Folktale

I grew up, for example, thinking that Jews were powerful, rich, and influential. This assumption stemmed from the oft-repeated family story about my maternal grandparents' long association with John Jacob Astor IV. For years, I believed that the Astors were Jewish and only quite recently found out they were not. My maternal grandparents were both young employees of the Astor family when they first met. Grandma Louise was an accomplished seamstress; Grandpa Randolph was an illiterate maintenance assistant. After marrying, my grandparents lived in Astor employee housing until they moved to New Jersey around the end of World War I. Grandpa Randolph worked for the Astors until he retired. During his employment he became the chief electrical engineer for Astor Court in lower Manhattan.

Mr. Astor, an avid collector of novelties, had one of the first elevators

in New York City. One weekend, while showing it off to a visitor, it
stalled between floors. None of the available workmen were able to
make it move. As the hours passed, Mr. Astor's temper rose, and he
began shouting and threatening to fire everyone. A Polish man kept
suggesting that someone should call the young Negro[1] who was handy
with mechanical things. When the situation seemed utterly hopeless,
my grandfather finally was called. He was lowered by rope down the
shaft to the top of the cage where he identified the problem and corrected it. With my grandfather still atop the cage, the elevator dropped
to ground level and Mr. Astor and his guest stepped out. Mr. Astor
wanted to know who was responsible for getting the elevator unstuck.
My grandfather was still atop the cage waiting to be hauled up, but the
Polish worker who had suggested that he be called immediately spoke
up. Mr. Astor was forever grateful for his release. He rewarded my
grandfather for having put his own life in jeopardy by advancing him to
positions of responsibility. On learning that some of his employees,
such as my grandfather (because he was colored) and the Polish man
(because of his lowly regarded immigrant status) were not able to take
night courses at the city public schools, he used his influence as one of
the most powerful landlords in the city. The Board of Education leased
many properties from him, which he threatened to cancel if the Board
did not open its courses to all. Thus my grandfather, the Polish worker,
and other Astor employees began to attend night classes, and my grandfather became literate.

At an early age my mother showed musical talent. She once accompanied her mother to deliver a special dress to Mrs. Astor. Although
instructed to sit quietly and not touch anything, my mother, who had
never before seen a piano, was attracted to it and began to pick out a
melody, astounding everyone. Soon thereafter, the Astors had a piano
delivered to my mother's apartment that had to be hoisted up the front
of the building and brought in through an upper-story window. Mother
often reminisced about taking lunch to her father at Astor Court and
receiving music lessons from the "March King," John Philip Sousa, who
lived in an apartment in Astor Court after retiring from the Marine
Corps Band. It was Mr. Sousa who wrote to the esteemed Mr. Tibbs, the
colored head of the music department at Howard University, to recom-
mend Mother's admission.

Recently, a colleague's firm insistence that the Astors were not Jewish
sent me scurrying to the library. To my amazement, as I checked various

reliable sources, I could find no confirmation of my lifelong belief. Indeed, Stephen Birmingham's book, *"Our Crowd": The Great Jewish Families of New York,* discusses the keen social rivalries and ambivalent relationships that existed between several generations of the Astor family and some of New York's elite Jewish banking families in the period from 1840 to the turn of the century. In 1892, Ward McAllister, called "Mr. Make-a-Lister," culled from the *Social Register* an abbreviated list of names of New York's "best"—dubbed "The Four Hundred"—that could be accommodated in Mrs. William Waldorf Astor's ballroom. Jewish names were conspicuously absent from both the *Social Register* and Mrs. Astor's Four Hundred.

I cannot explain why I thought the Astor family was Jewish. Since my mother, also an only child, died in 1988, there are no close relatives with whom to confer to ask whether this was their misperception or just mine. What I can say is that when I first read Birmingham's 1967 book about the "privilege, power, philanthropy, and family pride" of pivotal Jewish families such as the Guggenheims, it all resonated with what I had heard about the Astors.

Some Personal Background: November 21, 1933 — Scotch Plains, New Jersey

On this date, in the midst of the depression and three years before Jessie Owens's athletic feats at the 1936 Olympic Games in Berlin, I was born at home. My parents lived with my maternal grandparents in a comfortable bungalow set on a large lot on Plainfield Avenue. About eighteen years earlier, my mother's parents had had this house built for them. Instead of participating in the fashionable trend to relocate from lower Manhattan uptown to Harlem, they chose to move out to the Jersey countryside and become early residents of "Jerseyland"—a new, developing section of Scotch Plains in Union County where Negroes were able to purchase land and build modest homes. After my grandparents died in the 1930s, this property was held by my parents until the early 1980s.

Although delivered at home, my birth was carefully supervised by Dr. Howard F. Brock, general practitioner from the neighboring town of Westfield, who was trained at Howard University. He was assisted by his nurse, Alberta Banks. Such home deliveries were then the norm. Few, if any, Negro physicians had obstetrical privileges at local hospitals. In the 1930s, such discrimination was common in all parts of the country.

Because housing was strictly segregated, educated Negro professionals lived within the Negro community and provided a full range of services to their neighbors. Plainfield Avenue was a main thoroughfare that ran through Jerseyland, serving as a connecting link between the larger towns of Plainfield to the southwest and Westfield to the northeast. Directly across the street was Shady Rest, a golf and tennis club privately owned by Negroes that annually hosted regional and national Negro amateur and pro tournaments. My early memories of persons who met the social, physical, and spiritual needs of my Jerseyland community are that they were all Negro like me.

Both my parents were college graduates: my mother from Howard University; my father from Hampton Institute. They were both self-employed. Dad was an electrician/gardener. Mother was a music teacher. Both were active in church and civic organizations. For nearly forty years, my father was chairman of the Trustee Board of Calvary Baptist Church in Plainfield. For many years, Mother was the organist for the Saint Mark Episcopal Church in Plainfield, as well as the accompanist for the Male Chorus at Calvary. During the summers she ran vacation Bible school programs for churches in Plainfield and Edison, New Jersey. Dad was a 33rd Degree Prince Hall Free & Accepted Mason. Mother was a founding member of the New Jersey chapter of the Negro College Women's Club. She also participated in numerous YWCA interracial and interdenominational groups.

My parents' education and self-employed job status enabled both of them to assume leadership roles within the Negro community and to serve as respected liaisons to the larger majority community. They always sought out opportunities for me, their only child. Thus, although we literally lived in the shadow of the Scotch Plains elementary school that served our neighborhood and hence was nearly 100 percent Negro, my parents enrolled me in the Westfield public schools (then rated among the best in both New Jersey and the nation). For the next twelve years, they managed to pay tuition bills that rose annually.

When I started kindergarten at the newly built Franklin School in 1939, there may not have been a single Jewish child in the class. There was no Jewish temple in town. There may have been a few Catholics. The only Catholic church in town was on the south side of the railroad tracks. Westfield, a very well-to-do commuter town of New York investment bankers and other corporate officers, was mostly white and Protestant. All of this began to change after the end of World War II. For example, one of the first Jewish teachers to join the faculty of West-field High School was Melvin Michaels. The yearbook of the Class of 1951, my class, was dedicated to Mr. Michaels. The caption under his picture reads: "in hope that it will repay him in part for his faithful in-terest in teaching and his deep and friendly concern for his students." Today Westfield has a sizeable Jewish population. Both the Westfield Tennis Club and the various country clubs now are integrated racially and religiously. There is still, however, little socioeconomic diversity in Westfield.

Some readers might wonder how I felt or was made to feel as a mi-nority student in a predominantly WASP school system. Did I identify with my white classmates and de-identify with my family and the Negro community? How much of W. E. B. DuBois's oft-quoted lines from his 1903 classic, *The Souls of Black Folk*, apply to me? DuBois wrote:

> The Negro is a sort of seventh son, born with a veil, and gifted with sec-ond sight in this American world, a world which yields him no true self-consciousness, but only lets him see himself through the revelation of the other world. It is a peculiar sensation, this double-consciousness, this sense of always looking at one's self through the eyes of others, of mea-suring one's soul by the tape of a world that looks on in amused con-tempt and pity. One ever feels his twoness—an American, a Negro; two souls, two thoughts, two unreconciled strivings; two warring ideals in one dark body, whose dogged strength alone keeps it from being torn asunder.[2]

As the child of solidly established and well-respected business and professional parents, I never experienced any confusion about who I was or who I wished to be. Because of my parents' involvement in civic activities, I was well aware of the many inequalities, inequities, and in-justices that existed. I was raised, however, with the hope and expecta-tion that the position and status of the Negro would improve and that I had an obligation to make a contribution to that improvement. While I have a keen sense of "double-consciousness" or the feeling of "twoness" from being an American and a Negro, I did not and do not feel con-sumed by any "unreconciled strivings" or "warring ideals." A loving community embraced me and other Jerseyland children. All my pri-mary reference groups of immediate and extended family, close friends of my parents, and significant others within the Negro community encouraged and supported me in anything that I undertook. I always felt validated and special. Thus, I have never had to define myself "by the tape of a world that looks on in amused contempt and pity." I feel very fortunate for I realize that for personal safety and economic survival Negroes, if light enough, have sometimes "passed" for white, just as Jews at various times have either concealed their Jewishness or converted to other faiths. For me, unambiguous membership in my defining reference group of Americans of African descent has been beneficial—a blessing rather than a curse.

Because I had no early Jewish classmates, my initial introduction to Jews and their history came from two sources: the church, including Sunday school lessons and sermons, and my parents. Unlike some children, who may have been taught to revile Jews as "Christ Killers," my early awareness came from Old Testament stories about God's covenants with his people and his leading them out of bondage from Egypt into the promised land. Because some Negro Spirituals used these Old Testament stories as vehicles for conveying messages of hope for the future, I thought Jews were God's special chosen people. Sunday school classes portrayed God as being both gracious and loving, but also stern and demanding. As a child, I wondered if what I heard in church about Jews not accepting Christ as the promised King, and not complying with the New Covenant (Heb. 8:8) meant that they had invoked the wrath of God. A half century ago, many church writings and teachings had an anti-Semitic bias. As an adult, I am now unwilling to blame any inhumanity of man against man as being God's will, whether it be the long history of persecution of the Jews, the slave history of my ancestors, or current atrocities in the Balkans and Africa.

I have no doubt that I attended Wellesley College as a direct consequence of a friendship that developed between my mother and a Jewish woman from Brookline, Massachusetts. Mother met Clara Goldman, wife of a respected cancer researcher, while attending a women's world peace conference as a delegate from the Westfield YWCA. The conference was held on the Wellesley campus. Following the conference, Mother and Clara regularly corresponded. Clara's daughter, four years my senior, attended Wellesley, and Clara encouraged mother to send me there. When the fall of my senior year of high school arrived, Clara invited us to stay at her home while we visited Radcliffe and Wellesley. Throughout my student years at Wellesley, the Goldman's Brookline home was my "home away from home." Mrs. Goldman attended my Wellesley graduation. She accompanied my mother to confront President Clapp to protest the omission of my name from the program and to demand the public announcement and apology that was made during the graduation ceremony.

My experiences with Jews differ somewhat from those of my husband. He did not grow up in a small, fairly self-sufficient Negro community. Instead, he grew up in a part of the Roxbury–North Dorchester area of the City of Boston known as Cherry Valley. It was not yet mostly black as it is today. Then it was predominantly Jewish and a mixture of Scotch-Irish, Irish, and Italians, with Negroes, Cape Verdeans, and Chinese all together hardly constituting 2 percent of the population. When he was young, most of the merchants on Blue Hill Avenue, the major shopping thoroughfare, were Jewish. In the 1930s and 1940s, the shops on Blue Hill Avenue were all closed on the Jewish High Holidays.

My husband always felt safe living in this neighborhood or moving through other Jewish areas, in contrast to the open hostility he encountered in other white ethnic areas. He felt that some individual Jews did not like Negroes or did not wish to associate with him, sometimes because of having absorbed prevalent negative social attitudes about Negroes. He remembers how angry his father would become when he or his brothers, having been sent on an errand to a store, would come back having been sold something stale or spoiled. In some instances, the message was that their trade was not wanted out of fear that servicing Negroes might impact negatively on their regular clientele. With other merchants, whose stock did not move quickly, any occasional shopper might be sold old goods, while regular preferred customers got fresher produce.

On the other hand, some Jewish merchants such as the owners of a fish market and an auto supply store provided good services and were friends of my husband's parents. At the time, small neighborhood stores were the norm. Such store owners faced certain economic realities—no matter to which ethnic group they belonged. Many extended credit to their customers, but in order to stay in business they had to recoup their overhead expenses. For example, my husband remembers that a fee for credit accounts at local stores might add 10 percent to an outstanding balance—not so bad, given the high interest percentages that attach to credit card purchases today.

Some of my husband's schoolmates who lived in Lower Roxbury

(a heavily Negro area) had parents who worked as domestics for Jews. Unlike the "elite One Hundred" Jews whom Birmingham described as being "somewhat better-behaved than the elite Four Hundred" non-Jews, some of these relatively well-to-do Jews were experienced as demanding, difficult to please, and sometimes exploitative of their employees or customers. Other families in my husband's circle of Negro peers sometimes had hassles with Jewish absentee landlords. These experiences should be understood as products of a particular place and time and as descriptions of individual Jews, not as generalizations about all Jews, either then or now.

Because of our college experiences at Wellesley and Bowdoin, followed by graduate social work training, mine at Simmons College School of Social Work and my husband's at Case-Western Reserve University, we both have met and had relationships with Jews from many different backgrounds. Throughout our adult lives, we have maintained some very close friendships with various college classmates and work colleagues who are Jewish. For more than thirty years, my four children and my dear friend Alice Lowenstein's three children have interacted with one another as though they were part of an extended family. Because social work and law are professions with many Jewish members, we both have had many Jewish colleagues. My first instructor at Boston College Law School, Sanford N. Katz, has been my mentor, colleague, and friend for more than twenty-five years.

Notwithstanding these positive personal relationships and interactions with individual Jews, I am very mindful that since the late 1960s, an uncomfortable tension has developed in this country between certain Jewish and African American groups and organizations. I know that Jewish lawyers played significant roles in the civil rights battles waged by the NAACP Legal Defense Fund leading up to the 1954 historic Supreme Court school desegregation decision of *Brown v. Board of Education.* During the early 1960s many Jews worked as volunteers in voter registration drives in the South—some making the supreme sacrifice of their lives.

However, beginning with the Reagan years and since, it seems as though earlier supportive alliances between African Americans and Jews have eroded to some extent. Although many Jewish individuals and organizations continue to work for affirmative action, a few in collaboration with the conservative Christian Right now work to discredit and dismantle affirmative action policies and programs. I am probably not alone in wondering about these more recent initiatives. Does acceptance by the governing white majority require conservative politics from some Jews, as it seemingly does of some upper-middle-class African Americans?

Visit to the Slave House of Gorée-Island

I now turn to a relatively recent experience in my adult life, my 1995 visit to the Slave House of Gorée-Island, which raised my consciousness about certain similarities and contrasts between the African American and Jewish experiences. I probably received an invitation to attend the Third African/African-American Summit Conference, held in Dakar, Senegal, from May 1–6, 1995, because for nearly two decades I had been a faculty member of an American law school. The purpose of this third coming together of Africans, African Americans, and friends of Africa was to formulate a program of Principles, Declarations, and Actions to assist in meeting the economic, educational, and human development needs of sub-Saharan Africa.

I felt extremely privileged and excited by the prospect of being able to visit the Slave House Museum of Gorée-Island. I was eager to learn more about the history of my people. I relay the story of this visit in order to convey the complex feelings toward both Jews and Christians that it evoked.

MAY 1, 1995: DAKAR, SENEGAL

The crowded ferry slowly pulls away from the wharf to make its way out into the harbor to the historic Ile de Gorée.[9] Less than two miles from the mainland, Gorée is a small, balsatic lump of rock just 44.47 acres in size. From establishment of the first Portuguese slave stations in 1536 to 1848, when France abolished the slave trade, upward of twenty million persons from the whole of West Africa passed through stations such as this on their way to the Americas—more than one-third dying in transit.

Though the day is clear and the temperature is in the eighties, I begin to shiver. I sense a degree of anxiety rising within me as I anticipate how I will react when confronted with the reality of my ancestral past. I recall the opening scenes of a film I saw in 1994 by independent filmmaker Professor Haile Gerima of Howard University. *Sankofa* opens with an African fashion model cavort-

ing and posing for a European photographer on the beach in
front of a slave-holding station—now considered sacred ground.
The collective spirits of the ancient African elders are so greatly
affronted that to teach her a lesson, they transform and transport
her back in time to relive the traumatic experiences of capture
and branding, then of being held and loaded onto a boat for the
journey to a Louisiana sugar plantation.

My recall of *Sankofa* is interrupted when the tour guide, who
is moving about the boat spending a few minutes getting acquainted with each of the fifteen persons in our party, stops before me. When he introduces himself to me, he asks: "Why are
you with us today?" Thinking that he is asking about my attending
the Third African/African-American Summit Conference, I start
to tell him about receiving an invitation in February from the
renowned civil rights activist, Rev. Leon H. Sullivan, and the pres-
idents of two African countries.

The guide, however, raises his hand to stop me. He again asks:
"Why are you going to Gorée this afternoon? What do you seek?"
I then explain that having the good fortune and opportunity to
come to Senegal, my top priority is to visit the Slave House of
Gorée-Island in order to pay tribute to the millions of persons
whose last contact with their homeland was this or a similar slave
holding station. The guide beams. He says that he is glad I am interested in history and in hearing the truth, not merely setting
out on a tourist outing. He promises to take our group out on the
upper balcony to talk privately with us before leaving the museum. There is a need, he says, for Africans to acknowledge their
past roles in the slave trade. He believes this must occur for
strong and lasting bridges to be forged between Africans and
African Americans. This will be his contribution to that healing
and building process.

When the ferry pulls within sight of Gorée, I spot a circular fort
and think that this must be where *Sankofa* was filmed. After we dis-
embark, the tour guide leads us to the left, across a small open
plaza facing the water. Before starting down narrow Saint-Germain
Street, running parallel to the shore, he stops and announces that
although May 1 is a Muslim holiday and the Slave House is closed,
Boubacar Joseph Ndiaye, principal curator of the museum, has
agreed to give our party a private tour.

In response to the tour guide's knock, Curator Ndiaye opens

the door and quickly ushers us into the open, ground-level court-
yard of the last slave station built on the island in 1776. My first
thought is: This *is* where *Sankofa* was filmed. Later, however, I
learn the movie was filmed in Ghana, but that the designs of the
West African coastal slave stations were similar. Straight ahead, at
the end of a central dark corridor, is an opening to the sea—a
"Doorway of No Return"—through which thousands passed on
their way to the Americas. Immediately in front of us, on either
side of this corridor, two curved, pink, cement-railed staircases
sweep up to a balcony porch surrounding rooms with high ceilings that served as living quarters for the slave trader/masters and
their mulatto mistresses, known as "signares."

Curator Ndiaye first shows us the ground-level holding cells
into which family members were placed on arrival. Men, women,
and children were held in different rooms, seated with their backs
to the wall, with shackles around their necks and arms. The largest
room is the weighing room. Here young men were kept to be "fat-
tened up" before being weighed and auctioned off. For those reluctant to accept their plight, there were oubliette-cells for solitary
crouched confinement under each horseshoe-shaped staircase,
and a large, perpetually damp room on the far right side.

Sometimes as many as 150 to 200 persons might be in these
rooms awaiting arrival of the next ship. They were freed only
once daily to relieve themselves. The despicable health conditions at this station led to a plague that ravaged the island in
1779. In amazement, I wonder how the trader/merchants and
their mulatto mistresses could have lived just one floor above this
misery. How could they have been unaffected by the stench?

As our party moves about the ground level, stepping in and out
of the rooms, crossing the corridor to peer out at the sea, I feel en-
gulfed by an unseen yet palpable source of energy radiating up
from the floor and out from the walls. Instead of revulsion or fear,
I feel a surge of awe welling up inside me. How magnificently
strong and resilient my ancestors were to have endured this!

This Slave House of Gorée-Island, in the words of Curator
Ndiaye, epitomizes three hundred years of enslavement that removed from the African continent some of its most beautiful people. Whole families were separated and dispersed. Fathers might
be purchased and sent to Louisiana, mothers to Brazil or Cuba,
and children to Haiti or the West Indies, all stripped of their Afri-

can names and assigned registration numbers. Once in the Americas during slavery and since emancipation, however, the descendants of these former slaves found ways to survive, to reconstitute families and communities, to become, in Curator Nydiaye's eyes, a "single people : the AFRO-AMERICANS."

In closing, Curator Ndiaye speaks of the many different groups of Americans presently traveling abroad. Reportedly, more African Americans have come to Dakar for this Summit than ever before have returned at the same time to any single place on the African continent. Many other Americans, World War II veterans and Holocaust survivors, are journeying to Europe to revisit battlefields and Nazi death camps to pay homage to lost comrades and kin on the fiftieth anniversary of the end of World War II. Curator Ndiaye asks us, as we stand in the last slave station built on Gorée-Island in 1776, to remember that the entire history of the slave traffic through Gorée-Island spanned slightly more than three hundred years.

As the curator speaks, I feel intense heat rush from the soles of my feet and up my spine. Like a thunderclap "Never again! Never again!"—the oft-repeated refrain of Jews such as Holocaust activist Elie Wiesel—starts to reverberate in my brain. First, I realize that there is a consciousness about the atrocities and casualties of the Holocaust that has been engrained in the American psyche. Most Americans probably know that about six million Jews died in the death camps. However, there seems to be no such consciousness about the extent and magnitude of the horrors of the slave trade. Angrily, I think: "How dare folk forget, ignore, or deny the realities and legacy of this history of slavery—the history of my ancestors whose unsung and long, uncompensated labors subsidized not only the founding and development of the United States of America, but of all the modern economies of the Western World!"

Taking Responsibility

My visit to Gorée-Island made me realize that the task of remembering, commemorating, and celebrating the survival of African Americans is a personal task that I and other African Americans must undertake. It is a task that the Jews have already undertaken for themselves. I deeply respect and admire the way in which Jews as a group strive to preserve their religious views, values, and traditions. The flip side of such admiration is the sense of envy and outrage that I experienced at the end of my visit to the Gorée-Island museum. I wish that more African Americans were as assertive as activist Jewish survivors of the Holocaust have been in changing public consciousness.

Before our party left the museum, the tour guide took us out on the upper porch and explained that it was a common practice among warring African nations for members of a defeated kingdom to be enslaved. He said that those Africans who participated in marauding inland villages may have been enticed by personal greed, but that they could not have known the circumstances into which they were sending people. He said that defeat in war did not traditionally entail a denial of a person's humanity, nor was it a static condition to be passed from generation to generation. While there is no accurate count, it is estimated that from ten to twenty million persons were brought westward across the Atlantic during the four centuries that the slave trade prevailed. Some scholars estimate that between thirty and sixty million Africans were subjected to the horrors of the trade. Approximately one third, however, died on the torturous marches to the ships and another third died either in holding stations on both sides of the Atlantic or on the ships themselves. But no one knows how many countless others died in battles resisting capture.

The task of remembering, of bearing personal witness to suffering, is not something to be expected from others. However, I believe that it is important for everyone to understand the horrendous consequences that can occur when people see other people as so unlike themselves that all manner of inhumane behavior can be justified, such as the "ethnic cleansing" that has occurred in the Balkans and in Africa during the 1990s. As our party left Gorée, the idea began to take shape that just as there is now a Holocaust museum in Washington, D.C., there also should be museums, in D.C. and the various states, that appropriately and accurately document and record not only how our African ancestors were brought to the Americas, but how strong they were to have survived and what important contributions they made to the development of this nation.

Participation in this project has given me the opportunity to look for commonalities among Jews and African Americans. Initially I may have only focused on perceived differences between anti-Semitism and the racial prejudice and discrimination I experience in this society as an

African American. I have come to appreciate that being Jewish in American society is a minority experience, even though *minority* today usually means being non-white. To be a minority also means being deemed to be "outside" of the American mainstream, to be of inferior status, and to be posing some kind of threat to the status quo.

For many years following the Crusades, Jews in some European nations were considered to be "outsiders" because of their migrant status, religious beliefs, and mixed cultural and racial background. Yet most Jews in the United States today are perceived to be members of the dominant white population. Perhaps for that reason, it seems to me that Jews as a group have been invited to sit at the American societal table and to partake fully from the menu. In contrast, while individual African Americans may get invited to sit at the table (for example, General Colin Powell, President Bush's Chairman of the Joint Chiefs of Staff), African Americans as a group have yet to be accepted and welcomed.

I earnestly hope that color and the response to it are not the defining differences between African Americans and Jews, which will make raising public consciousness about the African American experience impossible. I see now that it is not productive to get sidetracked into debates or disputes about which group's pain is the greater. I feel wary that as the momentum grows to incarcerate ever larger numbers of African American men and women that another "final solution" might one day be justified as the only reasonable societal response to the inordinate expense of warehousing persons deemed to be nonproductive and unfit. From my perspective, activist American Jews, because of their wariness and sense of vulnerability, are ever vigilant in working to ensure that they never experience in this country a repetition of the Nazi Holocaust. I cannot say the same about the awareness or vigilance of many African Americans.

As the twenty-first century nears, I believe that the biggest challenge for Americans is to give up blind adherence to a "melting pot" ideology that values assimilation and engenders a static, prejudiced, and discriminating society, and instead to embrace an ideology of "pluralism" that recognizes, is comfortable with, and accepting of multiculturalism. At the end of my days, if God offered me the opportunity to return to this life, I would choose to come back as an African American to work on this challenge, to live out the words of sociologist Howard Winant, "[To attain] democracy: more of it, better varieties of it, and the further extension of it into every realm of cultural, economic, and political life."[4]

From Horse Carts to Quantum Mechanics

DENISE FREED

Stories of My Grandmothers

M Y GRANDMOTHER'S EYES gaze back at me from her wedding portrait. Although I'm looking at a xeroxed reproduction of a black-and-white photograph, I still see the color of my grandmother's warm brown eyes, a trait that I share with her. My grandmother at the time of that picture and I, staring at her now, could very well be the same age. (I'm thirty-two, and we don't know for sure how old she is.) However, a large gulf separates us. Grandma Anna was born at the turn of the century in a small Jewish shtetl in Eastern Europe, and I was born in the middle of the twentieth century in an American university town with a small Jewish community. She worked first as a milliner and then started a business in women's clothing with my grandfather. Years later she was the business manager for the apartment buildings they rented out. My career is in a very different sphere. I am a theoretical physicist, married to a mathematical physicist. Because Grandma Anna is my mother's mother, there is one thing I have automatically inherited from her—we are both Jewish. In many ways, what it means to be Jewish has changed from her lifetime to mine, but it is still part of a common thread that holds our family together.

My grandmother passed away two summers ago. Because she was the last remaining relative of her generation, her passing signified the end of an era. However, she will always be with me and remains a part of my earliest memories—I can still see her, my grandfather, Grandma Pauline, and Aunt Ray (my maternal uncle's mother-in-law) towering over me, looking very solemn, but also loving, while they awaited news of my sister's birth. Later, as a young child, I was fascinated by hearing stories about my grandmothers' and my mother's childhoods, which all seemed so foreign to me. I have learned from my mother that in the Jewish tradition a person lives on in the memories of others. Writing these tales about my grandmothers is a way for me to honor them and keep their memories alive. I feel lucky to have had two grandmothers who lived long enough to share with me stories from their lives, but at the same time I know there are many stories they were unable to reveal or never had the chance to tell. Their stories influenced who I have become as a young adult and, along with stories from my mother's and my own childhood, make up the fabric of my Jewish identity.

Grandma Anna. Grandma Anna was born around 1900 and was the youngest in a family of seven children. She grew up in a small town in Galicia, which is now part of Poland, and came to the United States between the two world wars. My parents, my sister, and I used to visit her and my grandfather in their apartment in the Bronx several times a year, especially for the holidays—Thanksgiving, winter break, and Passover. I have early memories of celebrating Passover at her house and of meeting much of my mother's extended family during our visits. Also, I remember being very upset when my grandmother would not let me use the scissors on Shabbat, because she was still very observant then. At other times, I was very appreciative of her generosity to her grandchildren, especially when she gave me the large jars of pennies she had saved so I could sift through them for specimens for my coin collection (and use the rest of the pennies at the candy store). Even at an early age, I inherited from my grandmother a sense of family and Jewish life.

In time, I also developed a sense of history and would often ask her for stories of her childhood. At that time, she would only tell us the good stories, of her house by the stream, of the beautiful fruit trees that grew on the local nobleman's estate. One of her favorite stories was about the time when the stream by her house overflowed. Her house was in danger of flooding, so her family packed all their belongings in a cart and left for drier ground. When they arrived, they realized she was missing and searched all over for her. They even sent someone back to the house to look. Finally, they found her; she was curled up, fast asleep, in the back of the cart.

It wasn't until much later that she started telling me the other stories, her sad and painful stories. While I was a junior in college, my parents went on a sabbatical to Paris. I called my grandmother every weekend, and, in my parents' absence, I became her confidante. In addition to telling me of her concerns about her health, she would complain to me about my sister dating someone who was not Jewish. I began to understand why my grandmother was so upset when she started telling me stories of pogroms and other anti-Semitic incidents she had experienced as a girl. One story she told me was about the time she and her father were on line to buy train tickets. Her father was dressed in the traditional Jewish clothing of the time, and several men began beating him just because he was Jewish. The ticket seller closed the window in his booth so he wouldn't have to see it. While my grandmother, a young girl at the time, begged them to kill her instead, they continued beating her father until they thought (incorrectly) that he was dead.

Another story she tried to share with me recounted how she and her female cousins and some of the Polish (i.e., non-Jewish) boys in the town used to put on plays together. The boys and her cousins had been on friendly terms, but during one of the pogroms, the boys "did what they had to do." At this point in the story, she'd pause and engage me with a meaningful stare. I never knew exactly what she was referring to, but, because of her inability to elaborate on this memory, I was led to believe that the boys did more than just beat her cousins. My grandmother also lamented the fact that during some of the pogroms, even the people who worked for her family were reluctant to protect them. These stories made it very clear to me why my grandmother felt so unsafe about being related to someone who was not Jewish. I still felt my sister had a right to make her own choices in her life, but at the same time these conversations put a lot of pressure on me to date only Jews. Years later, though, when my sister finally married her non-Jewish high school boyfriend, my grandmother had learned to accept him and grew to love him.

Just how vivid and strong my grandmother's memories and fears were became clear later that sabbatical year when my parents started planning a trip to visit my grandmother's hometown in Poland. When my grandmother heard about this, she called me up and started crying. "How can they go back there?" she sobbed. "There's nowhere for them to stay; there are no more Jews left." She continued, "They [the Poles in the town] will remember they owe my father money, and they'll kill them [your parents]." As it turned out, the trip was postponed for several years. By the time my father did visit her town, my grandmother was no longer as distressed by it. Grandma Anna was right about one thing, though—there were no Jews left.

In the United States, my grandmother and her family made a new life for themselves. She and my grandfather worked very hard and saved as much as they could for their children and grandchildren. Education was extremely important to them, and both my uncle and my mother went on to obtain higher degrees.

Grandma Pauline. Education was also extremely important for my father's mother, Grandma Pauline. She was also born around 1900 in Rizshe, a town near Kiev. After she learned to pray and write in Yiddish at the Jewish school, her father would not send her to the Russian elementary school because he did not believe that women needed to be educated. She was very persistent, though, and found educated relatives who could tutor her. She also learned the skills of a seamstress, to help bring in income so that she could "see the world and study." Once the Russian Revolution started, she became very involved in it. Despite her dreams and commitment to the Communist cause, when she finally had the opportunity to emigrate to Canada after many years of unsuccessful attempts, she left with her mother in 1922. She eventually made it to the United States, where, among other activities, she was very involved in unionizing. When I first asked her for stories about her childhood, she would tell me about her education. When she felt I was old enough to understand her story, she wrote me a letter describing the kind of education she had and what it took in those times for a girl to obtain a good education.

By the time I received her letter, though, I had learned about her involvement in the Russian Revolution, and I became interested in hearing stories about that. In her next letter, she told of her reaction to hearing about the start of the revolution. She was extremely enthusiastic and idealistic and felt she had a chance to make the country better for everyone, including the Jews, whom she especially felt needed a change. In her letter, she described how the Jews lived in a segregated section of the town and were not allowed to farm the land. They were also subject to "horrible sufferings," which I did not learn about until much later. My grandmother wrote about her exhilaration when one of her friends returned from the army smiling, a visible proof that the Romanov dynasty had fallen. Inspired by the "new feeling of freedom," she and the other youth from her town opened a library and founded a theater. When peasants took over the palace belonging to the town's wealthy gentleman and destroyed it, she regretted that they would not be able to use the building to house a school or hospital. However, the grounds with the beautiful gardens remained intact and were finally opened to the public. My grandmother believed that all property that had been misused by a few should be turned over for the common good. She never lost her idealism because she came to America before things went "sour" and many of her heroes were killed by the Bolsheviks. She could never bring herself to believe that the revolution did not turn out the way she had wanted.

In junior high school, I typed and edited her two letters for a history project, and I sent copies to her. She was going to send me a third letter, telling me what happened once she left her small town to go to the city to become more seriously involved in the revolution. Unfortunately, she died before she had a chance to finish it. I knew how important our correspondence was to her, however, because my two typed letters were found in her handbag after she passed away.

It wasn't until many years later, when a cousin was transcribing and translating my grandmother's old letters, that my family learned some of the stories she had never told us. The correspondence between her mother and brother describe all the financial and logistical difficulties that beset them in their thwarted attempts to join her brother in Canada. My grandmother was not officially registered in Russia, so she could not obtain a passport and had to sneak out of the country. At one point, she and her mother had finally managed to complete all the proper paperwork (with the exception of my grandmother's passport) and buy boat tickets to America, just to be turned back when they reached the harbor in Germany because World War I had started. Through these letters, we also learned for the first time of my grandmother's first marriage and how she lost her husband shortly after the wedding when he was killed in a pogrom while visiting his family. We were stunned to learn about this part of her life that she had kept to herself for so many years.

Unlike Grandma Anna, Grandma Pauline was not at all religious. The contrast was striking at a Passover seder at my Aunt Ray's house. Aunt Ray was like a third grandmother to me. She had six children and many grandchildren, but she still always found room to welcome my family at her Thanksgiving dinners and seders. One night at a seder, Grandma Anna kept shaking her head and clucking her tongue in dismay because of all the parts of the seder we skipped. Meanwhile, Grandma Pauline was browsing through the Haggadah to see what was in it while saying, "Interesting, very interesting." Although Grandma Pauline was not religious and not at all observant, she still identified strongly with being Jewish and with Yiddish culture in particular. She gave me books on Yiddish and recommended books on Jewish history as well as on the history of the Russian Revolution. In fact, Grandma Pauline encouraged my education and learning in all disciplines, and her activism and desire for social change were an enormous inspiration to me.

My Mother, Renee

My mother, Grandma Anna's daughter, grew up in a strong Jewish community. She lived in a one-bedroom apartment in an immigrant neighborhood in the Bronx with her older brother and parents. From her stories, I grew up with an idealized picture of how all the neighbors talked with one another and the children played together in the street. She had many cousins and loved spending time at a favorite aunt's house. Her parents were observant, and most of the people in her neighborhood were Jewish, so that both being with an extended family and practicing Judaism were a natural way of life for her. In college, she shed some of the religious beliefs and practices of her childhood, but belonging to a Jewish community remained important. It was extremely difficult for my mother when she and my father moved to Ithaca, New York, where he accepted a faculty position at Cornell. She was very unhappy being isolated from her family, and she missed the life and excitement of the city. It was also difficult for her because Ithaca's Jewish community was very small. My mother worked hard to re-create the close, extended family she had in New York by finding a group of Jewish families with whom we celebrated the holidays (when we weren't traveling to New York City). When the first set of friends ended up leaving Ithaca, my mother eventually found a second group of friends who formed a new Jewish family away from family. As a tribute to how successful they were in creating a sense of community, most of these friends, including those who had left Ithaca many years before, attended both my wedding and my sister's wedding.

It was also very important to my mother that my sister and I grow up with a strong Jewish identity, even though almost all of the people around us were not Jewish. We attended Sunday school and had Hebrew lessons. My mother kept a kosher home, largely so that her parents would be able to eat there when they visited. We actually had to have our meat shipped in from outside Ithaca, sometimes from as far away as Albany, which is about a three- or four-hour drive. We did not keep kosher outside of the home (except that, to varying degrees, we avoided pig meat and shellfish). This combination had the effect of making our home and our meals there feel special to me. We were rather anomalous in Ithaca; not only were there very few families that kept kosher, but at times we were probably the only ones who kept kosher and did not regularly attend Shabbat services.

My parents followed my grandparents in valuing education highly. To make sure that my mother obtained a good Jewish education, my grandparents sent her to Talmad Torah, a daily religious Hebrew school, in addition to the public elementary school. This was a strong indication of my grandparents' commitment to my mother's education, because most parents did not send their girls to Hebrew school. My mother went to Bronx Science High School, where she gained an appreciation for the excitement of scientific discovery and a belief in the value of basic research. She wanted very much to go to Barnard College, but my grandmother did not believe in paying for a woman's education. Luckily for my mother, my grandfather decided that because they were investing money in her older brother's education, they should also pay for hers, so she attended the school of her choice. When my mother learned about other religions and cultures in college, she rejected the teachings and influence of her Orthodox cousins. After college, my mother had several interests she wanted to pursue, but my grandparents, who believed strongly that a woman should have a trade to support herself with, insisted that she get a teaching certificate, in addition to whatever else she chose to do. After receiving her master's degree in education from Harvard University, my mother found that the only careers open to her were either to be "somebody's assistant" or to teach. The latter carried greater responsibility and was much more creative, so she chose to be a teacher. Having acquired a sense of history from her mother, my mother taught advanced placement American history (among other courses) for many years at Ithaca High School. In this course, she focused on teaching the students how to write and think. My father is a chemistry professor at Cornell, where he leads a very active research group. Because of my father's expertise in his field and his widespread knowledge in general, and my mother's deep respect for science, both my sister and I grew up thinking that authority and effectiveness resided in science. I also inherited from my parents a love for the world of ideas.

Denise: My Jewish Childhood in Ithaca and Around the World

While I was growing up, I was aware of what felt like an insidious pressure to conform to the non-Jewish majority culture. At times I also felt isolated, in part because there were very few Jewish children in my elementary school in Ithaca, and I was often the only Jew in my class. In first or second grade, I was very upset when my best friend came back from winter break and started bragging to me about the thirty Christmas presents she had received. After that, my parents gave us eight Chanukah gifts, one for each night. Later on, during Passover, which falls around Easter time, they also had to leave us kosher-for-Passover candy overnight, so we would not feel deprived. At the same time, though, I was adamantly against singing any songs in school that had Christian religious content. I think one year they even made us sing Christmas carols in school, and I strongly opposed it. Usually, though, I would just be silent during the "offending" words or lines. It bothered me that everyone took these religious words and songs as a matter of course and did not realize it might conflict with someone else's beliefs.

Toward the end of elementary school, I had a very unsettling experience. I was on the school playground playing with some of my friends after school. A woman approached us and asked what our names were and what church we went to. After my friends answered, I was silent. I felt very uncomfortable. I did not go to a church, and already I had an ingrained sense that it was not wise to reveal that I was Jewish. My friends were protective of me and said I did not speak English. I think we somehow made up the story that I was from Denmark and spoke only Danish (which I did know how to speak because my family and I had recently spent six months there). The woman then started to tell us stories. It turned out that she was from a nearby church and often came to the playground to try to convert the children. She had a bag full of picture books, all about dying children who accepted Jesus into their hearts and went to heaven and got to sit on Jesus' lap or wear a crown. Afterward, both my non-Jewish friends and I were angry that this woman was trying to influence us in this way. This experience certainly augmented my feelings that society was putting pressure (usually subtly) on us to conform to its Christian norms. It also helps to explain why I continued to feel so uncomfortable singing songs with religious words because, according to the woman at the playground, you just had to say a few simple words to be converted. Since then, I have had dreams influenced by this event (and possibly also by science fiction stories). I dreamt that people were being taken over by an evil force, but they were all happy so they didn't mind. By the end of the dream, I was one of the few remaining "unconverted" people aware of the danger, trying to devise plans to protect myself and my friends.

Even before elementary school, I was accustomed to being different and not fitting in. When I was quite young, my mother decided she wanted to travel around the world, so we took a year long sabbatical when I was in kindergarten. We spent the first six months in Japan, where I attended a Japanese kindergarten. In many ways I felt I was in an alien world. We lived in an old neighborhood in Tokyo where the sights and smells and customs were so different from anything to be found in Ithaca. Much of the food, especially the seafood, seaweed, unusual spices, and strong pickles, were so foreign to me that at times my mother even let me eat bologna (which contained pork) because it was one of the few familiar foods available. Luckily for my sister and me, we loved rice and delighted in eating rice balls. Every so often, the boys in our neighborhood would form a procession through the streets, carrying the shrines of the local gods and banging on loud drums. On the holiday honoring young children age three, five, and seven, the priests at the temples where we went sightseeing welcomed us warmly, since at that time it was still so rare to have Western visitors. At the next big holiday, my sister and I wore our new kimonos, and we were surrounded by a wall of Japanese men with fancy cameras who all wanted to photograph the young American girls in ceremonial Japanese dress. At school, I did manage to find some playmates. My family was welcomed into their homes by their parents, which was quite unusual at the time. They had visited America and wanted to reciprocate the hospitality they had received in the United States. However, at times I felt left out by my classmates. The strangest of these times was when the girls in my class would play a game that looked like follow-the-leader. They would weave through the room, single file, and touch different objects. I can't remember how I felt as each of the girls filed past me and tapped me.

We spent the second six months in Israel. Even there I did not really fit in, largely because of language difficulties; I spent most of my time in kindergarten playing with the other two girls from English-speaking countries. However, I did learn to identify with Israel and became very aware, firsthand, of its vulnerability. For example, one day my class took a trip to the local elementary school, and, among other things, we watched a movie showing us what the different bombs looked like that sometimes were planted by militant Arabs on the school playgrounds.

During our trip, I also learned of the Israelis' pride in turning desert into fertile ground again, and by the end of the stay I was speaking some Hebrew. This knowledge of Hebrew (and my many Hebrew lessons later on) has helped me to appreciate religious services more than my husband and some of my non-Hebrew-speaking friends do.

Throughout high school, college, and graduate school, the isolation and the assumption of conformity is something I have continued to struggle with. For example, Christmastime can be an especially lonely time. Some of my favorite Christmas days have been spent cross-country skiing on the Ithaca golf course, where fellow skiers smile and wave as they pass each other by. My first year in graduate school at Princeton I lived in the cloistered dorms. Before our month-long winter break, everybody kept asking me whether I was going home for Christmas (not what I was planning to do over vacation). This question made it clear to me that they just assumed everyone was like them in celebrating Christmas. Something about the way they asked the question and something about the general atmosphere in the dorms bothered me so much that I would often just answer no, instead of telling them that I was going to Paris with my family for the month. The atmosphere for me there was strongly shaped by one of my close friends that year, the only other woman in my otherwise all-male class in the physics department. She believed that one could be a good person only if one believed in God (any god). She did not realize that Judaism encourages questioning and allows ambivalence, and that, to me, being a good person does not depend on having a notion of God that others find acceptable.

My Jewish Education. For me, Judaism has been a mix of cultural, historical, and religious aspects, with different features taking prominence at different times. Early in elementary school, when I felt different from my classmates, I started to identify it with being Jewish. I thought there was a mythical Jewish community that valued learning and ideas where I would fit in. In Sunday school, I decided I wanted to be observant when I grew up, and I was also strongly affected by the stories of the Holocaust. For a year or two, I even regularly attended the small junior congregation. In it, my Hebrew tutor led a Saturday morning service for middle-school-age children. He taught us many of the songs and prayers. He made it interesting by telling us about their origins and the stories surrounding them and also by teaching us alternate melodies. At one point, he also brought in some sample discussions in the spirit of the Talmud, the rabbinic commentary on the Torah. I was particularly interested in this aspect after having read *The Chosen* by Chaim Potok, also because it was a way of applying logical thinking to questions of ethics and other human affairs. In American history in public school I identified with the founders of Rhode Island and Pennsylvania; those were the two original colonies that allowed religious freedom, and I valued religious tolerance very highly.

In seventh grade, I was the only one in Ithaca studying to be a bar or bat mitzvah at the temple. There was no class at the temple Sunday school for my grade, so I had to attend the class for children a year younger than me and study on my own with the new rabbi. In more recent years there have been several bar or bat mitzvahs during the year. The students have a chance to go to several to see what they are like and to start learning the services. I did not have those opportunities. The year of my bat mitzvah was also the rabbi's first year at the temple, so the whole experience was new for both of us. Before the rabbi came to the temple, women were not allowed to participate fully in the most important part of the Saturday morning service, the Torah reading. At the time, it was just becoming acceptable for women to take full part in the services of Conservative synagogues, but the extent of their participation depended very much on the beliefs and wishes of each congregation. Once the rabbi came to Ithaca, our congregation was going to consider the matter, and it looked likely that women would become fully accepted. However, at the time of my bat mitzvah, the issue was not yet decided. Some of the men who were the most active participants in the temple did not feel comfortable with having women read from the Torah, which is usually an essential part of a bar mitzvah. I did not feel right making waves, especially since I had heard that one of these men was quite ill. At the time it seemed reasonable to respect the wishes of the people who had contributed so much to the temple, and I did not feel compelled to protest the unequal treatment of women in the synagogue. Instead, I opted to do my bat mitzvah at the Friday night services, where there is no Torah reading, but where one can still chant from the Haftarah, which is usually a selection from the Prophets.

I could not personally relate to my particular reading, so the rabbi gave me a list of psalms from the Book of Psalms that he thought would also be appropriate for a bat mitzvah. In spite of my active participation in and strong identification with Judaism, it was through my deep appreciation of the beauty of nature, rather than anything learned in Sunday school or religious services, that I believed in God or had any spiritual inspirations. I tried to pick a psalm that conveyed at least some of those feelings. The closest was Psalm 8, which contained the lines:

> When I behold Thy heavens, the work of Thy fingers,
> The moon and the stars, which Thou has established;
> What is man, that Thou art mindful of him?

Two hundred people showed up at my bat mitzvah, a record for the temple at that time. They included both family and friends, both Jews and non-Jews. My bat mitzvah was a way of affirming my Jewish identity and sharing it with others.

It was also a turning point for me. Subsequently, I began to distance myself from the more formal aspects of the religion. Through all my studying for the bat mitzvah, I never felt truly connected to the temple. My growing awareness of inequality between men and women in the Jewish tradition was starting to alienate me from the religion. I was especially bothered by a prayer we learned about in junior congregation that thanked God for "not making me a woman." In the years immediately following my bat mitzvah, I started to resent a religion that did not give equal treatment to both men and women and did not really allow women to participate fully in the religious practices, even if this was supposed to be countered by a deep respect and honor for women taking care of the home and family life. I no longer wanted to grow up to be very observant, and I didn't have much interest in continuing to go to services (except on the High Holidays). I still planned to keep kosher but eventually decided that if I had a choice between keeping kosher and doing all the cooking myself, or sharing the cooking with my husband and not keeping kosher, there was no question: I'd share the cooking.

Around the time of my bat mitzvah, I also became disillusioned about the existence of an ideal Jewish community. I had joined the Jewish youth group Young Judea. I found the older leaders in the group very inspiring, idealistic, and intellectual. I think the high point of my participation in Young Judea came on a retreat, where the leaders had designed a very creative role-playing game that helped us to understand what the culture gap between the Israelis and the Arabs must feel like. Unfortunately, we didn't get to spend much time with the older kids, and the leader for the junior high children was much more interested in playing silly ice-breaker games. I lost my interest in Young Judea when I went to an intercity retreat and could not relate at all to the girls from the neighboring larger city. They were not interested in ideas and did not have the same values that I had and that I associated with Judaism. They were more interested in their clothes and makeup and with playing mindless games. Although I lost my dream of an ideal Jewish community, I still had a few close Jewish friends with whom I celebrated some of the holidays, especially Yom Kippur and Rosh Hashanah, and I remained a member of and later led the Young Judea Dance Group. In fact, sharing the holidays (and the Israeli folk dancing) probably brought me and my friends closer together, and to this day I still celebrate some of the holidays with two of my old friends. It was not until recently that my husband and I began finding more people like the ones I had originally envisioned, and we are slowly trying to build and become part of an intellectual Jewish community.

Life Choices and Current Perspectives. The feelings and history I have described so far have greatly influenced the choices I have made in my life. The intellectual values, the importance of science, and my love of and desire to understand nature helped me decide to become a physicist. It was also a way for me to do something creative while following a career that at the time seemed somewhat practical. By being a physicist, I also felt I could continue, in my own way, my grandmother's work in changing society. This is because there are very few women in physics; when I started graduate school, there were no permanent women faculty in the Princeton University physics department. If I were to advance in the field, then, by my presence alone, I would be changing the face of physics and giving the message (at least to some students) that women can do whatever they choose and can be taken seriously in various positions of authority in our society.

My Jewish childhood has also prepared me in other ways for my experiences so far in physics. Growing up in Ithaca, I am no stranger to being in the minority, and as a woman in physics I am a very noticeable minority. During my first few years in graduate school, out of about one hundred students in physics, only four were women. Since then, the number of women among my peers has not improved significantly, especially because I focused for a few years on quantum field theory, a very theoretical branch of physics that is especially underrepresented by women. I am also used to being on my guard for prejudice, which usually has not confronted me head-on, except for the occasional swastika in graffiti and sexist comments about my success in physics. My childhood resistance to conformity has probably helped me choose and continue along a career path that so few women follow.

My Jewish experience has also strongly affected my choice of spouse. I have married a Jewish man who shares many of my values. He identifies with being Jewish and is happy to celebrate some of the holidays with me. He pursues a life of the mind and, like me, is a mathematical scientist. Social issues are very important to him, and he would like to make a difference in the world.

My Jewish identity is very much a part of me, but I can go for great lengths of time without giving it a thought. I celebrate some holidays and follow some rituals, while ignoring others. I find meaning, community, and sometimes even spirituality in these holidays, while at the same time I do not have a firm belief in God and certainly do not observe holidays because God has commanded us to. At times, I feel very much in the minority, and yet, as a white, middle-class American, I do not suffer from many of the difficulties we associate with minority status in this country. I feel very hesitant to reveal my Jewish identity to non-Jewish acquaintances and colleagues, and yet I personally have not suffered much by anti-Semitism. I more easily feel at home socializing with other intellectual Jews, but I cannot fully explain what distinguishes them from people of other backgrounds, including my many non-Jewish friends. As I carry on the Jewish heritage of my parents and grandparents, my life contains many such contradictions, but it is all the richer for them.

Finally, Our Own Minyan:
A Coming Together

LESLIE BRODY

M Y SENSE OF MYSELF as a Jew has been enriched and transformed during the course of participating in this collaboration,
which often demanded more time and energy than I had originally bar-
gained for. This project took root in my consciousness in a way that few
others have done, affecting and shaping the course of my identity.
Many of the other Fellows also changed and expanded their visions of
themselves and their own ethnicities. In the process of writing, we discovered forgotten memories that had critically shaped us, and we were
able to see ourselves and others from a different perspective.

We developed a sense of trust as we listened to each other and read
each others' essays, which enabled us to re-evaluate our thoughts and
feelings. We carefully scrutinized our definitions of Judaism, the stereotypes we held about Jews, and the distinctions we drew between what
kinds of remarks constitute anti-Semitism and what kinds don't. We
analyzed the process of communicating about these issues and tried to
assess the kinds of interactions that worked to facilitate or block a
meaningful conversation. We also shared our hopes for improved interethnic communication and relationships in the future.

Although we frequently disagreed, sometimes resulting in heated
e-mail exchanges or face-to-face debates, the high level of motivation in
our group to bridge interethnic divisions and the close relationships
we had formed helped us to develop a communication process that
effectively changed at least some of our views. In this concluding chapter, I often quote the poignant and passionate exchanges we had after
reading each others' essays. Helena Meyer Knapp ("Half-Breed or Hybrid") describes our evolution as a group in this way: "The fact that we
understand how different our perspectives remain is a sign that we are a
genuine community."

Getting Over It

When Rachel Kadish ("Living for Export") first read about my fearful reaction to her openness about being Jewish, she was surprised. She wrote:

> And then I felt . . . well . . . weary. An odd sensation. As if, rather than being younger than everyone else, I were the old woman clucking her tongue. I grew up around a lot of ardent Jews: relatives, family friends, teachers. . . . Sometimes I hear their counsel in my mind, a medley of Polish, Russian, Israeli, and American accents. In my imagination they shake their collective heads: "Here they go again, trying to get away from being Jewish." I was not only surprised but also impatient when I read of your discomfort. "Honestly," I wanted to chime in, my own Generation-X vocabulary joining the mix. "Get over it."

Get over it. The image that comes to mind is a children's pantomime I saw recently: two fists held straight out in front of your body; one represents "you," the other "it." The first fist crosses over the second. That's all there is to it—you get over it.

And actually, I think that's what I've done. Gotten over it. Gotten over some of the pain and fear I associated with being Jewish, I mean. It's not so much that I was trying to get away from being Jewish as it was that I was simply frightened to be Jewish. In fact, I winced when Rachel wrote, "One can choose to hold memory high, or to bear it quietly, to bear one's pride on one's sleeve or in private. The only unhealthy reaction is to be ashamed of one's own Jewishness." Her sentiments were echoed by some of the other Jewish Fellows, such as Barbara W. Grossman ("Embracing *Tikkun Olam*") who said to me, "I was distressed, at times, by the negative feelings in some of the Jewish women's essays, surprised when I realized how uncomfortable they were with their Jewishness. As someone for whom Judaism has always been profoundly meaningful, I can't imagine being afraid to acknowledge my Jewish identity or embarrassed about embracing a rich and rewarding heritage." In response to these sentiments, I can only say that I did not choose the pain I felt about my Judaism. It was, however, a burden that has lightened some by sharing it with others.

I now openly acknowledge my Judaism more frequently. Recently, in an aerobics class, one of my classmates, known to me only by virtue of exercising next to me twice a week, naively asked if I had finished my

Christmas shopping yet. "No," I said, "I don't Christmas shop. I'm Jewish." This is an announcement I never would have considered making before working on this book. I waited with a mixture of pride and trepidation for her response. I don't know what I expected: Rejection? Distancing? Disdain? At the very least, I expected some change in her attitude or behavior toward me. Instead, she said, "Oh, how interesting. My husband is Jewish, too, but he celebrates Christmas along with me. I've tried to get him to keep up Jewish traditions, but he's lost most of them." From there developed an interesting conversation about the assimilation of American Jews, and since then she and I have become closer to and more respectful of each other.

More interesting to me is the fact that I now feel pangs of sadness and loss when I meet people who have abandoned their Judaism and who no longer identify with their Jewish background. A gifted folksinger I heard not long ago, currently residing in Appalachia, soulfully sang tunes accompanied by colorful stories from almost every American ethnic group except one: Jews. Although he was obviously Jewish, not once did he mention Jews or Jewish music. His identity as an "American" folksinger was of the utmost importance to him. His silence about Jews left me feeling restless and sad. I stifled the longing to go up to him, to try to convince him that he had pushed away a rich legacy, wanting him to see the disservice—yes, the disservice—he was doing to other Jews. I actually found myself thinking that his difficulty in coming to terms with his own Judaism made it worse for the rest of us. He made it harder for his Jewish listeners to speak out.

You see, Rachel, I am getting over it.

It's also possible that the reason I've been able to get over it is that anti-Semitism has actually waned in this country over the past forty years. Alan Dershowitz, in *The Vanishing American Jew*, makes the argument that anti-Semitism is now promulgated by powerless and marginalized right-wing groups, in contrast to a long history of it being acceptable and even mandated within this country's most powerful institutions. Rachel and even Denise Freed ("From Horse Carts to Quantum Mechanics") may have had an easier time acknowledging their Judaism than I simply because they are twenty years younger. We grew up in two different Americas. It is humbling to realize how much a product of our historical times each of us is. As participants in this project, our often fervent interchanges helped us to realize that we each had unique histories from which our feelings about being Jewish emerged. Not only when but where and how we grew up were formative for our experiences. For the Jewish Bunting Fellows, communicating our differences was the first step in acknowledging Jewish diversity, in understanding that being Jewish is far from a one-dimensional experience. Our heated group discussions and essays allowed us to understand these issues and to believe that change was possible. Personal change does not always translate into social change, but this project at least made the possibility of personal change a reality.

Trust and Reaching Out

Many of us also recognize that there continue to be risks inherent in speaking openly about our various ethnicities. Although I am more at peace with myself both in speaking out about and exploring my Jewish roots, I still pick and choose the settings in which I do so. I measure a setting before venturing forth in public with my "differentness." I ask myself, does it consist largely of non-Jews? If so, is it worth the work it might take to explain my Jewishness to them? Often the answer is no; not every setting is equally safe nor is every setting open to a discussion about difference. To put it simply: it's not necessarily useful or even appropriate to talk about being Jewish everywhere. I don't always announce, "Oh, I'm Jewish," to the ubiquitous, "Have a Merry Christmas," I am greeted with every December.

Paula Gutlove ("Going Back to Bocki") recently told me a moving story that illustrates that being public about one's Jewishness is not safe everywhere, especially in Europe. The story also acknowledges her own new ability to acknowledge her Jewish identity:

> Dawn was breaking through gray clouds and drizzle as I boarded the train in Graz heading toward Vienna. I was leaving my Austrian colleague Sonja and a group of Bosnian physicians with whom I had been working for the last four days. I was on my way home after two weeks of travel throughout Central Europe. I sank into my seat and closed my eyes, weariness washing over me. As I put my feet up on the seat facing mine I imagined the Austrian train conductor scolding me in loud staccato German, as has happened before, but I was too tired to care. A sharp knock on my window forced me to open my eyes to see Sonja pointing with her umbrella toward a slight, brown-haired woman boarding the train. "I want you to meet her," she mouthed to me on the other side of the glass. Sonja, ever the organizer, networker, still keeping me busy as she had done during the past four days.

I reluctantly moved my feet off the opposite seat, thinking that now I certainly wouldn't be able to sleep during the three-hour train journey. The woman put her small suitcase on the seat, stuck out her hand and said, in excellent English with only a hint of a German accent, "Hania Friberg. Sonja says we have a lot in common."

We did have a lot in common. Close in age, we were both married, mothers, both engaged in social change, peace-related work. We exchanged anecdotes, theories, references, citations. We were handing each other our business cards, when Hania said to me in a soft voice, "It is hard to be Jewish now in Austria. I can speak to you about this because you are Jewish. My family has had some very hard times." She told me about the small Jewish community with whom she met in her corner of Austria and their Sabbath celebrations in her uncle's bookstore. She described recent difficulties she and her family had experienced: harassment, property damage, a bomb threat that caused them to be evacuated from their home. She described hostile attitudes and actions of the police and other officials. "The others in my Jewish community are all older, survivors of the war," she told me. "They are telling me to get out, now, that this is how it started last time. But I say to them, it could never happen again. Besides, this is my home, my life, where should I go? And they say to me, 'Yes, that is what we said then.'"

I had chills on the back of my neck where I felt my hair standing on end. I reached out and held her hand, crushing her business card and mine both as our hands embraced across the chasm of the train seats. It briefly occurred to me to wonder how she knew I was Jewish. But then I recalled Karen Fraser Wyche, who described the special quality of eye contact and the nod of recognition that can pass between strangers, two women of color. Perhaps between Jewish women there is also an energy of recognition, a connection through an invisible thread. Somehow, it seemed obvious that Hania would know I was Jewish, and I realized I wasn't at all surprised when she told me she was Jewish. I had known it in some part of my mind. There was a kinship bond between us that I never would have noticed, much less have acknowledged, before meeting with the women who wrote their stories in *Daughters of Kings*, before reading their stories, before writing my own. But now it was important to me to acknowledge this bond—no, to embrace it. I had lived for forty years without overtly denying but without expressly acknowledging a key part of who I am. I marveled at what happened when I was open to seeing, hearing, and feeling the intensity of the Jewish parts of my identity, a legacy of culture and custom, beauty and pain, spirituality and connection. I held on to Hania's hand and told her, "No, we, all of us, won't ever let it happen again."

Paula's story reinforces the message that Jewish parents inculcate in their children: no matter how secure they feel, anti-Semitism is ever-present, and persecution can return at any time. The German Jews are often held up as an example not to follow. They were highly assimilated into German culture and secure in their acceptance by German non-Jews before World War II, and we know what happened to them. Jewish parents tell their children, "You can never be too careful. The tide can turn at any time." An American friend of mine who recently relocated to London echoed Paula's story about the prevalence of anti-Semitism in Europe. He told me that the parents of children who attend his six-year-old son's British Hebrew School take turns every Sunday patrolling the school vicinity for potential bombs and troublemakers. The parents are assigned in pairs to carry walkie-talkies and to check in every so often with each other, monitoring both the school's entryway as well as the surrounding streets. Apparently this is typical. Jewish families in London feel they need to protect themselves when they gather in a visible, public setting. Although I react to my friend's and Paula's stories by trying to reassure myself that America is not now and never has been similar to Europe in its level of anti-Semitism, the moral of these stories is impossible to ignore—anti-Semitism still exists. Neither I nor any of the other Jewish Fellows feel that we can fully let down our guard about the possible return of discrimination against American Jews.

Group Think: The Dangers of Vigilance

Part and parcel of the vigilance against future persecution of the Jewish community, the vigilance Ruth-Arlene W. Howe ("Reflections") admires in her essay, is the constant need to be on the lookout for anti-Semitism. The unwritten code to Jewish watchfulness is that any images that smack of historical anti-Semitism should be immediately stopped dead in their tracks. These include images of greed, wealth, and power, reminiscent of those used in the propaganda generated by Hitler's Nazi regime. Jews know these images to be dangerous, because historically they have been used to oppress us.

Yet the ironic consequences of this vigilance were all too clear in our group when the Jewish and non-Jewish Fellows attempted to communicate about some of the less than desirable characteristics of some individual Jews. For the Jewish women to admit that some individual Jews have characteristics such as greed or lust for power, just like members of any other ethnic group have, was sometimes too frightening to do. Partly, we worried that there would be an immediate generalization from any one Jewish individual's behaviors to the entire group of Jews.

I am reminded here of how horrified some of my Jewish friends are, especially those who are older, when a crime is committed by a Jewish perpetrator. The Jewish criminal's behavior is seen to reflect badly on all Jews. It is easier to flatly deny that Jews commit crimes than to convince others of the complexities behind the motivations for a particular Jew's criminal behavior. This reluctance on the part of the non-Jewish women to acknowledge individual fallibility limited the degree to which our exchange about interethnic relationships could be open and helpful.

For example, it was hard for the Jewish women to accept that the Jewish shopkeepers and landlords in the 1940s and 1950s described by Ruth-Arlene and Karen really were exploitive of their clientele. Ruth-Arlene and Karen did not intend to promulgate anti-Semitic stereotypes when they described the relationships between African Americans and particular Jewish shopkeepers and landlords in Dorchester and Harlem. They were trying to understand and to come to terms with their own or their family members' experiences. They described African Americans and Jews who were both affected by a complex set of interactions among race, class, and economic factors, each rooted in a particular place and time. Yet, despite our intellectual understanding of the complexity inherent in the factors influencing these relationships between African Americans and Jews, it was hard for the Jewish women not to perceive some of the images that Karen and Ruth-Arlene described in an anti-Semitic light. Indeed, my first reaction to their essays was to conclude that some individual Jews were seen as exploitive because Jews have been historically stereotyped in that way. Yet this reaction ignores how complicated these issues really are. Karen wrote to me, "It is important for readers to understand that we are talking about our experiences growing up, not present-day experiences in that community (at least for me). The stores owned by WASPs were in segregated communities that were not even accessible to African Americans during the time that I described." She adds, "There is racism and exploitation on the part of many merchants and landlords who make their living in low-income areas, not just the particular Jewish ones whom I describe in Harlem. Today the same exploitative relationships that existed in Harlem occur between black customers and Korean and Asian Indian merchants in Brooklyn."

In conversations I had with Karen and Ruth-Arlene, we acknowledged

that socioeconomic and class differences between Jews and other minorities are probably as powerful, if not more so, than race differences
in affecting the quality of interethnic group interactions. And certainly
the point in time in which such interactions occur, representing the
convergence of various historical forces (legal, social, economic), is also
powerfully formative. Black-Jewish relations in urban areas have shifted
dramatically over the past thirty years, as Jews have moved out of the
inner cities and into the suburbs; undoubtedly they will undergo similarly dramatic transformations in the next thirty years. When we are living in a particular moment, it is almost impossible to understand how
this multiplicity of factors converges to influence our relationships with
others. We simply respond to what we experience, moment by moment
and day by day.

To put it succinctly, one of the downsides to the vigilant search for
anti-Semitism is that it continues to lead to "group think," in which it's
hard for Jews to publicly admit that there are negative characteristics of
any Jews. This reluctance to acknowledge any negative attributes on the
part of members of one's own group is certainly true of other ethnic
groups as well. Karen writes: "For me as an African American woman, I
need to realize that African Americans can be racist, although I do not
like to acknowledge this fact. Obviously, there are individual differences in any group, and to assume that because one is Jewish he or she
will not discriminate, or because one is African American he or she will
not discriminate, is naive. This 'group think' issue is still alive and well.
For example, it took me a long time to trust white people with Southern
accents or whites from South Africa because I assumed they were racist."
(Ironically, most of the South African whites whom Americans are likely
to meet are those who left South Africa because of their antipathy to
apartheid. Many are Jews.) Individual Jews are no more spared from
racism than are individuals from any other ethnic group, despite their
proud commitment as a group to civil rights and despite their own long
history of being discriminated against. Karen reflects: "It is these tensions in finding out about ourselves that make this a good book. What a
struggle."

In the course of the conversations among our group members, I realized that there is always a trade-off in confronting prejudice. By being
ever-watchful for anti-Semitic comments, we may perceive anti-Semitism
even when it isn't there, leading to unnecessary and confining catego-

rizations and distortions about ourselves and others. When one gets used to listening for gun shots in a war zone, it's hard to hear the sound of the plane flying overhead as a routine flight. On the other hand, we can't be nonjudgmentally accepting of all comments about Jews either, even comments about individual Jews. In doing so, we run the risk of ignoring real anti-Semitism when it rears its ugly head, and we may unwittingly allow the poison of anti-Semitism to spread.

Even stereotypes that sound positive, for example, "Jews are smart," can be potentially dangerous. As many of the essays indicate, people frequently do not know who is Jewish and who is not and may make assumptions about Jewish identity based on stereotypes. The reverse is also true: Once they confirm that someone is actually Jewish, they may assume that the person does indeed have certain stereotypic characteristics, such as intelligence.

The pervasiveness of the link between Jews and intelligence was poignantly captured in the film *Nobody's Fool*, starring Paul Newman in the role of a working-class ne'er-do-well with a big heart who learns for the first time that a close friend of many years, an unsuccessful lawyer, is actually Jewish. "You're Jewish?" he repeats in astonishment. He pauses for a moment, puzzling over this new information. "Then how come you ain't smart?" he finally says, with a mixture of affection and good-humored devaluation of both himself and his friend. Nancy Jones ("Confessions of a Shiksa") and I chuckled while reminiscing over that moment. She e-mailed me, "I think the overwhelming majority of Jews I know are highly educated professionals, in other words, 'smart.' I don't think this stereotype (whatever its relationship to reality) is always the product of envy or hostility."

Yet stereotypes, both positive and negative, limit our abilities to see the humanity of individual Jews, each struggling to play the hand he or she has been dealt in life. Although Jews are disproportionately represented in many fields relative to their actual numbers (including medicine, law, and higher education), this doesn't mean that every Jew is an intelligent professional. Once we strip people of their individuality, there is no reason to treat them with respect or compassion. Stereotypes pave the way for discrimination and persecution.

The balancing act for Jews or any other minority group is to be able to discern when a stereotype accurately characterizes an individual (for instance, any particular individual Jew may be intelligent), or when it imputes characteristics to individual Jews based on generalizations, and not on individual experiences. An example of this is Paul Newman's dilemma: "Well, since he's Jewish, he must be smart." To distinguish between characterizations based on actual experiences and those based on general stereotypes is actually more difficult than it sounds. This is because our stereotypes not only mirror some aspects of experience, but they also create them. Psychological research, for example, suggests that if we interacted with all Jewish children as if they were smart (based on our stereotypes that they were), they might well actually become smart, in a self-fulfilling prophecy.[1] The complexities of these issues do not easily lead to the possibility of social relationships free of categories and distortions, or to nondefensive and open interethnic exchanges.

The Up- and Downsides of Open Communication

Both our ability to be open with each other and the time and motivation we devoted to this project helped shift many of our stereotypes and images about Jews and non-Jews. Stereotypes that had previously loomed as large as icebergs, frozen not only in space but in time, melted somewhat, allowing more water to flow around and through them. I think of the water as new information that lapped at the edges of our icebergs in little waves, slowly transforming their shapes and sizes. Nanci Kincaid ("Not a Jewish Woman") sent me a letter in which she said, "This project has been a real discovery process for me. Full of contradictions, but I have a strong sense of the distinctiveness of the Jewish experience. It's so intriguing to me." Many were amazed by how vulnerable to persecution some Jews feel. Ruth-Arlene wrote that she was initially quite surprised by the degree of wariness and insecurity that Jews revealed about their experiences. Karen too wrote, "It never occurred to me that the assertive, accomplished, smart, feminist women that I knew also could have ambivalence about their Jewish identity or that they would assume that anti-Semitism is everywhere." Nancy contributes:

> Reading other essays and receiving comments on mine showed me that however much I think I know about Judaism and Jewish culture, I still have lots to learn about them and my own cultural assumptions. For example, essay writers used a number of Yiddish and Hebrew terms that were new to me; and I found that a Jewish reader can have different historical horizons from my own. I assumed, for instance, that everyone knew that the Counter-Reformation was a Catholic anti-Protestant move-

ment, and that Protestants reject the cult of the saints, just as my Brandeis colleagues assumed during a discussion of the Book of Genesis that I knew what the term *Midrash* meant. A new humility.

Nancy Jones's images of her own Protestant ethnic background shifted over the course of this book project, too. After writing her essay, it occurred to her that

> WASP (how I dislike this acronym!) culture is often portrayed as so homogenous, bland, and hegemonic as to become itself invisible in the current discussions of multiculturalism—it becomes the blank background against which all other ethnicities seem to define their putatively more authentic, vibrant, and conflictual cultures. As I tried to convey in the early part of my essay, there was more than white bread in the world in which I grew up, and I miss the unassuming decency of that world. (Which may be a thing of the past, for who really is a WASP anymore?) My desire to reclaim the best of my heritage is intertwined with my desire to scrutinize it through the critical lens of Jewish culture and experience. I've spent many years living among cultures and subcultures other than my own, by choice, but recently I've been trying hard to integrate elements of my Indiana childhood into my life. While I don't wish to idealize and sentimentalize the past, I don't want to forget all the rituals and folkways that would otherwise die with my parents. In this, I feel one with those Jews (like my husband) who wish to reclaim parts of their Jewish heritage and family ways. I'm so conscious of the fragility of my parents' WASP culture—I see it disappearing so rapidly. Thank you for getting me to write this essay—it's been an important part of a personal discovery process.

These quotes illustrate that for both Jewish and non-Jewish Fellows, our conversations and essays helped us to formulate new links between ourselves as Jews and non-Jews. The project also helped us to see the diversity that exists within any ethnic group. Ann Olga Koloski-Ostrow ("Hannah's *Teshuvah*") writes,

> Wallace Stevens once urged that we should learn to see "the lines between the stars" and not the stars themselves. The stars are just so many bright spots in the night sky. But the lines between the stars give us whole constellations, whole new perspectives on the stars. All of us as authors in the collection drew lines connecting our experiences of being Jews and non-Jews in our stories. We discovered some essence about being or not being Jewish. As we searched our memories for both the stars (the important moments that had shaped us) and the connections between

them (or tried to but couldn't) I think we were finding (and trying to find) new constellations of meaning for ourselves and for each other.

Ironically, although this project shifted some of our images of Jews and non-Jews in more positive directions, it also had unanticipated disappointing consequences. Some of the non-Jewish women now feel more cautious about what they can say about or to Jews than they did previously. Perhaps this should not be a surprising consequence. They are "outsiders," running the risk of misreading signals, of offending others if and when they speak out honestly and openly. They also run the risk of being blamed or even attacked for making anti-Semitic comments that they might not have realized were indeed anti-Semitic. Nanci concluded: "Even cloaked in all this good will I feel less free to stumble around in my clumsy search to know more. I feel that my improved sensitivity to issues of Jewishness and anti-Semitism will likely silence me when I'd like to ask another question, cause me to act satisfied with my limited understanding, while I secretly remain curious. Now I'm forced to wonder, 'How many times have I misspoken and misunderstood? How many times has my ignorance offended?' There is something in me that reluctantly vows to be more careful in both word and deed out of respect for all that I don't yet understand—and may never."

The non-Jewish women may also have become more guarded in the face of the Jewish women's anger, which was sometimes openly acknowledged and displayed, sometimes only implied. We have acknowledged our anger about many things: about the pervasiveness of anti-Semitism; about the long history of persecution the Jews have suffered, including the devastation of the Holocaust; about the traditional subservient roles that women have played in Judaism; and about many aspects of the assimilation attempted by our parents' generation, which for some of us led to a failure to learn about our Jewish heritage. This anger was both uncomfortable for non-Jewish women to hear as well as uncomfortable for the Jewish women themselves to express.

In expressing their anger, minority groups risk alienating their audience. There is some social psychology research[2] that shows that when victims demand justice in a mild and friendly way, then members of non-victimized groups are sympathetic. When victims up the ante, and are insistent on justice, frequently repeating the ways in which they have been persecuted, other groups begin to turn a deaf ear. It's as if they say to themselves, "Since we can't possibly make up for all the wrongs we have done, what's the point in trying at all?" Their defensiveness begins to overpower their empathy. Victimized groups always run this risk: how much anger to express, how much to complain, how much to ask for, without alienating those they want for allies. Speaking out may not only result in alienation (a passive acceptance of anti-Semitism) but at worst may actually result in more active persecution. Denise captured this dilemma when she told me, "I was initially uneasy about the project because it called attention to ourselves as Jews and as minorities in this country. At times when I explain the project to a colleague or acquaintance this sense of uneasiness returns."

Yet even with these unintended difficulties that were inherent in our discussions, Rachel repeats the importance of continuing to try to communicate:

> I'm not naive about the consequences of speaking out: I know that some people may immediately become more careful in how they approach me. That's unfortunate, but true. Ideally, everyone would feel comfortable asking me about the issues I've raised, but I know that's not the case. Still, the alternative is to guarantee my own discomfort by hiding an enormous part of my identity. So I speak openly, and I follow that up by trying to be as approachable as possible about Jewish subjects. In the reverse situation, I eventually summon the courage to blunder toward that outstretched hand offered by a new friend. Eventually, I find the temerity to ask my ignorant questions about Greek-Orthodox churches, Palestinian cooking, African American music, Italian American sayings. I stumble my way toward learning, sometimes at the risk of my own composure. I frequently get myself into situations (German-Jewish dialogues, etc.) where I spend hours upon hours explaining the most basic things about Judaism. Yes, it's exhausting. But I feel it's worth it. Timidity seems like something we as citizens of a multiethnic nation can't afford. Timidity seems like a cop-out : the wrong lesson to learn from "political correctness." Ultimately, it preserves the notion that certain people are after all "diverse" and one shouldn't mess with them lest one get one's head bitten off.

Trying to Understand Jewish and Ethnic Identity

One of the many unanswerable questions we dealt with in this project was what it means to be a Jew. It is interesting to note that this is not only our question but one under debate throughout the world Jewish community. Is Judaism a cultural, religious, ethnic, or spiritual identity, a set of values, a particular stance toward life, or all of the above? Perhaps the most remarkable thing about this process for the Jewish Fellows was the realization of how much diversity there was among us. Not necessarily diversity in our historical backgrounds: We were all Ashkenazi Jews, with Eastern European immigrant parents or grandparents, as are most American Jews. Even Ann, who converted to Judaism as an adult, had an Eastern European immigrant background. (An interesting aside here is that one historical theory suggests that most Ashkenazi Jews are descendants of non-Jewish Russians who converted to Judaism at the beginning of the sixteenth century.[3]) But there was so much diversity in how we regarded Judaism and in our experience of it, in whether we viewed Judaism as a cultural or a religious identity, and in the extent to which we believed in God. Nancy was surprised to hear one of the Jewish women "talking about saying Hebrew prayers and going to synagogue, but adding that she didn't believe in God. This was very strange to me, having been raised as a Christian!"

For many of us, we are Jewish because we had Jewish parents and grandparents who exposed us to Jewish rituals and history, who told us intergenerational stories of suffering and joy that they and their ancestors had experienced as Jews. We internalized these stories and learned the intricacies of the rituals, making them a part of ourselves and of how we respond to other people and events. We learned to value education, achievement, tolerance, a questioning spirit, family loyalty, and the expression of feelings. The distinctiveness of Judaism's rituals, values, and history were formative for our identity and serve partly to define Judaism as an ethnicity and a culture, as opposed to only a religious or spiritual identity.

The repeated stories we were told by parents and grandparents shaped the identity of almost every woman in our group in powerful ways. For Jews, these included stories about members of the European Jewish community who had perished during the Holocaust. Writing about her trip to Auschwitz enabled Lois Isenman ("The Other Side") to realize that

> More than a year after I started my essay, when I was almost completely done with the process of revising, slowly it dawned on me that the destruction of Eastern European Jewish culture was so significant to me, not just because it represented the loss of an important part of my Jewish cultural heritage, but because it represented a very personal loss as well. This feeling of personal loss came to a head one morning in tears: I had

a poignant, thoughtful cry, which had a surprisingly sweet quality to it. Apparently in feeling the loss, I gained some sense of continuity with the past that I longed for more or less unconsciously. I now see that this longing was indeed one of the motivations behind my trip to Poland and my need to write about it.

This identification with distant members of our own ethnic group was formative for the non-Jewish women's ethnic identity as well. Ruth-Arlene, in her visit to Senegal, made powerful connections to her African ancestors who were taken as slaves. She now finds these connections a riveting source of strength. Both she and Lois independently describe uncanny, surrealistic sensations of being able to sense the continued presence of the people who suffered and perished at Gorée-Island and Auschwitz, respectively.

Yet a Jewish identity, unlike some other identities, is more than ethnicity shaped by a common history, passed down by repeated family stories. Although this has not always been historically true, Judaism today is an identity that is fluid: one can choose to be or choose not to be Jewish. Ann, who has chosen Judaism, was raised with a set of Catholic rituals and intergenerational stories different from those of Judaism. The ethnicity she grew up with was not the one she later drew on for her identity, although she emphasizes that her immigrant family always shared many ideals and values in common with those of Judaism. Her experience casts a different light on what it means to be Jewish. She writes:

> At some point in my life—in particular, when I thought of bringing my own children into the world—I realized that I *was* Jewish. *That was* my identity. That *was* an important identity I wanted for my children. I'm not sure how "conscious" my so-called "choice" to convert to Judaism was. If there was a "consciousness" about anything, it was that the choice about being Jewish was already made, and therefore, there really was no choice for me. I was, in a sense, just acknowledging a deeper understanding of myself and my reality. Therefore, I engaged in two and a half years of "Jewish study" before the "official" conversion ceremony in order to educate myself in the finer details of Jewish culture, religion, philosophy, and history.

Ann's essay clarifies what a Jewish identity means to her. She emphasizes that unlike some other religious traditions, Judaism encourages people to ask their own questions, not to passively memorize dogma. She also describes Jews as "guilt ridden, ambivalent, compassionate, and forgiving." Reading Ann's essay highlighted for me the fact that the burdens involved in being Jewish, including our long history of suffering and persecution, lead to empathy and tolerance for the suffering of others, characteristics far too rare in this world. Ann's descriptions of Judaism embrace not only spiritual and cultural dimensions, but also the personal values that the religion encourages in shaping individuals' lives. In converting to Judaism, people choose to pass on to their children a different intergenerational legacy than they were exposed to as children themselves.

Other Fellows, too, emphasized a Jewish identity as one in which ethical values are prominent. Barbara writes,

> I credit Judaism with my unwavering commitment to ethical activism in a very personal sense. Judaism has taught me that it is never too late for a new beginning. Each year on Rosh Hashanah and Yom Kippur (the New Year and Day of Atonement), it is possible to reflect on the events of the past year, ask forgiveness for any thoughtless action, and vow to do better in the year ahead. There is never the sense that one's fate is sealed or that the opportunity for atonement has passed. Forgiveness and redemption, hope and possibility are part of the Jewish calendar and central to Jewish life. I consider Judaism a "precious legacy" (to use the title of an exhibit I saw several years ago at the Jewish Museum in New York that featured Nazi-confiscated Judaica) and feel privileged to perpetuate it.

Some Fellows grapple with the spiritual dimensions of Jewish identity. Lois writes: "My essay has played an important part in my spiritual odyssey. I am struggling to find a deeper level of commitment to Jewish spirituality than I have had in the past, and this may well involve some aspect of Jewish mysticism. And yet as the call for commitment grows stronger, my resistance grows as well. I am a participant as well as a fascinated spectator in this dynamic, unfinished process."

In reading these essays Nancy remarked on how diverse the experiences of Jewish women have been: "The variety of experiences recorded here about Jewish women also makes me want to know more about the different kinds of experiences Jews have had in this country." As she thought about raising her daughter in the Jewish tradition, she continued to want to know more about Jewish women's identity struggles: "Is there anything that Jewish women feel ambivalent about, or critical of, in their own traditions, besides the lingering sexist elements? Does it feel safe to be openly critical of Judaism or Jewish tradition when you're part of an embattled, tiny minority?"

Letting Go and Looking Forward

The book has helped us to envision a different kind of future for ourselves and for our children. Partly this involves the increased recognition of the commonalities among us, regardless of our Jewish or non-Jewish backgrounds. Nanci writes: "I hope that the bond of what it is to be women in the larger culture can help us to overcome, but not eliminate, the specificity and rich history of our smaller cultures. It is clear that there is so much difference to celebrate. And so much likeness too."

One of the things that struck me in so many of our conversations and essays was how each of us felt "different" in some way, whether because of religion, or race, or our family backgrounds, or the geographical region we came from. I recently heard a non-Jewish woman describe her fear when she entered a Jewish temple meeting. She was terrified that she would not be welcomed; that she would do or say the improper thing; that she would cause offense. Her description of her experience saddened me. Is there any way we can recognize each other's "otherness" and yet still retain an open and welcoming connection to each other?

Part of the difficulty in opening ourselves up to "otherness" is that the power of our collective ethnic memories threatens to overshadow and distort the reality of our present and even our future interethnic relationships, just as I suggested our ever present vigilance for anti-Semitism often does. This relentless process of history repeating itself in a self-fulfilling prophecy can be stopped partly by sharing our memories with others, as well as by attempting to integrate and understand these memories in a meaningful historical context.

We found this to be true in our project. By writing our essays and disclosing our feelings to others, we were able to gain a new perspective on our history and our identity. The burdens of the past lifted some, and previous hurts that we had experienced were able to heal. Rachel explains how the process of writing her essay and showing it to others allowed her to let go of some of her pain:

> Some of the focus on memory that guided my essay has lessened for me in the past year. It's not that I grant any less importance to the issue of memory—it's just that I find myself concentrating more and more on looking forward. I find that the more I write and speak about the question of memory, the more at peace I am with it. In the past year, as I've struggled with many of the issues of modern Israel and the ways in which people (mis)use memories of tragedy to inhibit progress, I've come to

feel more and more strongly that the important place to focus is on the future. I will certainly always carry a great burden of memory—and don't get me wrong, joy in the Jewish past as well—but memory cannot be the beginning and end of anyone's Jewish experience. It certainly isn't the beginning and end of mine. Rereading my essay, it occurred to me that I'd written down those words so I wouldn't have to carry them around any longer. The issues certainly aren't gone—I continue to speak at German-Jewish dialogues and to write about some Holocaust related stuff—but they do feel lighter.

And Lois, too, in the process of remembering a long forgotten, poorly processed, anti-Semitic incident from her childhood, began to let go of her anger. Though she chose not to include this incident in her essay, she writes, "I am very angry, but I think I have been angry the whole time since it happened. I feel somewhat softer for letting this anger finally see light and live."

Writing our essays entailed a process of trying to understand why and how formative events in our families had occurred. In gaining clarity, we gained some freedom over the power these events had had in our lives. Often the consequence of the process brought us closer to our current family members. Paula wrote:

As I sat on the train, with Austria's withered November landscape blurring past me, I realized that since I learned of my father's birthplace in Poland, I have been on an unusual journey of discovery and connection. It started as a way of discovering my father, to begin to learn something, finally, about who he is and where he is from. Part of the impetus for searching for my roots in Bocki came from my excitement at uncovering a way of connecting to my father, a man who does not confide, does not relate, does not connect. The search then propelled me forward and beyond him. Unearthing the ghosts of Bocki tangled me in a web of connection not only to the Jews who died in Bocki, but to the Jews of the Warsaw ghetto, to the Jews of Poland, to the Holocaust itself. The web further wove me to connect with others, non-Jews, who were victims of genocide in Bosnia, in Croatia, in Serbia.

I first wrote my story about going to Bocki for my father and other members of my family, to share the discovery and the connection with them, and perhaps to draw them into the web. My family responded with curiosity and growing fascination. My two sisters, my daughter, and one of my cousins, in particular, plied me with questions, requested copies of my story and of the photos I had taken. My cousin eventually began her own exploration with her parents, seeking more information about their lives as Jews in Eastern Europe. I began to share the story with selected friends, Jews and non-Jews, and later I shared the story with our group of Bunting Fellows who were thinking about the identity of Jewish women.

And Helena too noted: "I am delighted that working on this book has given me the opportunity to talk to my mother in new ways. We have clarified some historical details, and the scholar in me is pleased to correct inaccuracies. We also have talked more openly about the challenges each of us faced and the opportunities we encountered in our multicultural lives. Writing this chapter has brought me closer to her."

These shifts in our relationships to our family members promise to allow the future to unfold in new ways, without being quite so distorted by its tenacious association with the past. Understanding our histories more clearly leaves us with more energy to devote to ourselves, to our work, and to those we care about.

Hopes and Doubts

My own feelings about the future are mixed. I am newly proud of my Jewish identity, and I have become more open to learning about the beauty of Jewish traditions. Each of the Jewish women's perspectives on what constitutes Judaism left me with a renewed sense of what I value about my own identity and why I myself might choose to convert to Judaism had I not been born Jewish.

Perhaps what I learned to treasure most is the centrality of the idea that it's what you do in this life that counts. And that how you live your life becomes eternal, not necessarily in a hereafter, but in the memories of your loved ones who survive you. Jews traditionally name their children after their deceased family members as a way of honoring them and symbolically keeping their relationships with them alive. To me this is a lovely tradition that encapsulates many of the important themes in what it means to be Jewish: that what you do on earth matters, that what you do will live on after you in the way it affects those around you, especially those whom you love. This rich sense of intergenerational continuity, and the accompanying righteous and moral actions needed to sustain it, comes closest to representing the spirituality of the religion for me, perhaps even closest to representing my idea of God.

I also feel connected to Judaism's premise that religious principles are open to question. Especially in Reform Judaism, rabbis are available as guides to the basic tenets of Judaism, but they do not dictate how any

Jew chooses to express her faith. It is easy to see how this idea would promote inner thoughtfulness and resourcefulness, rather than a dependence on authority figures, even idealized or revered ones, to serve as guides through life's alternative pathways.

I have chosen to join a Reform congregation and am experiencing for the first time the joys of being part of a Jewish community, not the least of which is the joy of not having to explain to other temple members that indeed I am Jewish, as I often feel compelled to do in multicultural settings. Ironically, the congregation I have joined and in which my husband and I feel comfortable is one in which many of the couples are interfaith and have chosen to raise their children as Jews. We were attracted to this temple because of its openness to diversity, its tolerance and liberalism, and because of its strong and creative educational program for our children. Its name, Shir Tikvah, translates as "Song of Hope," quite an apt expression for what I feel after participating in this project. I'm not yet sure where my new feelings regarding Judaism will take me. If the future is anything like the past, I anticipate that there will be twists and turns in my Jewish identity that are impossible to foresee right now.

How non-Jews view Judaism is less important to me now than it once was, having taken second place to the importance of how I myself view Judaism. Nonetheless, non-Jews' reactions to Jews still remain an integral part of what it feels like to be Jewish in a largely Christian American culture. To put it bluntly, whether non-Jews are accepting or persecuting can mean the difference between a meaningful and fulfilling life or, at the extreme, torture and death. Through some of the essays in this collection I have gained a renewed belief in a part of non-Jewish America I had learned about in elementary school and had long ago decided was largely mythical: an America where people truly do care about diversity, equality, and religious freedom. The legacy not only of the Holocaust, but also of my own coming of age in the tumultuous 1960s was that I grew up with the suspicion that most of society was to be mistrusted and that most Americans were anti-Semitic. Somehow, I never questioned this assumption, confirmed by the anti-Semitic remarks people made to me, not knowing that I was Jewish. Because I was afraid to "come out" as a Jew, I never saw the positive, welcoming light from many Americans that was there all the time and in which I could be embraced by many non-Jews. I was surprised at how important the issue of Judaism was to the non-Jewish Fellows writing for the book. In fact, at least one (Nanci) had already started on her own essay when I approached her about writing one, and she was thrilled to have the opportunity to expand on it. And many Fellows whom I had assumed to be non-Jews actually had a Jewish parent, or a Jewish grandparent, or were married to Jews. The sense of isolation I had felt as a Jew in America was one that I had partly created. This project opened up the possibility that I could begin to trust non-Jews, and the message of diversity in America, once again.

Yet even though I have a new trust in many non-Jewish Americans, I continue to feel that I can never take my blessings as an American Jew for granted. I can never fully relax. My continued vigilance is partly a consequence of some of the more demanding aspects of this project. It was sometimes difficult and frustrating to communicate accurately about interethnic issues, even with the best of intentions. I also sometimes shuddered at the Jewish stereotypes I encountered, even within this group of close and highly educated and motivated women. My major enemy in combating what I perceived to be anti-Semitic stereotypes was fatigue: I would sometimes get tired of being vigilant, would sometimes let a disturbing remark pass rather than muster up the energy it would take to counter it. However, the support of others who shared my views sometimes helped alleviate my weariness.

My hope is that Jews and non-Jews can come to terms with their differences, yet I continue to worry that they can't. Given the amount of time and effort required to unlearn distortions and negative stereotyping of ethnic groups different from our own, I feel somewhat pessimistic about overcoming in-group/out-group distinctions and, in particular, anti-Semitic stereotypes. Most people don't have enough time to commit to issues that they don't perceive will benefit them directly.

Ironically, my pessimism is related to the power of family stories that shape our ethnicity: stories that have the power to heal but also the power to hurt. The essays in this book powerfully demonstrated to me that our ethnicity is molded by the stories passed on to us by previous generations. Unfortunately, our parents and grandparents don't usually tell us stories about other ethnic groups' histories. We remain largely ignorant about anyone's past but our own. Even when we take the required time and energy to hear stories about other groups, we may react differently to them than the original group itself does. Why? For one thing, we lack the personal identification that makes the stories especially meaningful. For another, ignorance is often combined with distortion: not only do we know very little about other groups, but what we have learned is often wrong. We may actually have been educated, even encouraged early in our lives to feel negatively toward groups other than our own. Some of us may have been told family stories which cast other ethnic groups in a negative light. And a final difficulty: ethnic hatred is often related to social and economic inequalities, with inequality and hatred each feeding off of each other. These difficulties have undoubtedly been part of human history since Cain and Abel. It is overly optimistic to think that they will be completely washed away by sharing our ethnic stories, as dirt washes away with soap, leaving us fresh and clean.

To Rachel's wonderful image that stories are the doves sent out from the ark to test whether the storm waters have receded, I add that the dove may survive or it may be shot to death before realizing its destination. What happens to the dove depends on how much people care about it. To put it simply, the quality of interethnic relationships largely hinges on how much empathy people have for each other. It is not just our stories, but the feelings that accompany them that are critical to convey. How do people develop empathy for the feelings of other ethnic groups? This is an extremely complex question, with a partial answer embedded in how children are raised by their parents. For children as well as for adults, empathy seems most likely to develop when their own feelings and struggles are acknowledged by others. The others, in turn, must have their own struggles acknowledged before they too can feel empathy. I am describing here a mutual process of noncritical listening and openness that has no real beginning or end. Perhaps we can begin to make this process happen between ethnic groups not just by being open to each others' stories, but by being aware of the preconceptions and biases we bring to the listening process. These sometimes present formidable barriers to hearing the truth of someone else's experiences.

My pessimism about the possibility of widespread interethnic communication makes me uncomfortable, and my discomfort motivates me to try harder. I am resolved to educate my children not only about the beauty and the suffering in their own ethnic background, but also about the beauty and suffering found in the backgrounds of other ethnic groups. In fact, my children are already being exposed to more cultural diversity in their public school system than I was at similar ages. And although I think that sharing our experiences with others may not be the perfect solution to building interethnic bridges, it is only through projects like these that our shared humanity becomes palpable to others. Telling my own story and listening to those of others certainly helped me both to reclaim my Jewish heritage and to better appreciate the heritage of my sister Fellows.

Some of my friends and colleagues have already read parts of *Daughters of Kings*. For many of them, reading it has generated a powerful impulse to tell me their own childhood stories relating to ethnicity. Some have even written down their own poignant stories about their ethnic backgrounds, asking for my response. I have been moved and touched by their narratives. I hope that this project will continue to serve as a fruitful springboard, not only conveying what it feels like for Jewish women to grow up in America, but creating a dialogue among people of different backgrounds, and motivating readers, no matter what their ethnic background, to speak out more openly.

NOTES

NOTES TO LESLIE BRODY, INTRODUCTION

1. Langman, P. (1995). Including Jews in multiculturalism. *Journal of Multicultural Counseling and Development*, 23, 222–236.
2. Dershowitz, A. (1996). *The Vanishing American Jew*. Boston: Little, Brown.
3. Crocker, J., & Major, B. (1989). Social stigma and self-esteem: The self-protective properties of stigma. *Psychological Review*, 96, 608–630.
4. Siegel, R. (1986). Antisemitism and sexism in stereotypes of Jewish women. *Women and Therapy*, 5, 249–257.
5. Beck, E. (1990). Therapy's double dilemma: Anti-semitism and misogyny. In R. Siegel & E. Cole, *Jewish Women in Therapy*. New York: Harrington Park Press.
6. Siegel, R. Antisemitism and sexism.
7. Lewin, K. (1935). Psycho-sociological problems of a minority group. *Character and Personality*, 3, 175–187; Lewin, K. (1940). Bringing up the Jewish child, *Menorah Journal*, 28, 29–45; Lewin, K. (1941). Self-hatred among Jews. *Contemporary Jewish Record*, 219–232; Lewin, K. (1946). Action research and minority problems. *Journal of Social Issues*, 2, 34–46.
8. Siegel, R. Antisemitism and sexism.
9. Weiner, K., & Moon, A. (1995). *Jewish Women Speak Out*. Seattle: Canopy Press.
10. Greenwald, A. G., & Schuh, E. S. (1994). An ethnic bias in scientific citations. *European Journal of Social Psychology*, 24, 623–629.
11. Romer, N., & Cherry, D. (1980). Ethnic and social class differences in children's sex-role concepts, *Sex Roles*, 6, 245–263.
12. Ruddick, S. (1982). Maternal thinking. In Thorne, B., and Yalom, M. *Rethinking the Family*. New York: Longman.
13. Rosten, L. (1968). *The Joys of Yiddish*. New York: McGraw Hill Company, 204.

NOTES TO RUTH-ARLENE W. HOWE, REFLECTIONS

1. In this section I use the term *Negro* because that was the term commonly used at the time.—Au.

2. DuBois, W. E. B. (1989). *The Souls of Black Folk: Essays and Sketches.* New York: Bantam Books, 3. For a recent compilation of essays that ponder the meaning of DuBois's passage, see Early, Gerald ed. (1993). *Lure and Loathing: Essays on Race, Identity, and the Amibvalence of Assimilation.* New York: Allen Lane/ Penguin.

3. A slightly revised version of this narrative appeared in (Winter 1997) Old Prejudices and Discrimination Float Under a New Halo, *Transracial Adoption* (TRA) 6: *B.U. Pub. Int. L.J.*, 409–412.

4. Winant, Howard. (1994). *Racial Conditions: Politics, Theory, Comparisons.* Minneapolis: U of Minnesota P, xiii.

NOTES TO LESLIE BRODY, FINALLY OUR OWN MINYAN

1. Brody, L. R. (1997). Beyond stereotypes: gender and emotion. *Journal of Social Issues,* 53 (2), 369–394.

2. Walster, E., & Walster, G. W. (1975). Equity and social justice. *Journal of Social Issues,* 31, 21–43.

3. Dimont, M. (1962). *Jews, God and History.* New York: Simon and Schuster.

About the Contributors

LESLIE BRODY is an Associate Professor of Psychology at Boston University. She has a Ph.D. from Harvard University and has published extensively in the area of gender differences in emotional expression. She is also a child and family therapist and has taught courses on family psychology, child and family therapy, abnormal psychology, and counseling. She served as the Director of Boston University's Ph.D. program in Clinical Psychology from 1991 to 1996 and was the Marion Cabot Putnam Fellow at the Bunting Institute from 1994 to 1995. She is working on a book about gender and emotion, to be published by Harvard University Press. Leslie would like to dedicate her work on this book to her parents, Shirley D. Brody and Sydney W. Brody, whose love has sustained her, and to the memory of her grandparents, Jennie Dym Davidowitz, Louis Davidowltz, Rebecca Friedman Brody, and Harry Brody, whose courage as immigrants has inspired her.

DEIRDRE CHETHAM is the Associate Director of the Fairbank Center for East Asian Research at Harvard University. A career Foreign Service Officer for ten years, she worked in China, Hong Kong, and East Germany, as well as in private business and journalism.

DENISE FREED is a research physicist who grew up in Ithaca, New York. She received her B.A. from Cornell University and her Ph.D. in theoretical physics from Princeton University. After finishing graduate school, she held a postdoctoral fellowship from MIT and then taught at Wellesley College. The following two years she was a Science Scholar at the Bunting Institute. She is currently a Junior Fellow at the Princeton Materials Institute, and this fall she will be embarking on a new stage of her career as a research scientist at Schlumberger-Doll Research. She has published technical papers in both particle theory and condensed matter theory. The first of these fields involves trying to understand the

223

nature of the fundamental particles and the forces between them. The second is the study of materials (such as metals, liquid crystals, or sand piles), which are made up of many particles and exhibit collective behavior due to interactions between these particles. Her essay is dedicated to her grandmothers, Anna Strauch and Pauline Freed, whose lives, although so different from her own, still shape and inspire hers.

Theatre historian and director BARBARA W. GROSSMAN, a *magna cum laude* graduate of Smith College, received an M.A. in English Literature from Brandeis University, an M.F.A. in Directing from Boston University's School of Theatre Arts, and a Ph.D. in Theatre History from Tufts University, where she is a member of the Department of Drama and Dance. The author of *Funny Woman: The Life and Times of Fanny Brice,* she was appointed by President Clinton to the National Council on the Arts (Advisory Board to the National Endowment for the Arts) for a six-year term beginning in 1994. She is active in many civic, cultural, and social service organizations in the Boston area, including the American Repertory Theatre, Anti-Defamation League, Combined Jewish Philanthropies, Jewish Women's Archive, Klezmer Conservatory Foundation, Massachusetts Foundation for the Humanities, and People for the American Way. Winner of ADL's Distinguished Community Service Award (New England Region) in 1991, she received the Dean's Arts and Humanitarian Services Award from Boston University's School for the Arts in April 1995, a Leadership Award from the American Association of Jewish Holocaust Survivors of Greater Boston in July 1996, and a National Community Service Award from the Jewish Theological Seminary in May 1997. Barbara writes: "I am grateful to have had the opportunity to express my pride in being a Jewish woman and awareness of the many ways in which Judaism has enriched my life. Writing this essay has been profoundly satisfying and has left me with a deep sense of emotional tranquility about the choices I continue to make on a daily basis. I have been blessed with wonderful parents, in-laws, siblings, relatives, and friends. I am thankful for my husband, Steven, and our dear sons, David, Benjamin, and Joshua. In addition to the mutual love and respect we share, our strong Jewish values bind us as a family and keep us morally grounded. Giving something back to our communities is one of the guiding principles of our lives."

PAULA GUTLOVE is the director of the Program on Promoting Understanding and Cooperation at the Institute for Resource and Security Studies in Cambridge, Massachusetts. The program works with people of diverse perspectives and interests to improve communication, build understanding, resolve conflicts, and promote cooperation through such projects as the Young Wallenberg's Project, the Balkans Peace Project, and Health Bridges for Peace. The Young Wallenberg's Project seeks to promote a culture of caring, courage, and activism in young people in the United States through concrete, experiential, classroom-based programs that engage high school and college students. The Balkans Peace Project promotes the use of nonviolent conflict resolution processes with parties from Serbia, Croatia, Slovenia, Bosnia, and Macedonia in order to contribute to a sustainable peace in that region. Health Bridges for Peace links health care with the prevention and resolution of intercommunal conflict by using the common desire for improved public health as a bridge between conflicting communities. Health Bridges for Peace projects are being organized in the Balkans and in Europe.

Paula received her B.S. degree from Cornell University and her D.M.D. degree from Boston University. She was a postdoctoral resident in Oral Surgery at Mt. Sinai Hospital in New York. Through her eclectic career path she has both taken and taught courses in negotiation and conflict analysis and resolution at Harvard University and has been a lecturer in the Department of Psychiatry, Harvard Medical School, for more than ten years. She has organized numerous workshops and seminars to explore the potential for collaboration between governmental, inter-governmental and nongovernmental groups in conflict management and has facilitated dialogue and conflict resolution training with international groups in the United States, Soviet Union, Japan, Australia, Europe, and the Balkans. She wants to dedicate her contributions to this book to her father, Benjamin William Gutlove (May 15, 1900–June 17, 1997), and to her lost relatives in Bocki.

RUTH-ARLENE W. HOWE is an associate professor at Boston College Law School. She received her A.B. from Wellesley College, her M.S. from Simmons College School of Social Work, and her J.D. from Boston College Law School. She specializes in family law, and her current research focuses on transracial adoption. A former chair of the American Bar Association Family Law Section Adoption Committee, she has served on a number of Massachusetts gubernatorial and judicial commissions and advisory groups concerned with the unmet legal needs of children and presently is a member of the U.S. Department of State's Study Group on Intercountry Adoption. She is coauthor of *Child Neglect Laws in America* (American Bar Association Press, 1976). Ruth-Arlene believes that these personal stories and reflections by Jewish and non-Jewish women demonstrate how wide-ranging and diverse views and perspectives not only can be stated openly and shared in a trusting group environment—free of defensiveness and fears about difference—but can be heard, understood, acknowledged, and respected.

LOIS ISENMAN is an independent scholar who studies the process of intuition and its role in scientific endeavor. She received her B.A. from Brandeis University and her Ph.D. in Cell Physiology from University of California at San Francisco Medical School. She worked as a biologist for many years, primarily at Tufts Medical School, studying membrane permeability to proteins. During this time she became aware that her cognitive style was heavily weighted toward intuition, and she became more and more interested in understanding what intuition is and the role it plays in the scientific process. She wrote an article on the topic during her year as a Bunting Science Scholar, which is published in the journal *Perspectives in Biology and Medicine,* and is currently working on a book. She is still involved in two interesting scientific collaborations and does not rule out the possibility of eventually returning to biology full-time. Lois writes: "I am amazed at how intact some of my memories are of my trip to Poland and Auschwitz and even more amazed that some of my childhood memories survive. Certain of these memories returned immediately, others only later. Some came back with great clarity, yet others required progressive refining over time to get closer to the actual experience. Moreover I found the process of working with memory to be extremely pleasurable, and surprisingly, this was true even when the material itself was very painful. These experiences, and the additional experiences they sometimes pointed to, have had a strong influence on my life; yet for the most part this influence lies outside of my consciousness. Bringing such experiences back to consciousness and reflecting on them helps me become aware of who I am. Indeed to reconcile, or to celebrate our differences with others, we must first become aware of who we really are. Participating with my 'sister Fellows' in this project on identity and difference has been an extraordinarily rich experience." She dedicates her essay to the Jews of Eastern Europe, past and present, and to her father George Isenman.

NANCY A. JONES is a Resident Scholar in Women's Studies at Brandeis University. Her scholarly work focuses on women and gender issues in medieval literature and culture. She is co-editor, with Leslie Dunn, of *Embodied Voices: Representing Female Vocality in Western Culture* (Cambridge University Press, 1995), and the author of articles on medieval French, Italian, and Latin literature. Her current projects include studies on women and textiles in medieval France and the female voice of lament in medieval literature. She lives in Cambridge, Massachusetts, with her husband and daughter. Writing her essay has moved her to explore family membership in a local Reform congregation that welcomes interfaith couples.

RACHEL KADISH, a twenty-eight-year-old writer, grew up in New Rochelle, New York. She attended Princeton University and has lived in Jerusalem, where she worked for the Israel Women's Network. In 1994 she completed her M.A. in Fiction at New York University and the following year was a fiction Fellow at Radcliffe's Bunting Institute. She has received grants from the Whiting Foundation and the Rona Jaffe Foundation and has recently been a resident at Yaddo. Rachel currently teaches fiction at the Harvard University Extension School and is literary editor for "The Radio Play" in Boston. Her short fiction has appeared in *Story*, *Bomb*, and *Prairie Schooner* and has received a Pushcart Prize as well as a nomination for the 1996 National Magazine Award in Fiction. She is at work on a novel set in Israel and in the United States, titled *From a Sealed Room*, forthcoming next year from G. P. Putnam. She is grateful to the family members who discussed these issues with her, and to the friends—both Jewish and non-Jewish—who read what she'd written and responded with such understanding.

NANCI KINCAID has written two novels, *Crossing Blood*, published in 1992, and *Balls*, forthcoming, and a collection of short stories, *Pretending the Bed Was a Raft*. *Crossing Blood* was nominated for the Lillian Smith Award and was selected by the American Library Association as a Recommended Book. Her work has been anthologized in *New Stories from the South* and other anthologies. She is presently at work on a new novel, *Against Regular*. Nanci has received an NEA grant and residency fellowships at Yaddo and MacDowell Artist Colonies and in 1996 was honored as an Alabama emerging artist. Nanci Kincaid was born in Tallahassee, Florida, but claims Alabama as her home state. A generic Southerner, she has also lived in Virginia, Massachusetts, Wyoming, and North Carolina. She now lives in Tucson, Arizona.

ANN OLGA KOLOSKI-OSTROW is an assistant professor of Classical Studies at Brandeis University. She was the 1988–1989 winner of the Louis Dembitz Brandeis Prize in Teaching and more recently was a recipient of the Perlmutter Award for excellence in teaching and research. Her major publications include *The Sarno Bath Complex: Architecture in Pompeii's Last Years* (L'Erma di Bretschneider, Rome, 1990) and *Naked Truths: Women, Sexuality, and Gender in Classical Art and Archaeology* (contributor and co-editor with Claire L. Lyons, Routledge, 1997). She is currently writing a book on the archaeology of health and sanitation in Roman Italy. "Hannah's *Teshuvah*" was written especially for Rabbi Albert S. Axelrad, Chaplain and Hillel Director of Brandeis University, and Rabbi Laurence L. Edwards, Chaplain and Hillel Director of Cornell University, Ann's two learned rabbis, most valued teachers, and close friends, who helped her convert to Judaism in 1981. Ann's essay is about her realization that her conversion did not happen once, but is rather an ongoing process of *teshuvah* (turning or repentance). The life of the woman inside the story, however, is not a minute-by-minute account of the details of what happened at Ann's conversion ceremony, nor the exact thoughts she had as she delivered a sermon at Brandeis University. She created the character Hannah as an exercise in remembering selectively, in balancing reality and fiction, in re-evaluating emotions, and even, at times, in suppressing aspects of her real life that were too painful to recall in full. Hannah, the character, now has her own life— and even her own spirit—and certainly her own completed story. Ann's real life, as a Jew who was once not a Jew, is in a way the first draft of another story. Ann herself is still happily discovering what it means to be Jewish. She offers warmest thanks to Leslie Brody and her fellow Bunting Sisters for patience, unending support, and encouragement. Steven, Aaron, and Benjamin Ostrow provided the inspiration and love that make *teshuvah* possible

FLORENCE LADD, psychologist and author, was director of the Bunting Institute of Radcliffe College from 1989 to 1997. Earlier in her career (1970–1972), she held a fellowship at the Institute. She has a B.S. in psychology from Howard University, a Ph.D. from the University of Rochester, and has taught at Simmons College, Robert College in Istanbul, the Harvard Graduate School of Education, and the Harvard Graduate School of Design. Florence was the associate dean of MIT's School of Architecture and Planning and dean of students at Wellesley College. She is a coauthor of *Different Strokes* (Westview Press). Her novel, *Sarah's Psalm*, was published by Scribner in 1996. She lives in Vermont, where she is affiliated with the School for International Training in Brattleboro.

HELENA MEYER-KNAPP's work has long been shaped by the grandparents, whose story is central to her essay: From her grandmother, Maria Meyer-Cohn, she inherited a passion for research. From her grandfather, August Weber, she inherited a commitment to respond actively in the face of war, oppression, and cruelty. She spent a decade as an activist and scholar working with organizations such as the Nuclear Weapons Freeze Campaign to end the Cold War. These days she works on the wider problem of how and when people and nations at war become willing to seek a permanent ceasefire. She is currently writing a book, provisionally entitled *Altered States: People and Nations at War.* She also teaches about war, peacemaking, and citizen involvement in political processes at the Evergreen State College in Olympia, Washington. Helena dedicates this essay to her mother, Paula Quirk, who fortunately has lived long enough to share in its creation; as well as to the memory of her father, Roger Quirk, and grandparents, August Weber and Maria Meyer-Cohn. It is her hope that generations of Knapps, Snapps, Webbers, Nutbeams, Eleys, and Rawsons still to come will value the courage of these four, each of whom crossed cultural boundaries and worked in her or his own way for a better world.

KAREN FRASER WYCHE is an Associate Professor at the Ehrenkranz School of Social Work at New York University. She has a master's degree in social work from the University of Maryland and a doctorate in clinical psychology from the University of Missouri-Columbia. She is a fellow in the Division of Psychology of Women of the American Psychological Association. Her research and writings focus on strength and resilience in women of color who live under stressful life circumstances. Karen wishes to acknowledge her Bunting sisters for the community they continue to create in helping her conceptualize her work; the women in her family whose courage, love, and spirit are always present; Bunting sister Ruth-Arlene Howe, whose conversations about race enriched the dialogue in this book; and Bunting sister Leslie Brody, whose vision, tenacity, humor, editing, advocacy, organization, and friendship made this book so wonderful.